T0354818

CIVIL STRIFE
UNITED STATES
AFFAIRS

BASIC ASSUMPTIONS OF TRUST

PARADOX AND CONTRADICTIONS

PRESIDENTS, POLITICS, AND OTHER PERSONALITIES

OF REAL INTEREST

THE STAND/THE GROUND.

STEVEN SWAZO

BALBOA.
PRESS

A DIVISION OF HAY HOUSE

Copyright © 2018 Steven Swazo.

All rights reserved. No part of this book may be used or reproduced by any means, graphic, electronic, or mechanical, including photocopying, recording, taping or by any information storage retrieval system without the written permission of the author except in the case of brief quotations embodied in critical articles and reviews.

Balboa Press books may be ordered through booksellers or by contacting:

Balboa Press
A Division of Hay House
1663 Liberty Drive
Bloomington, IN 47403
www.balboapress.com
1 (877) 407-4847

Because of the dynamic nature of the Internet, any web addresses or links contained in this book may have changed since publication and may no longer be valid. The views expressed in this work are solely those of the author and do not necessarily reflect the views of the publisher, and the publisher hereby disclaims any responsibility for them.

The author of this book does not dispense medical advice or prescribe the use of any technique as a form of treatment for physical, emotional, or medical problems without the advice of a physician, either directly or indirectly. The intent of the author is only to offer information of a general nature to help you in your quest for emotional and spiritual well-being. In the event you use any of the information in this book for yourself, which is your constitutional right, the author and the publisher assume no responsibility for your actions.

Any people depicted in stock imagery provided by Getty Images are models, and such images are being used for illustrative purposes only.
Certain stock imagery © Getty Images.

Print information available on the last page.

ISBN: 978-1-5043-9976-0 (sc)
ISBN: 978-1-5043-9977-7 (e)

Balboa Press rev. date: 04/13/2018

"THE United States of America's military is the reason we even have a country. The Army, Navy, Marines, Air Force and Coast Guard- they are the reason we can get up in the morning and do pretty much any goddamned thing we want. They, not their Political bosses. Our armed forces are the reason we are Respected and, yes, feared throughout the world..."

"It is the soldiers, grunts, truck drivers, medics, mess sergeants, Special Forces, Rangers, and SEALs who make us great..."

-----Colonel David Hunt, *On The Hunt*

"It is no more possible for me to do my work honestly without giving pain than it is for a dentist. Because the nation's morals are like its teeth: the more decayed they are, the more it hurts to touch them." -George Bernard Shaw.

CONTENTS

PART I
SPLITTING ATOMS
Some basic elements of social life

PART II

1896 THROUGH 1932

PART III
1937 THROUGH 1955
World War II Era, Korea, & Vietnam

PART IV
1980 THROUGH 1992
End Of Cold War Era
Latin America & The Middle East

PART V
EXPERIENCING

Challenges And Coping With An Emergent World Disorder

PART I

SPLITTING ATOMS

SOME BASIC ELEMENTS
OF SOCIAL LIFE

1

MEANING & VALUES, FUNDAMENTAL CONSIDERATIONS

ANXIETY

I AM ANXIOUS, BECAUSE I AM deprived of something I would like to have or experience now.

It is not always personal doubt that undermines a political social system and drives the system empty of *ideas, values,* and *meanings*. In most cases, and en mass, it is the fact that these core *values* and *meanings* are no longer understood in their original power of expressing the individual human condition, and answering or solving existing socio-economic, political, moral, and personal problems. The present period is so different from those in which their inspirational or spiritual contents were created and absorbed, and so modifications and new creations are ever needed.

Creation is a ceaseless human activity; while all our individual being and fulfillment in society is dependent on our relations to their purpose and meanings. As such, we are only human by understanding and shaping the social reality of both self-world, and outer world environment, according to shared *meanings* and *values.*

Meanings and *values* are the relative satisfaction and fulfillment we strive for, arrive at, achieve, and experience in social life. They are the building blocks of culture and self-worth. When they are attained or experienced, we feel a sense of relief, fulfillment, continuity, and purpose. Through their agitation, disruption, disintegration, and dissolution from demands on the individual from the outside world of self formation, we

1

automatically experience the all-pervasive and dominant mood of human *anxiety*.

Anxiety must be experienced, simply because these *meanings* and *values* to which we have attached ourselves and become accustomed to are derived from others who share, or don't share the same *meanings* and *values* of the community or society in which we live. Also, our interpretations of what is revered are highly varied. Although each individual's and social groups' value differ in one quirk, extreme, moderation, or another, there are core values which all people share in any human community we may find on the planet.

These core values and meanings are universal, specie-wide, and cannot be questioned without disruption to the individual self; simply because they relate to individual or group survival. Further, communication systems are wired or connected between the outside and inside the individual human, and non-human world of events and incidents- most of which we have absolutely no control over. It is the inside world of our selves which concerns us most, for it is the one we take for granted to be the real *me*. My likes and dislikes, pleasures and displeasure. It is always the sum total of my experiences or feelings in, and about social life at the moment.

COOPERATION

Core values, and communication, or the expressions of meanings that pertain to individuals' and groups' survival cannot grow, develop, or mature without the agency of human cooperation. The individual is a weak animal, who is not strong enough to live well alone or in isolation. Therefore, the highest premium on human behavior that we have come to attach *meanings* and *values* to, has been paid and placed on *cooperation*. Otherwise, advancement of the species beyond a Hunting-and-Gathering mentality would be absolutely absurd, and inconceivable. We adapt, attach, give our loyalties to, cling, or hang on to each other. If for nothing else- to enhance personal survival, pleasure, leisure, and status.

At its most nascent level of organization, cooperation begins with the biological family. And at its widest and highest level of function, it is the human family of individuals, social groups, and organizations- seen and experienced in the structure of the political state, its institutions, and industrial organizations. In all ways, all societies are fundamentally and essentially a *cooperative enterprise* to help us fulfill our basic needs satisfaction, keep us in touch with one another, and to actualize our goals and dreams.

Communication and E*ducation,* or learning is the most primary universal tool of value that we share as a cooperative enterprise. Communication is the tool we use to arrive at understanding that learning. Learning, or education encompass preparation and use, for/of the arts and techniques to social life. It involves labor or work, along with the production of goods and services. Our learning and communication systems go hand-in-hand with this understanding of social life. It shows our human interdependence, how to constructively expend, or progressively use our energies; and it relates directly to the formation of self, industry, and the political state we live in.

WHY WORK? WHY LABOR?

The fundamental rewards of *work* or *labor* is freedom- more accurately, freedom-from want. Human freedom involves our capacity to make intelligent and accurate choices. *Choice* is burdensome, because it involves labor or work, which is a conscious and deliberate pause or inhibition between any given stimulus and sensation we are likely to respond to. In that pause we may consider alternative responses. And following this sequence, we ultimately do make an irrevocable choice. That is, a value is attached or placed on interpretation of the stimulus or sensation we absorb from people, objects, or problems encountered in our social environment- be they good, bad, useful, waste, or irrelevant.

The *pause* our brain-function makes involves labor or work. This labor or work is an evaluation to determine or obtain the best possible outcome of choice, or the avoidance of pain. In its application to a way of life, as an economic function in any form of interaction, social structure, or human community. This unavoidable intellectual *work,* or *labor* is the basic means humans use to earn and maintain our basic health, subsistence, and the enlargement of our freedoms. It is what we *have to do, must do, and ought to do,* in order to develop, achieve our goals, and grow to our fullest potentials.

Because our *basic needs satisfactions* are dependent on others, and on our individual relations to *industry* as a reliable means to earn the rewards for our basic subsistence and other growth needs, the most basic, most universal, and inescapable *anxieties* of all are our personal social relationships, and relations with work; since it concerns our individual, overall fates and health in society.

Our personal fates and hopes are what evoke the meanings and values we struggle to attain, arrive at, or get out of social life. In fact, meanings and values are what gives vitality to individuals' and groups', social lives. Therefore their loss reflect our frustrations and down moods as actual loss of some kind of *hope.* The condition of unemployment is one prime example.

Meanings and values must now be looked at as being primarily economic, psychological, spiritual, and social security, because they constitute our sense of form and continuity. In this interdependent cooperation, in and with society, they amount to personal health, satisfaction, fulfillment, and well-being from points of accomplishment- the awareness upon which our current sense of self experiences are built. These we refer to as *success* or *failures* in: living standards, employment, measure of suitability, material resource, comforts, and sociability.

Another primary source of our fundamental anxieties results from our ultimate consciousness of death- through accidents, injuries, prolonged illness, diseases, and our ongoing desire for unfulfilled longings. The constant reality awareness of these two recurring human conditions, probabilities, and possibilities that revolves around all of us in social life, accounts for what produces the most profound striving and struggles in each and every one of us; as we feel our sense of security or livelihood threatened.

Large portions and areas of human civilizations have given us some measure of safety, security, and spiritual institutions against the many forms of *anxiety* produced by these inescapable conditions of existence that befalls each and every one of us. The organized constitutions or working ideologies of political states today, and their five major institutional organizational forms of: *family, education, industry, religion* or *moral-beliefs,* and *government,* validate this observation and experience.

These institutions must be regarded as our basic humanitarian or cooperative mores. They provide simple and routine answers to the complex problems of social life, presenting themselves as unchangeable, by the patterning of human behavior. This base justification of everything, and anything we encounter or come in contact with lies in the sense that when we awoke to consciousness of social life as children and onwards in our bringing-up, we found them as *facts* and *logic,* which already now hold us in bond to custom, habit, and tradition.

Government, industries, formal education, religion, moral beliefs of specie-wide virtues or Philosophy, entertainments, sports, play, and the human world of art and science are all created specifically to serve this purpose.

In spite of these attempts at making life full of hope and meaning, we grow weary and worry. And our anxieties run high every time we feel unsafe and insecure. Not only this, sooner or later, every conscious person come to realize that no absolute or final *security* is possible anywhere on the planet, or in any political state we find ourselves in. We may vainly search. And as we do, we also come to realize that social life demands again, and again, the courage to surrender some- or even all conscious sense of *security* and freedoms, given or attained, for the sake of mere survival!

These existing sources of anxiety and insecurities that arise from agitations, failures, doubts, mistrust, ignorance, through no faults of our own, incompetence, and the frustration of human efforts, drive us toward resentments, anger, rage, bitterness, feelings and acts of retribution.

Our sense of being is lost from time to time, or is overwhelmed. The anxieties we fell are temporary, but as they wear-on without relief or resolution, we feel a threatening sense of eternity- life on the edge, permanent rootlessness, disorientation, and insignificance.

We are then lead or driven to reckless daring, radical or revolutionary alterations, re-organization, or re-construction of our accustomed and habitual mental processes and thought patterns. We feel like the perfect mythology: "driven out of the garden of Eden!" The balance we once knew and were used to went bye, bye. We now search desperately for the foundation of an individuality that can withstand the rigors, ravages, and demands of a social world into which we evolved from NO-Choice of our own, but that of a female parent willing to carry on the human process of reproduction- Pro-Choice for self.

RESEARCH

The conscious, painstaking, undertaking of this human condition is called *research*. Work. Research is a continuous process we must all *do* and go through, if we are interested in living well, or accomplishing anything meaningful and worthwhile having in social life.

Genuine *research* involves the unbiased accumulation of relevant facts or evidence for our projects or pursuits; their sorting and selecting, organization, and re-organization into ideas, and concepts; and making the necessary adjustments of our behavioral approach to our projects, and the surrounding social realities of others we must address or respond to.

This calls for an aptitude and attitude towards *active-learning*. In this pursuit, we routinely encounter dysfunctional forms of values and meanings of our own choosing or making, or those provided for us by the formal set-up of society, which must be rejected, replaced, or even neutralized.

These are the forms and configurations which we have become accustomed to, especially cultural stereotypes, based on our ethnic grouping, which often dominate or overwhelm our thinking patterns, especially when the behavior of selected individuals are magnified to control desired responses from members in larger spheres of the community, but do not conform to the true or actual conditions of the environment in which we may find ourselves. In many cases, stereotyping serve the expedient purpose of strangers, as well as exploiters.

In other words, the bane of human reasoning could always be found when the action and deeds of an individual of a defined ethnic group is superimposed on every other member of that ethnic group.

Simultaneously, in the overthrow or modification of such dysfunctional values and forms, there must be creation, the affirmation of truths, and a new value system replaced into the same dominant systems of meanings which already exist and is supported by the constitution, culture at a particular time in our personal histories, tradition, or trustworthy authority. These are the works, discoveries, demonstration, and observations of research or science that may be hidden, unexplored, ignored, or repressed, rather than expressed.

The rejections of dysfunctional forms which do not give vitality to individual and group social life allows for the making of cultural deviations by persons engaged in some form of occupation or industry. Our productive crafts and forms, of our own makings and ideas, within the same dominant system of forms, hinges on the observation of rule of law as our guidance, and does not return the individual to re-live the past of outmoded forms. A kind of freshness is eeked-out and reinjected into a system now transformed.

Individual detachments and take-offs, look at, and continue to improve on the unfinished business that have caused human errors and imperfections, human tragedy and misfortunes, and more than anything else, the unnecessary sufferings which we often undergo to reach or acquire our goals.

Cultural deviation or the rejection of dysfunctional forms are fundamentally take-offs from what has already been learned, transmitted, practiced, used, established, and can be verified as *true*, and a clear pattern easily discerned. His hamburger taste better than Mc Donald's next door. He serves his with plenty of garlic. Well, well!

Consequently, in an individual's or social groups' search of greater freedoms, human creativity in its re-formation or new formations is both an affirmation and defiance- which is also a disruption, and a challenge to give birth to more relevant truths, discover new meaning, and continuity to social life. This is the spirit of human creativity and the production of artifacts that confer upon a psychology- a *how to* strategy and approach to all-around social living.

The creative process is thus a human struggle and expression against disintegration of self and meaning in social life, as well as the struggle to bring a new kind of being into existence that will give harmony, integration, balance, and continuity to both self-world, and the outer world of other humans.

CREATIVITY & CHOICE

Truths we seek already exist, and many more than what each and every other individual has, will ever discover, possess, or experience. And however they are gathered or ascertained- whether through pain, work, wit, whim, pleasure, conscious curiosity, experiments, the frustration of our efforts, or just by consciously experiencing social life- unless these *truths* are reduced to some form of order as a serviceable commodity, and also as to offer a basis of comparison and objective analysis for current and future problem-solving, they may bear little upon events we are consumed with; since change of conditions and contingencies will more than likely impair their relevance.

Randomness of both the human-made and nature-given universe impose constant change in any existing form, body, or substance we can verify, think of, or hold in our perceptions- however visible or invisible, audible or in-audible, touchable or untouchable. Changes can be very subtle, and often are when they occur below our daylight consciousness. They can be volatile, violent, or radical without any single one of us alive having any perception, much less control, over them, their quality, source, or their occurrence.

Moving through these omnipotent forces in social life, and in search of constant relief, fulfillment, balance, and resolutions is the sole human individual. We are always in need of company, rest, or recuperation. And no conscious adult individual can be at rest, and stay at rest self-assured of anything, unless some kind of order is imposed on this random and haphazard universe.

Simply because shit is happening! It is going to happen! And will continue to happen. Because more than likely, the dice will not roll in our favor if we do nothing. Everything we don't want to happen in all probabilities is likely to, or will happen. If we don't do anything to prevent them from happening to us, then we have set ourselves up for extinction. Even if the dice is loaded.

The adopted or biological family structure of our individual evolution into society provided us a seemingly perfect structure, imposed on the haphazard nature of both the human-made, and Nature-formed Universe in our early years as children and adolescents. Now it is up to us conscious adults to do it for ourselves.

Order, intelligibility, and understanding- which are the main ingredients of *standards, meanings,* and *values,* must thus be imposed on the chaos or randomness of the Universe, by individuals, or some forms of social organization created by them, and for them.

Order on the planet in any nation state or human society can only be imposed according to some form of discipline in mental and physical organization. Since the world we now live in was created before we individually came on the scene, our individual task at hand, as conscious adults, is to choose intelligently those things or *truths* that are already here with us and are functional, and inherently good for our individual selves; create new ones which benefits and enhance community survival. Ones that will remain constant, meaningful, and undergo minimum or slow change. These are the things that keep us and the communities we live in, whole and fulfilled.

Self-creating is actualized by the shaping of our hopes, ideals, images, and all sorts of imagined constructs that we consciously or unconsciously inherit, work-out in our heads, work with, consume from others as their products; choose, or hold from time to time in the forefront of our attention.

I participate in my creation because I am able to shape my feelings, sensibilities, enjoyments, and hopes, through *choices,* into a meaningful pattern that makes me aware as a male or female. I can only do this as I am related to the immediate objective world. The key word here is *relation-* my relation to disorder, antagonisms, or randomness in occurring and recurring events of the moment- the world of people I must move around.

Choices we are likely to make results from our apprehension of concepts laid down in our human historical evolution by our ancestors' successful response to their environment, which are instinct, impulsive and mostly stereotype. These truths are laid down in our concepts of language, symbols, and myths as mental implements, and represent condensations of their experience; constituting summaries of the class, type, and variety of knowledge they had acquired and used, and other tools that they had to invent, perfect, and learned to handle themselves.

The concepts are laid down as images, facts, logic, symbols, myths, and metaphors in our everyday usage of language, and must be regarded as the cornerstones of our cultural *values, meanings,* and *standards* in our native learning, against which all things are judged or evaluated in our daily carrying-on.

They are also the native intelligence we inherit that inhibits and confer upon contexts of an intelligent human act, which involves the understanding of relations that exist between elements of a given situation or problem, and the invention or production of an appropriate solution.

Our individual selves are constructed on this growing body of models, forms images, myths, metaphors, and all other kinds of idealized psychic content of our local culture, and human ancestors' accomplishments, as well as our present human communities' struggles, which aids or obstructs our individual selves in its self-creation and direction. This process goes on forever. The major challenge ahead for each and every one of us is to choose intelligently. This is the objective of all human undertakings. Again, it cannot be overstated that choice is burdensome, and all intelligent human choice that yields desired outcomes usually involve *labor* or *work.*

SELF-AFIRMATIOM

Most of us who have reached the age of maturity in consciousness have discovered rudely, crudely, painfully, and sometimes severely that, beginning with *labor* or *work,* biological self-affirmations, or the acceptance of self under the randomness and chaos of the human and non-human social worlds are necessary, and universal to the entire species or race.

Again, if we are still interested in living, and living well, in trying to maintain our overall health, which encompass all the physical *standards, meanings,* and *values* which we have given and attached our selves to; the rewards they yield, and what we can reasonably expect from our struggles or investments in social life, we must take a stand and affirm them. We must!

This reason for self-affirmation comes as we continue to struggle for a better life-form of existence. In these trying times and moments, we routinely encounter the inescapable realities of our own ignorance of not-knowing, pain, discipline, privations, insecurities, despair, losses, and even some brushes with near-death situations.

There is the uninvited, unappreciated, new neighbor, their children, in the apartment or house I just moved into, and must make adjustments to, whether I like them or not. Then there are all the constant challenges and intrusions of technological inventions, based on the discovery of new knowledge, inventions, and products forced upon us for use- whether we understand them or not, like them, or not!

To move us forward toward our goals, objectives, and self-development, we had to learn to accept or affirm these things as part and parcel of our socio-biological struggles with *Nature* and *Nurture*. *Nurture* involves other humans like our individual selves.

Whatever their impressions and the consequences of their acts are or may have been on us, from personal experience, upon reflection, these were some things we now believe we *had to bear and do* in response or reaction to the situations we found ourselves in. We had to learn one way or another, or absorb the shocks of displacements, in order to preserve our individual selves, allowing or buying ourselves time to make further advancement in adaptation.

It is not that we couldn't or would not do otherwise, we just believed that any other considered alternative behavior would have been inappropriate, and the *act* or *choice* we made was the best thing under prevailing circumstances. Upon reflection, was this bad faith? Bad choice?

No. Bad fate! But our faiths always convince us to choose more-life!

We know that we are going to die, and because of this, we must have, or develop the courage to rebel against, or confront death. This is the trigger point of human imagination and ceaseless creativity. Creativity in the negation of death is called *courage*.

Courage is the foundation that underlies and gives reality to all human virtues and personal values and sacrifices in our struggles in, and with social life. The creative process that occurs within the realm of our imaginations is what gives *form* and *meanings* to social life. Courage, by doing meaningful things constantly, and however small, is the necessary element to make *being* and *becoming* possible.

Being and *becoming* are impossible without commitments and obligations. Courage is therefore the ability to stick with our duties and commitments. It is our ability to hold together forms of ideas to be imposed on what we feel to be discord, chaos, void, emptiness, or lacking.

Whatever these choices and things are that we commit ourselves to; their combinations will be the true social identity we become or bestowed upon us as creators.

It becomes the grounds of social life that we stand on, and for. This identity as it were, is a productive and dynamic developmental resistance to the aversive forms of discord in the environment. We cannot be anything more of self-worth, other than that which we have given our selves to- what we have worked-up our individual selves to become in the midst of discord or the randomness of both the social world of *Nurture* and *Nature-*

GROWTH

ABOUT OUR PRE-VISIONS

The human growth process requires a constant willingness to learn, to give, and take risks; make intelligent guesses, and eventually choices. This activity also requires that we develop a pre-vision of the social world in which we live. Developing our previsions require the outreaching of our imaginations to its greatest lengths and depths, and is the individual capacity to accept the bombardment of his or her conscious body-mind with ideas, impulses, images, and all other existing psychic filth or shit from the living environment.

It would have been biologically destructive to our individual growth, were we not able to accept this human fate, developing a capacity of tolerance to consider alternative and diverse possibilities, and to endure the tensions involved in holding, molding, and transforming them according to our wishes and desires.

Projecting ourselves into non-existent situations, making intelligent guesses and inferences from historical or factual evidence, taking calculated risks of insecurity; making, and testing of *forms* and *ideas* to move us further- these are all parts and parcels of our imaginations' and pre-visions' struggle to create forms, in order to put meaning and value into existence. A healthy person remains conscious of these processes.

Some people regress to infantile safety where the creation of artifacts and things of necessity for personal fulfillment and growth was done for them. They lack the drive, motivation, initiative, or developmental resource to generate the process of creativity. Or, the level of creativity reached is no more than imitation and vulgarization of what has already been established, and the stereotyping by status quo. Instead of going forward toward personal growth, and taking care of their own personal development, a learned dependency and reliance on others is created or adopted.

You can live without a father or a mother who accepts you. But a person cannot live without a *world* that makes no fucking sense to him or her. Although infantile, by comparison to others who have taken control and responsibility for their lives, the search for meaning and values are less demanding and burdensome on such individuals' mental capacities who remain in a sort of parental protective custody. This lethargy is in direct contrast to the vitality which others show for taking personal responsibility for their social lives.

If the scene we are in or will be exposed to is to have any meaning, all the gaps must be filled to form a whole. Our need for *form or wholeness* expresses our yearning to make the social world adequate to our needs, desires; and to experience ourselves as having some significance. However misleading or inaccurate our imaginations may arrive at filling gaps in scenes in order to form a whole perception, it is compulsory. Because the human body-mind has an inherent need for *closure*, in order to create and arrive at *meanings* or *forms*.

However vague these pre-visions of *forms* and self-affirmations are, or may be, they allow us some measure of assurance and control, based on what we have learned, accomplished, and established to this point in social life. They have also given us our state of well-being; making the possibilities of our investments, growth, and the continuity of our diverse interests.

Thus, our pre-visions, along with our self-affirmations, are states of consciousness and its deliberate organization, that enables us to be somewhat prepared for all possible and probable outcomes in the random events of the social world. Our pre-visions are developed to its fullest and most accurate capacity through education or learning, practice and experiments, which brings about the eventual organization of ideas, creation of symbols, tools, and their outward application.

Given to ignorance and instincts by contrast, our response to the social world without looking ahead is blind and careless reaction, or pure unscrutinized emotional energy. This kinetic energy flowing through us are units of thought stimulations in the ocean of human consciousness, that are always in need of adequate development for proper or accurate response to any actual situation we are facing in social life.

The kinetic energy we hold is the resistance we began developing when we were yet infants, and does not stop in our development until we die. It is the reservoir of the sum total of human experience and learning. This basic component of our individual resistance or body-mind's constitution is stored information, used as intelligence to respond successfully and adequately to our surrounding environment- consciously or unconsciously.

INSTINCTS VS HUMAN INTELLIGENCE

Without the conscious human brains' deliberate sorting, selecting, matching, coding, and decoding endless patterns and combinations of energy information absorbed from the outer and inner environments of our individual physical worlds, we would remain imbecile-like humans.

Nonetheless, it is this raw, emotional kinetic energy of ignorance, inherited instincts, and sometimes arrogance, or whatever *qualities* of discharge it may make upon others that powers us toward many goals, disappointments, and frustrations blindly. Through habits of thinking, whim, fancy, and hunches- however accurate or inaccurate. It, (referring to the quality energy-content potential in us), is what we call *human instincts*. They are activated automatically, virtually requiring no thought, and they basically cover our every reaction and response.

In concentrated forms, our instincts may narrow the scope of our awareness of any particular object, substance, or thing we may come in contact with in the Universe. But if and when we set or apply them in motion as conscious curiosity, they can enlarge the scope of our visions and imaginations in great depths, heightening sensory processes, intensifying memory, and the capacity to think, only because they are guided by conscious intelligence.

Otherwise, instinctual Energy in human feelings and its *quality nurture* revolves around two polar extremes of painful or negative charges; and positive or favorable charges. Painful, or negative flow in charges is likened to an underdeveloped balance in carrying on the burdens and business of individual survival. By contrast, the other end of the pole which revolves around the positive or favorable flow of energy, is a well-developed and balanced self, in a dynamic relation, and in response to the surrounding world of people and things.

To avoid painful or negative consequences in our every reaction or response to energy surges or lows in our being, the entire range of social learning we take up must be re-examined from time to time. This implicates an inherent need in us for constant research, evaluation, revision, development, formulation, and reformulation of our ideas and concepts in the apprehension of our surrounding social realities.

It summons an aptitude to consciously *stop* the motions of kinetic energies, in order to examine or understand its *contents,* then regulate its flow of motion going through us. This is the purpose of the agency of human thinking, which involves analytical considerations and alternatives. Inhibition. The *pause* or *stop* situation.

The primary elements of our analytical considerations are always directed toward the avoidance of painful experiences or costly consequences. If this is not possible, our last resort is to do anything we can within our powers or energies to make the outcome and condition of our choices and decisions less severe.

Without the capacity or ability for conscious intervention or inhibition of kinetic energy, which is e-motion, (literally what we commonly refer to as "emotion"), there will be no free flow, nor breadth of *reason* in us, that we may need in our human mental operations to arrive at adequate judgment for anything.

The whole process of analytical thinking is what is considered to be *human intelligence.* It involves understanding relations between the elements of any given problem or situation, and the invention or production of an appropriate response or solution. Whenever we try or make an attempt to do or accomplish anything based on inadequate learning or insufficient considerations, we experience frustration, a loss, or pain. These experiences often teach us that the reflexive actions of our individual instincts must be consciously developed through learning or education in order to satisfy our most basic, and vital support for survival or any of our wish-fulfillments.

Learning or education, which cannot be separated from cooperation, must thus be placed as the foremost human value. It is the separation of the *content* of our accustomed to, or assumed individual mental processes, of the flow of energies from the external audible and visible world of objects which we are confronted with, matched against a memory, history, or developed library of *contexts* that takes place as results of failure, pain, frustration of efforts; or accretion in the successful responses we have made up to this point in social life. The truths we arrive at through crude experience or conscious learning now becomes a formula or standard that will be an affirmation of, or the denial of something which verifiably exist, or doesn't.

It is this dual external objective nature of environment, and the nurture of our community, which is its mode of organization, that prepares the grounds for our success, anxieties, personal failures, pain, and frustrations. Again, this is so because of our mutual dependencies on each other, having dissimilar habits, customs, and ways of social life to fulfill *basic needs*.

Another consideration is our inherent and absolute inability to control the multiple layers of variables and subjective experiences in environments external to our bodies upon which the fulfillment of our planning, and goal acquisitions are all contingent. An earthquake, tsunami, storm, hurricane, tornado, atmospheric caused fire, or a volcanic eruption may obliterate our sanest planning forever! A social upheaval that bears the semblance of destruction or war in extremes can do the same. A dishonest person can ruin the life of another or many persons forever!

LEARNING

If we look for simple answers to these highly complex events of *Nature* and *Nurture* that: eliminate, mutilate, and humiliate our loved-ones, family, friends, and godly alliances in and out of our existence, it would have to be a direct *cause* that we are satisfied with. If not, we all become interested now in knowing our human ancestors' state of awareness in dealing with events like these, other people of other cultures, other teachings, other learning. Their models of social reality, their successful responses, and how adequate they were.

This puts us- the living and survivors, on a basic level of awareness from where they left off in civilization. In order to avoid the errors and fates that befell them, we do research and experiments and try to improve on their models. It turns out that the most persisting and demanding quest in social life is *to know* and *to understand* causes. For if we do know and understand most causes, all our plans, moves, and actions would be perfect. But we err, stumble, bumble, fall short, and make big goddamn mistakes.

The nature of environment in its unity combination with re-curing events does not give a hoot, or a damn whether you are a master or slave, rich or poor, pretty or ugly, a somebody or nobody, already sick and suffering, have or have-not, or still enjoying a healthy lifestyle. *Nature* has no respect whatsoever for any of us individual humans alive!

It therefore forces each and every one of us to confront three of humanity's fundamental and eternal problems in order to achieve some kind of predictability, balance, or some form of social harmony. These problems are: *ignorance* (not knowing), *irresponsibility*, and *false perceptions or apprehension of social reality*. The command of Nature and Nurture is:

Understand me! Which humans can only make ambitious and fantastic attempts at trying, but none of us could ever completely do it. Nonetheless, we must understand something about these three fundamental elements of human existence, at least to maintain and enhance our survival chances.

Conscious older folks are rest assured that of the twenty or more meaningful and realistic goals that they had once aspired for, and believed they could have been convincingly achieved within a day, week, month, or year, have found out that only about three or five of these goals can actually be attained or fulfilled within their consciousness of a lifetime. Changing realties of the social structure in which we pursue our goals, and the inevitable potential of accidents, illness, and untimely physical death, works against all of us.

All hopes of fulfilling goals come alive, and stay alive, only in an atmosphere and environment of harmonious unity with *nature* and surrounding human *nurture.* Human nurture calls, and demands form all of us to learn and use available techniques for survival- to get as much understanding as we can from each other, and summons an aptitude and attitude of responsibility, active learning, as well as care-and concern-for other persons and things.

Therefore, no man or woman is happy, contented, free, or satisfied with social life under sates and conditions of *basic needs* privation in human nurture. Being subjected to extremes of basic needs privation, most humans automatically show a willingness to facilitate learning, or education in whatever form, to relieve or improve their condition. It cannot be argued away that *learning* or *education* is most primary to human *Nurture*, and is a deliberate attempt to inhibit instinctual human reactions, in order to facilitate an adequate or proper response to challenges of both the human and non-human world.

One notable and peculiar thing about human learning is that once we have learned something about something- anything- that is, we have a tendency to think that we have learned all there is to know about that something. If we are adamant about our new-found, or old learned something, we will be shocked to find out different learnings, use, and improvement of the same something we know so very little about- even if we had invented it. More of this will be revealed as you read this treatise.

LEARNING & POVERTY

Learning and education as a circular mode, morally, and paradoxically- are often used as a *ritual,* rather than the active creation of symbols, forms, and artifacts to confront the problems which *Nature* and *Nurture* may pose for each and every one of us. This kind of learning is conservative, generally confined to the years of our primary development socialization processes. Its adaptation as a customary mode of interaction for the remainder of social life is commonly associated with a culture of poverty.

It stops, or slows down the advancement of learning by rejecting more relevant concepts suited for adaptation. This learning is not progressive. It is the closest thing to animal learning, credited to instincts or lapsed intelligence, which is an enduring tendency on the part of any living organism to act or carry-on its adaptation in a particular, seemingly fixed manner.

As opposed to the lower races of animals, the human species and its wide variety of individual ethnic group members are not biologically fixed to adopt to, or act in any single or particular manner, or mode of adaptation. But we can be programmed to do so. And most of us are in innumerable cases with re-enforcements; as Psychologist B. F. Skinner has so amply demonstrated in his experiments with pigeons.

We are endowed with the natural gift of choice, regardless of the rigidity of our determined outer imprisonment or conditioning, whilst an idiot, dog, cow, cat, horse and other races, have no choice but to continue acting and thinking as they do, for their particular species' survival. Wolves and sheep can never live peacefully in company, given to their own disparate race, and natural identities without any kind of human intervention. The main reason, if for nothing else, is that these two different animals are indeed of separate or different *races*.

Why can't black people and white people, and every other category and classification of people, based on our physical features live peacefully, and in company with each other today, when many have done so, and are still doing so, ever since time came into being?

We are forced to look at the individual. And the answer is: in America, african americans, and white niggers are definitely, and **officially** not of the same *race!* Black people and White people are. The former two categorized ethnic groups are intellectually, and physically looked upon as sheep and wolves, rats and cats, dogs, and horses. Some people just can't, and won't get the real concept behind this *race*-word.

We just can't be of the same *race!* Absolutely not! And so now, today all the inhuman roles a person or individual could engender is on. That is, to show the rest of the world what he or she thinks, and knows and how one is superior or inferior to the other.

We see the happy-go-lucky, relatively contented, and well-adjusted human animal, along with the herd, and family in his or her community, who needs no further learning, education, or adjustment, other than the common mode of community's social life they have come to know. Both biological and socially-learned behavior will now act as instincts- without any thought, as they have combined, creating a fixation, binding habit, and attitude in adaptation.

In the maintenance and upkeep of their values, most candidates of *poverty* consent to religious faith and fates, a completely false analytical mode of existence, generally the old Marxist ideology of inevitability, and are convincingly given to biological reproduction. Then there are the rituals and customs of ethnic group worship, or the exaggerations of their heroes, and heroines; all sorts of popular events, manias, and delusions to lose their wretched selves in, in search of hope, meaning and eternal values.

Today, these lives consist largely in doing work or jobs which help to maintain bare subsistence, that may consist of a small overpopulated apartment rental, an occasional break from the tedium of work, and a frantic search for better paying, more stable and steady job, that is justified by getting married and raising a dependent family; to go on doing the same kind of goddamn thing their parents did- wishing and hoping, without having the ability to lay down any sound foundation for the future of their sons and daughters, who would then reproduce and rear another family, in a continuous, vicious, and unbroken cycle of learning.

More than half a century ago, Eric Hoffer noted that not all people who are considered *poor* are frustrated with their situation. "Most are smug in their decay and familiar cesspool." Not only that, they consider the configuration of their biological and social evolution into society an *eternal order;* an ordering that is not likely to change under any kind of normal circumstances.

Easy access to sexual bonding and satisfaction satisfies the norm, along with the religious and political states' approval of the reproductive process, seals and re-enforces this vicious fate, *faith,* and a coherent belief-system that we call *poverty*. It is a complete institution with all its ethos of morality. This is the bare bone normal structure and institution of poverty.

Owing to the *fear of God* imbued in our ancestors throughout the dawning of our civilizations, and through the imprint and teachings of religions- world-wide, this reality of a decreed *eternal order* configuration is still commonplace for millions of American lives- rich or poor, haves or have-not. Whilst by contrast, all intelligent Americans, beginning with the nation's founders, have discovered this to be the very yoke and tyranny of human ignorance. In fact, it was the very essence of their rebellious acts against the *Old World Order.*

Today, most of our socially-learned instincts still have their roots in this crucible of elementary learning, owing to the repetitious scourge of religious concepts and precepts put forth by Judeo Christian bibles, and applied in most of our everyday government business transactions. It cannot be argued away. It is one of the cornerstones of our American heritage and tradition- "While 94% of all Americans believe in God, three out of four make no connection between religion and their judgment of right and wrong," stated, former U. S. President Gerald Ford.

EDUCATION

Whether a person chooses to accept it or not, *learning* or *education* is a continuous and ever-conscious process; and is a necessary burden and undertaking until we die, if we are all interested in living well, or leading better and more wholesome lives. To learn anything, or about anything is to know or have a broad scope of understanding on the nature of its being, use, or existence.

A better understanding of any *body,* phenomena, or *thing* allows us great breadth of awareness to make better use of its energies or energy potentials, including our own. We are rest assured of its main properties, identity, or parts of its functional use in our world of forms, constructs, and ideas that give value and meanings to our existence.

Through absorption and learning in culture, we develop a *memory* and acquire *belief systems* to help us function like majority of competent others we witness around us. This imprinting that began in infancy, which is the accretion or accumulation of useful knowledge, again and again, demands constant extensions, organization, modification, or complete reorganization in an individual's or social group's belief system, from time to time, and even over, and over again. The normal function of our human brain can accomplish this feat astoundingly with lightning speed. In fact, surrounding *Nature* demands this from all of us, as our biological nature responds automatically.

To facilitate intelligent responses to our common communal environments, most cultures have fixed and formalized our learning process or psychological developments. They are channeled through the medium and institution of *education,* and are used as the primary means of social selection. Our education involves the learning and use of language, symbols, and other physical tools, which are then used as *concepts* in resolving, building, and conveying meaning to us and others.

Most of our early developments are fixed and formalized, definitely according to some dominant, economic, hierarchical and structural order of society- mainly industry, handed down or dictated by the status of our parents. Although these fixations dictate at deeper levels of our consciousness where we are often unconscious in the moment, we are not damned, destined, determined, or cursed to follow this order or pattern of socialization, without options, choices, or alternatives.

The primary reason for psychological development or the institution of education in any society is to have the capacity and ability to organize the sensations we absorb from our surroundings into meaningful wholes or *forms.* These *forms* are tools that help us overcome obstacles, solve problems, get us the results we desire or need, and to avoid all possible undesirable or negative experience, that are more often results of instinctual reactions, sheer ignorance, or inadequate learning.

THE POLITICAL STATE

Education or learning may be the foremost tool applied and incorporated in our evolutionary response to successful social adaptation. However, the life of organizations and industries within a political state, which precedes our individual births or evolution, is where and how- (simultaneously), adaptation, imprinting, and the application of learning and education actually takes place.

While any form of industrial or social organization must recognize *standards* and *values* that define their boundaries of purpose, public service, and existence, it is the political state that hems us all in, allowing latitudes or variations in forms of organization. The political state is the ultimate boundary and recognized legal force of formal standards and values for its own survival. Its institutions stands as guardian of the social order, in which an individual is born or socialized, migrates, or assimilates and carries-on his or her own daily affairs and pursuits.

As members and citizens of society, it is expected from each and every one of us to establish a relationship with Industry, which involves *labor* or *work*. If for nothing else, labor or work is a *means* we utilize through compulsion or contract for financial gains or rewards. It is used to maintain our state of well-being, and to earn our basic life subsistence and leisure needs. *Labor* or *work* promotes the welfare of the state through contracts or mutual exchange of talents, goods, and services. This is the reality of the political state's social order.

Although education or learning is entirely a communal affair, owing to the use of language and other mutually understanding symbols of communication, its deepest connection is to the national political state, while its ultimate benefit is fundamentally an individual enterprise. Through learning or education, we create tools of domination to overcome obstacles, necessary to move us forward toward our goals.

Beginning with symbols, tools are the results and products created as the extension of our imaginations, and its deliberate organization through what we call *thinking*; while language and its many expressions is the means we use to share this social reality- the tools we are likely to create, or the ones we have already created.

What we stumble on and discover by accident in *Nature*, without forethought or the organization of thought, is what all humans have referred to as *pure luck, a given,* or a *freebie.* If human civilization had relied on these factors alone to move us forward, we still would be living in in the age of dinosaurs, and human organization never would have made the leaps and advancement it has reached today in all-around improvements of our condition.

In fact, even with the given and freebies, we must do something intelligent to keep them, and keep their availability going on. This can only be accomplished through some measure of conservation. And so, because there is no thrift nor conservation in *Nature,* the deliberate organization of thought, which is *work* or *labor*, is the primary requirement for the activity of human *conservation.*

Without this deliberate organization of our body-minds through *labor* or *work,* we can never develop the ability to build, to stay, and preserve our being or form; or to progress and be in possession of that which we wish to have, attain, or acquire. They are either wasted, taken by any whom, swept away by natural processes or disasters, or are forgotten. And so are we!

In a practical sense, we can come to say that: motion of a portion of the random world of events, must be frozen within a time framework- to facilitate the understanding of its whole movement, which none of us alive have been able to fully grasp. What we arrest, grasp, and control are the puny realities of self-fulfillment and successful adaptation, and the building of artifacts, within the framework of that great illusive social reality that exist before us, which is actually the time framing of a political state.

The political state was formed or framed for us before we came on the scene to consciousness of self, and our surrounding world relations. And this consciousness is a form of motion. Many *forms of motion* have been organized for us under the dominance of national symbols, standards, and values from which we derive and pursue our public goals- in fact, the entire range and scope our social life.

In another generalized and detailed sense, the forms of motion we are referring to are *freedoms-* freedom-from, or the freedom of human movement. All these *forms* and *meanings* are supported by bodies of logic supported by principles of our national constitution.

Logic, by definition is organized reasoning. However, in reasoning we can easily recognize the practices of a variety of people who have come to agree and understand the use, and purpose of forms and meanings of the same things in a different way. What is perfectly logical and proper in community A through C may be totally illogical and illegal in D through Z. This kind of reality we encounter as we move out and about different locales', states', time zones, or boundaries-

further broken down to written laws and accustomed rules, as we commonly refer to them, are agreements or understanding of the base tradition of forms, working, or operating consensus used by most people within a geographic area of occupation or locale, who have adapted to such forms, and require little or no questioning from their formal authorities or emergent populations.

These forms exist in our heads as learning experiences of day-to-day caring- on, captured, and stored in our memories. We can credit the acceleration and progress of all individuals', social groups', or cultures and their civilizations' directly to their particular configuration of dominant *forms* of logic, and symbols of organization used, from which, members derive meanings and satisfaction from consequences; established standards, and then redistribute these values to others.

Because we live in worlds of *meanings* and *values* that are logically valid morally- such as: love thy neighbor as you love yourself, and do unto others as you would have them do the same to you; *politically*- because of regulations we observe and standards of relation to others in society; *scientifically*- because these regulations and standards contain the life of *reason* and all trustworthy knowledge; *aesthetically* and enthusiastically- because of the free-spiritedness, and spontaneity it gives to human thought, vision, creativity, and action in every encounter with social reality in the community. The structures of our individual selves and social worlds are also interdependently present with these *meanings* and *values* that we have become habituated and accustomed to, under influence of the political state.

LANGUAGE

When we look at who we are, which is our individual *self-concepts'* makeup, we are looking at this part of the world to which the self has labored, worked, or absorbed to become and made its logical world. So, as far as any individual significance is concerned, the community world would not be what it is without the regulation of a moral conscience enforced by principles of the political state's constitution in this self-composition. Its influence on our thinking and self-creating, which accounts for the continuous development of our social lives, is also inseparable.

This awareness of *self, me,* or *I* develops and grows in society according to its scope of influence in the *organization of thought* and thought patterns. These are the action potentials we wish to effect, or have already effected in motion and forms.

The *organization of thought* is what focuses us to the physical surrounding world of action or inaction. It is what we use to interact with, in order to build our individual social lives, and is the immaterial material from which our ideas are influenced, constructed, molded, and also its director of outward physical acts performed or to be accomplished.

All the spheres of social reality and understanding in which we participate in the organization of thought and its pursuits in social life are communal. That is, they exist in the communities and environment we move about. The most fundamental expression of this fact is the use of the symbols of language, which is thought's most primary physical expression.

Language is not individual. It is communal, while its rules, grammar, and various symbols of accentuation are always evolving and changing to guarantee meaningfulness that are the meanings of change, discourse, or matters at hand between communicators or understandees, as it were- Meaning, those who understand the symbols and contexts of the communication.

I didn't say I love you. I said I love ya.

Language as the delivery of our thoughts in *words* is a convention; since *words* we often use are of social convenience. Quite similar to the use of money, *thoughts, words,* and *ideas* are *coins,* or the medium and modes of intellectual exchange for the real things we come to mutually use, manipulate, and understand. Some are not in and of themselves real things yet- *thoughts, ideas,* and subsequent *words,* and symbols just represent those *forms* and things we are likely to construct, effect, do, or must manipulate.

The things we humans create, produce, use, and manipulate in the environment are independent of the identity we give them in language or words. Cultural bias is the physical world of *Nurture* which human thought has analyzed, created, categorized, and sorted into groups or forms now called, *concepts,* and *things.* This is the *motion* mentioned earlier, that has been frozen for us by our past political leaders and administrators of the state, our early caretakers or parents, and continued by a national dominant status quo to act within.

The things or forms of concepts we use are given an identity by naming them with words, or giving them symbols that convey feelings. Feelings are the essence of human experiences, because they are acquired meanings with, or without effort, and most times easy to communicate between understandees, or people who are mutually in touch with each other, one way or another.

Our entire American history and nation *form* is a cultural bias, because of its unique Constitution composition, and language in a world among many other nation states' languages and communities, that are structured in radically dissimilar ways, and varying widely.

In spite of other nation states' or communities' cultural bias of any kind, understanding the contents and contexts of our thoughts, in the manner we intend and wish them to be, is our real goal and objective in all human communication or communication systems. Because tacit meaning of words, forms, other symbols must be learned in order for one person to communicate to the other clearly, and understandably.

In all its extensions, it follows that the *real* world we live in is built up on the language habits and patterns of individuals and social groups that give definitions, meanings, values, and action to social reality in different ways. And this fundamentally occurs at the convenience, ease, warp, twist, or flair, of individuals, social groups, organizations, and our broader social relationships.

Because it is physical, its development and invention through other symbols such as *writing* or *art,* the use of language has demonstrated more efficient use of our energies and emotions. Language and its extension of symbols ultimately serve the individual and human community as tools of domination, neutralization, and conquest of *fate,* which above all today, for the vast majority of struggling individuals and families, means economic and spiritual security, and in being a participant of the political-economic productive process in the state.

COOPERATION

Unless a person has a chance of gaining some direct benefits form his or her efforts in learning or education, there is not much inducement to think ahead and make the sacrifices necessary as an enterprise, to provide the tools for production and self-development, beyond the elementary and common social norms imposed through the rituals of *work* or labor, and the customary practices in the culture of poverty- just to earn basic subsistence needs. Masculinity and femininity are enforced through easy sexual bondage and the reproductive cycle.

Although it is always obvious to the simplest of body-minds to see the great benefits of *cooperation* in human exchange, and even though they may be educated as a class category of people, given to their adopted way of social life, lower homogenous and heterogeneous groups, of which the vast majority are the *poor* can never see mutually advantageous opportunities and rewards through voluntary cooperation. Individual and familial interests are too defensively volatile.

Their dominant mode of adaptation in relation to each other is often elementary, and one of antagonistic submission and domination. It is a fact that most societies with dominant homogenous populations show more cooperation in their routine state of affairs. However, the United States has always been a heterogeneous society ever since its inception. And as such, more demands have always been made on our physical and intellectual abilities to cooperate in forming amicable alliances in our adaptation. Our communication forms and systems are fundamentally and constitutionally developed this way.

ATTRACTION & PERSUASION

The most dynamic leaders in society who have achieved a measurable quality of education, and who understand the agency and benefits of human cooperation, exert more vitality in their affairs, and their service to society are always given to be the creators, designers, producers, and manufacturers of goods, for the greater masses of the human population.

Scientists, educators, physicists, chemists, inventors, physicians, business executives analysts, administrators, or men and women who have specialized knowledge in all fields of defense and medicine, routine affairs of the political state, and industry are the model representatives of our cultural forms and structures.

Most of these representatives, creators, and producers of our needed goods and consciousness, which the vast majority of human populations have been dependent on, consist of at least two dominant categories of people: the first and preeminent classes and category are the genuine producers of all goods or human artifacts. Their intentions are also all good and neutral for any random consumer. These *goods* could be labor, craftsmanship, or artifacts. No matter how, or in what way this category of people produce their goods, their ultimate intentions remain the same- for the good of all.

whether the quality of goods produced are mediocre, substandard, naturally perfect to our use, or superior by comparison to other competing producers offering a similar product that meets the ends or expectations in our use or consumption of It, matters not. "I don't build a bridge for whites or blacks only, or for any other specific ethnic group members to cross. I build a bridge safely to accommodate all humans to cross." -US Engineer, Robert Cook.

The second category of our representative leaders, creators, and producers of goods and consciousness are who are commonly called *suckers*, mostly *salespersons* who are a shit stock of skilled and educated people, by which vast majority of populations are led, tricked, and fooled. We may conveniently call this category of people the *color* people of society.

These are the people who specialize in the organization, exaggerations, and manipulations of our senses, imaginations, and legitimate interest through base fears and needs- especially in those goods and artifacts produced by genuine producers that we are dependent upon, and who never had such intentions, thereby misleading us.

Just as the ones who led majorities of people in the nation to vote for Hillary Clinton to be President in the 2016 election, subscribing heavily to surface culture- something I will comment about much later in this treatise.

Long ago, this category of American *color* people were aptly called: *hidden persuaders*, opinion molders, sociopaths, or suckers at best- as we know them today!

These are the people who continue to connive and convince us of *needs* in order to think in certain ways, consume specific products, deliver useless information deemed as essential, but which we actually have no need for- among other things, just to maintain and aggrandize their status. With guile, guts, and glorious cunning, and evermore variety of influential and attractive devices are used. These are the kinds of people who would knock on the door of an Eskimo's igloo trying to sell him a California snow cone.

In short, sociopaths need to be shot or locked up.

Taking it a tad closer to home, our hidden persuaders are the real *rulers* and *governors* of our conscience when we give them our trust. They are the *common man* and *common woman* exerting influence and control over each other, in all forms of human interactions and relationships we can think of, or form in social life.

How is this made possible?

We individually yield to what we feel, sense, and believe to be true, favorable, or genuine. If we do not believe, feel, or have that sense of certainty, we may still often yield, maybe because of being convincingly attracted to, or owing to fears of loss, deprivation, destruction, pain, punishment, or death. Otherwise, we will always make a choice of maintaining our grounds, enhancing our positions, or remaining neutral.

Obvious, or hidden persuaders- unscrupulous, deceitful, corrupt, contemptuous, and dishonest men and women, in their quests for control over others' fate, and amassing resources, or the maintenance of a class feeling of superiority, through the ceremonial identity degradation of another individual or social group- character defamation, or any form of undermining, often thrive and thread on the uneducated and unaware consumer. This could be you or me- it matters not to sociopathic behaviors.

In whatever manner, form, or disguise, our persuaders of the second category of human producers always want us to make decisions that are not guided by conscious thought, but by an individual's or social group's instinctual reactions to feelings of fulfillment of the artificial needs that they have created, supplied, and maintained for them through sayings, language, images, designs, symbols, arts, pictures, signs, colors, human poses in advertisements- whatever our senses are likely to respond to immediately, and instinctively, and are associated with their full intentions, wares, designs, or products.

Seduction in the most spontaneous, convincing, and persuasive forms is always employed in millions of ways by millions of people upon billions of people. The seducers' base research is to find and invent tools to induce, influence, cajole, or manipulate the greatest amount of people to cooperate with, buy, join the consort, company, party, club, or consume their wares.

The prime medium and solution used to elicit this insatiable human desire, plea, and merging of feeling is *attraction*.

Attraction is a total human thing. We humans are basically and fundamentally moved from within when something attracts us- whether we show it or don't show it. Whatever a person is attracted to at first sight or experience, just cannot be argued away. Again, because we are persuaded and convinced by that which we believe and feel to be wholesome, genuine, and true- even if temporary, or for the moment, these become the real ingredients of the symbolic and technical props used in the various communication mediums of persuasion, that not only our professional and skilled hidden persuaders study and employ, but also the average common man and woman who inherits and perpetuate them.

Because it is personalized, the fact of individual freedom is that you can cheat as much as you want to with all your social relationships in the world. Conversely, you can be as honest as a pig, or as you choose to be. In both cases, you will reach limits set by other individuals, organized groups, greater society, the political state, or *Nature* itself. This is simply so because we can never escape existence without sharing an environment. And this sharing requires that we *give* and *take* according to limits imposed by their consensus, cultivated logic and forms, or social reality.

However vain- our lovers, hated ones, family members, enemies, associates, co-workers, friends, and broader social relationships- they cover the entire scope and province of our *hidden,* and *obvious* human *persuaders.* They supply and employ the entire range of suggestions continuously being put forth for our considerations, to take hold in our perceptions, and for the underlying analytical energy motion in us to respond accordingly.

Ritual is the process by which our deepest values are developed, formed, and established. It is a perfect form of drill, or regulated habits of an individual, organization, or social group. Rituals are often enacted or initiated by persons who enjoy statuses of autonomy or social pre-eminence. This is the hub of attraction.

The status of social preeminence begins with property ownership, the autonomous individual, the well-salaried and paid, a parent, the pretty, the handsome, good-looking, and attractive; the authorized, privileged, licensed, popular media personality, jocks, and sassy females who push nonsense with their influence - all their private and public acts freely dictate to the masses, and are often repeated mechanically, without any conscious thought, intelligence, or reflection.

This contagion, which is the ready transmission and spread of their eases or diseases, (their ideas, acts, attitudes, and emotions), are concerned with all the symbols of human communication and association. Since we come to understand and regard people of authority, the autonomous, and those who enjoy the statuses of social preeminence as a natural dominant human cultural given.

Beginning in our earliest years of self-developments, it is not an uncommon thing for most people to look toward each other sometimes, or most of the times, as guides, role models, and orientations to the physical unexperienced world, as well as our immediate surroundings of social reality.

In this looking toward the *other* as a guide or model, especially in states of failing powers, when our maps reach dead-end roads, and more often when we are in states of severe deprivations and helplessness, in order to enhance our own survival, we willingly reach out to any-who person. This begins with the use of another human self in a modality of fantasy or social reality. In other words, everybody consumes everybody else's *body* or *goods* within the state, in one way, shape, form or another.

Meanwhile, the life and vitality of each individual depends on the *qualities* of his or her consumption of these *goods* or relational *selves* consumed. So, do people really eat each other up?

Well, Yes!

We do get on each other's nerve endings, here, and there- mainly because of our individual differences and our apprehension of social reality. There are millions of other reasons, but these two will do.

All the products- beginning with human actions- that we willfully, comfortably, and enjoyably imitate or consume, make their anchors and influence on our feelings, thoughts, and self-creation; because they are in and of themselves good company, fulfilling, and are therefore considered vital, important, and significant.

Some such people are sports personalities and the great pretenders, who are the actors of Hollyweird. Hollywood. Besides these popular and dominant personalities, there are a great variety of other human personalities and their artifacts of production, such as literature and art, which we have consumed and yet to be consumed, who are, and may be way, way, more interesting in furthering our personal interest and well-being.

These anchors or cornerstone of people we have chosen, or given to us willy-nilly- their products, and influence take hold on our conscience more easily when they are rhythmically concerned with our recreational activities, and core needs; Imitated, and intimated in action and the seriousness of social life.

Fashion is taken-up in dressing, idle curiosities, quality of music listening, entertaining others, attending sport events or playing; dancing, watching movies, attending concerts and theatres, listening to radio broadcasts, paying attention to the entire world of symbols and arts, in advertisements, entertainments, and so on are always suggesting sentiments.

And when you really get down to it, *Sentiments* are the chief element in all human social selection, or in the making-up of our body-minds for a positive choice; simply because sentiments yield meaning and fulfillment for any individual or a social group's purpose.

To beat the scourge of influence, intelligent choices are demanded of each and every one of us, and at every junction, turn, and twist on the road in our self-development.

2

CHOICE & THINKING PROCESSES AGAIN REVISITED

THROUGHOUT HUMAN CIVILIZATIONS, OUR RELATION to *industry* and the *political state* have been the two most compelling force of influence over individual and familial social life. They are the physical reality and vitality of the social order, and the most permanent institutions around which we come to organize our lives. So the threat of being excluded from the productive process for not having an economic base, the loss of one, or the anguish of getting one established, which generally is a state of privation or unemployment, is what *fate* in American society means today.

Our nexus of bonds, through the years of childhood, adolescence, and perhaps early adulthood, provided for our basic subsistence needs of food, clothing, housing, transportation, and so on. However, most American male and female adults are expected to have established this operating economic base or some kind of relationship with education, apprenticeship, or industry, before they are twenty-five years old.

As adults, our individual self-concepts' formations are often associated with roles or expected performance and rewards from industry that reinforce them. Roles are chosen or selected through a social selection process of education, learning, or training as: jobs, profession, trades, specialization, or craft; and they engender specific abilities, performance, discipline, and public expectations. Financial reward is the most important end sought in these positions, followed by status, and prestige, or they may all go together.

The political state on the other hand, through its laws, regulates freedoms of its individual citizens, as well as industrial community functions, in order to promote growth and development. Both individual

34

and industrial community's growth depends on the capacity of expanding freedoms. This is done deliberately through the scientific enterprise of education, and the deliberate organization of knowledge, or truth-seeking intelligence to improve the human condition. As such, new forms of industries are ever created to improve and meet these demands.

The most rudimentary conditions of human freedoms depend on the use of our intelligence and wisdom in making accurate or appropriate choices. This is the art and method of correct thinking. It is also the heartbeat of our better conscience. We are thinking correctly every time, and anytime our thinking processes and consequential action from it matches any form of social reality, or produce the desired solution to any random problem we may be facing, taking on, or is in our immediate experience.

Error, frustration, mistakes, failures, and misunderstandings, by contrast, are all results of incorrect thinking and *forms*, false belief or belief systems – wrong information. Period! To arrive at correct or accurate thinking in most of our trials and errors in social life, it is worthwhile knowing the meaning and importance of *thought* as it affects our entire state of being.

Human consciousness of any stimulation or sensation, object, or thing in the Universe is the organ point of all thoughts that takes place in the human brain. It is also the human will to continuity of purpose in creating *forms* and pleasure for self and others when deliberately chosen. Necessities of survival, influence, and desire, determines the course, form, or *content* that individual human thought will take, move, or groove in. And naturally, the sensations of sentiments will always flow stronger.

Consciousness, on the other hand, is neither a thing nor an entity, but is in a flux with thought and its familiar systems and sentiments of relations. In form, it is a point where sequences of relationships of memory thoughts coincide vividly in the human brain with harmonizing sequences of events we are experiencing in the now. It is what focuses us to the physical world, and what we use to interact with others and things we must use or manipulate.

Human consciousness is a form of energy within all the energies of existence. In us, it is *e-motion*. As such, it can be changed or express itself in an infinite number of ways. Change is a natural requirement for any conscious being to exist. It is a constant in all the components of *Nature* and human *Nurture*. To change is to mature as a process in human evolution; and to mature requires continuous learning or education, and ceaseless creation for our desires and fulfillment. Consequently, there is no knowable limit to change or human growth, other than death. The organizational form of human thought is the only vehicle to achieve, use, and maintain any desired end.

Thought is the material with which the human world of change and stability is created. And all our ideas for development and growth are constructed in the human brain. Our brain is also the primary source of all sensory data or information from both the outside and inside world of our physical bodies. From its sensory data, biased by our memories and sentiments, our brain develops a composite view on an actual, real, or imaginary basis of the surrounding world we live in, or wish to move in. These are the impressions, sensations, and stimulations we feel or absorb that it uses in projection, introjections, and its molding or forms.

Our whole composite view is now called a *perception,* composed of images, symbols, sound waves or vibrations, similar to images, symbols, and motions on a television or motion picture screen. These symbols and motions are what generate the forms or definitions of social reality in our understanding to which we respond. Outer Symbols carry shared and tacit meanings of experiences, tied to our understanding each other in our accumulated learning and familiar surroundings. This is habitually exercised and experienced as joint action, social harmony, wit, wisdom, failure, success, or misery in choices, social relationships, and general adaptation to social life.

Whatever our thoughts are, they are generally the results of an urge or push. They are drives of what we are *feeling* in the now- mostly, discomfort, fear, want, desire, and safety. These *feelings* are literally *colored* energies in motion, and their parlance interpretation is *emotion*. Rarely are we ever fully conscious of our true energy source of surges, push, lows, and urges, unless we choose to make a deliberate and conscious effort to do so.

The regulated flow of emotion that runs through us consists of different ingredients in our core self-concepts' make-up or historical formation. They represent equilibrium in energy vibrations and frequencies which we have become accustomed to, worked-out ourselves, feel comfortable with, and are always the choices and things we believe to be right- however wrong we may be in the moment.

One frustration and failure after another in human response have taught cultures and civilizations everywhere, that the real reason why we are more often unsuccessful in most of our emotional response to people and things in the social and economic world of Nature and Nurture is because *emotional energy,* in and of itself, never permits adequate thought and reason to facilitate a successful response to most of the challenging problems of which social life itself poses for our comforts and desires.

Again, this is the main purpose and need for psychological development or the pursuit of education. Human emotions are blind, and most of the conscious ones which surface are directly linked to our learned and cultivated belief systems that individuals' and social groups adopted and use in our early socialization and stereotyping process. They are thus taken for granted because they are the easiest to recall and apply in just about every, and any given situation. And furthermore, they are socially acceptable.

Often times, emotional responses are inadequate, and they very seldom address the real changes we seek to bring about in our current orientations, owing mostly to the limited breadth it allows us in the understanding of anything. Whether the responses and reactions are right or wrong action, and however gutsy or wimpy- they are always the product and direct result of an individual's acquired belief system, accustomed, or habitual response, and are the very constructs gathered and assimilated by human thought in choice of forms.

ABOUT BELIEFS & BELIEF SYSTEMS

Individuals' and groups' beliefs and belief-systems are acquired every which way, and from any, or every possible source and circumstance in social life - whether they are experienced or not, true or false. Beliefs, which are generally grouped into belief systems, always serve as a reference index to correct or right contextual action for any individual or social group, upon reflection of their positive or negative consequences.

Beliefs and *belief-systems* are really enabling human mechanisms. Even though they may not match social reality, belief systems serve as the anchors to all human behavior response or reactions, nonetheless. They reflect the integrity, wholeness, solidity, and unity of an individual's or social group's mental form of organization at any moment, in response or reaction, in an ongoing, changing social world. "Each of us seeks a truth that is true for me," noted Soren Kierkegaard.

Beliefs, or a belief may also be defined as what the human brain interprets as *fact*- even if it is truly *fiction* or false, and can readily be proven by others in the know. "The power of belief is the power of hypnosis," states Doctor Maxwell Maltz. Therefore, it is no exaggeration to say that human beings are hypnotized to some extent by ideas repeated in culture, and without any careful thought or scrutiny accepted from others, or convinced by self to be true. As William James puts it: I believe because it is useful. Not necessarily true.

The ultimate test and use of all *beliefs* and *belief-systems* is their ability to get us all the things we want, wish, or desire in this world. So all the belief systems that we acquire, use, and create which does not match social reality, or the social reality we are seeking, are automatically crushed, and must be modified or abandoned to meet the demands of the real world. Any argument contrary to this expressed purpose and use of any form of *belief*, or *sets of beliefs* held by any individual or social group, is futile and useless.

The relative ease or pain we experience as we move out and about, interacting with others in meeting our needs are often propelled by temporary or expedient belief systems. They are temporary and expedient because they normally don't express our deeper and truer feelings or sentiments about things in general. Also, reasons often prevail where they- the temporary beliefs we hold, can be easily modified for convenience. So they should be properly grouped and labeled *get-along* belief systems. They represent the give-and-take in the errors and corrections of our individual orientations and perceptions about everything and anything in our daily routines.

In a situation where beliefs may be based on an insistence that the *truth* is what a person wishes or wants it to be, the believer opens his or her body-mind to the real *truth* only on condition that it fits in with his or her own preconceived ideas and wishes.

The more formidable belief systems that concern us here belong to our deepest emotional attachments, and they reflect the solidity of each person's individuality. In religious terms, they are interpreted as the *most sacred part of us*. You touch them you touch us. Even so, the rigors of social life demands that all beliefs or belief systems undergo change or modifications. And some of these formidable beliefs that we hold so dear, do undergo change, but they do so sluggishly, stubbornly, and often, very, very slowly. They are also subjected to be repeated in use, again and again, even after adverse consequences- for the sake of *meanings* that are felt to be irreplaceable, extremely difficult, or impossible to substitute.

In fact, the longest lasting and most difficult beliefs to remove, or to let go of- if ever, are those which belong to religions and ethnic group survival values. Since both religious and ethnic group's core values surrounds clusters of symbols and mythologies held dear, around which most of us are socialized in youth, to organize our lives accordingly, even after maturing into Adulthood. At best, both individuals, ethnic groups, and religious members, believe in their rituals and systems only because they are useful in fulfilling some of their basic needs.

In spite of this fact, we cannot knowingly and intentionally kid ourselves for too long. Can we?

A myth can only work when it is thought to be the truth, accompanied by reinforcements. Both religious and ethnic groups' hold of myths and symbols lose their power and action in individuals' and group members' thought processes and action when they are unable to provide the basic needs satisfaction they are seeking. Naturally.

Just as we humans are able to learn very rapidly, we can also unlearn at the same rate of learning, if not faster. When behavior reinforcements and rewards are ever-present, and there are re-curing successful response to re-curing challenging events in the social environment, these become the key elements in the maintenance of any form of *belief* or *belief-system*, be they favorable or aversive, temporary, expedient, or formidable in our individual relations to any form, person(s), structure, or human social organization that may hold them. Negative and painful experiences also speeds up learning or its avoidance. The most common response to social learning is that of voluntary attention deficit- what we choose to pay attention to.

The most important thing to know about *beliefs* and *belief-systems* is that they provide the means to act on something we individually value, desire, or believe to be true. It doesn't matter what it is we are acting on positively, negatively, or with indifference to. If we don't believe, we are not going to move, flinch, budge, or act by our free-will, unless we are persuaded, convinced by trickery, or there is a direct application of some form of threat, pain, or force.

As independent members and producers of society, laborers, workers, and partners to contracts, the most primary and formidable forms of our individual belief systems comes from, and is linked to the political and economic base of the nation state. If this isn't so, where else are we willing to live-out our lives, fulfill our wishes, goals, hopes, and desires? No matter where we roam or reside, all the values we attach our selves to are based in this external currency and merit, which is the political state itself.

Personal values we inherit, chose, or incorporate, may be related to our individual resistances, such as *what we are not willing to do.* However, in the avoidance of life-threatening situations, injuries, privation, pain, punishment, or death- all personal human values or beliefs are compromised. By contrast, the most stable and everlasting value, as well as a burden for most of humanity's population is *work;* its merits, and rewards.

As members of the American political state we subscribe to a dominant political belief system called *free enterprise.* Free enterprise, and rugged individualism that began in frontier days, onwards to the formation of states through conquests of territory; the near-dissolution of the Union between and among the enterprising emergent states, through the Civil War; along with repair, and eventual breakdown of this form of political, economic, and social system during the Great Depression.

These conditions paved the way to the making and forging of a new American belief system, around which millions of lives are now organized.

This organization of social life has become commonplace for more than 30% of the American population, who also have become dependent on their representative form of government to mitigate the burdens of its poorer classes, in which citizens have invested their *interests, values,* and *meanings* in social life, and over which they have come to exert very little control.

As civilized Americans, we are always dominated by economic imperatives, regardless of the forms of government we are subjected to. These are commands and demands of superior powers such as: political forces- specifically laws. Powers of industrial enterprise, interest groups, and social organizations that the few and privileged owns, and can control.

Alongside this population of superior physical resources and capital are unlimited pools of intellectual ability and knowledgeable resource from the poor and middle classes, vying for, and trying to wrest control of the more stable physical values and resources of the above superior powers of the political state, which are fundamentally social positions, income, property, and money.

The most primary of virtue, value, and meaning to social life that economic imperatives and political forces of the state generate is this kind of *ambition*. The word means an earnest desire for a person to achieve a goal of some significance, distinction, control, status, or power in relation to all others in work, duty, labor, profession or craft.

Both the political state and industries' visible, ruling, and predominantly dictating ambitions are the rewards of money or property, rank, status, prestige, popularity, and fame. All confer on how a person is treated; or the relative satisfaction and fulfillment a person may attain and can maintain in social life.

Symbolic illusions fostered in these realms, for the lesser in rank and resource, and for those in its eager pursuits and aspirations, attest to the tyrannical, vulgar, egregious, and sometimes vomitous mechanisms by which the powers of *ambition* and commercialized fantasies of the nation's heroics are weaved, pursued, and sustained with status dramatizations.

When dishonest, deceptive, and eager persons who attain visible ambitions of rank and status wield power over masses using vulgar means to achieve their ends, it becomes infectious. Anyone can pull it off. It trickles down to the lowest classes and category of people. This is a stark definition of the word *contagion*. A contagious something. Once they are aware of it, the mechanisms that the ascendant classes use then become means of justification for lower classes to take like brutal action toward their common social relations.

Notions of: follow the leader, everybody's doing it, feeling left behind and the generation of guilt, feeling stupid for not taking like action, are all controlling suggestions; creating vicious cycles of a justification system of survival, for the lesser in rank, resource, and social class. This is carried on in a controlling atmosphere of mistrust, cynicism, and active deception, where like-others are forced, pushed, conned, and tricked below their level of consciousness and awareness to cooperate.

CONSIDER THE REPRODUCTIVE CYCLE

Yes, society is indeed a cooperative enterprise. Individuals who are weak to meet the challenges of social life alone always gather and find new strength in, and through *herd life*. Sexual reproduction is the most basic of these cooperative enterprises. By contrast, sexual companionship, which is also on the same side of cooperative enterprise, is a personal relationship for the consensual fulfillment of mutual human needs; while reproduction bears the need for self-transcendence of obstacles in social life, especially for the poor, such as being mother, father, or parent; or to establish the most primary form of authority of public recognition, hope of coping with the future, and the acknowledgement of a complimentary identity.

There are a million and one "holier than thou" reasons why humans indulge themselves in reproductive sex. Definitely not the concern of this treatise.

Our births are deliberate plots by women (*mothers*), who decide or choose to carry on the biological process, with the nurture or existence of a father, who may or may not be the true sperm donor. Sexual reproduction is public, because it is governed, ruled, and dictated by purely selfish human interests. The mere existence of any human life covers all human concepts of *morality, sacredness,* and *ultimate reasons*. It is one of the main answers to the problems and ills of social life for many females- especially to poorer classes, presenting itself as final, and unchangeable to the vast majority of still ignorant humans.

In any case, the continuity of a pregnancy's inception is a self-chosen event that a female individual consciously participates in, presenting itself to her as *the answer* to the practical problems and miseries that social life presents to her as final. Can you believe this continuous idiocy in today's social world? Well, Yes.

The old taboo on abortion now enters the great epic of American nonsense, God, the bible, and every strain of human feces.

When it becomes urgent in late teens to prove that an individual can do something, that is to make and control something in the person's own way, and command recognition, the easiest place for a young female to turn to is Herr Cunt. Uterus. The occupation of a baby-maker is always available. All her fears and incompetence of measuring up to the outside world is masked or hidden there. The mysteries of individual evolution is cooked-up here. She goes through having the baby to prove her competency, assert her gender, gain attention, and feel immortal. Motherhood gives her a clear sense of identity.

This *deliberate free-choice*, from the time of a female's awareness of conception is now taken on and interpreted as something very natural, and yet mysterious, as by the creation of God, and should continue undisturbed, with reverence, and should not be aborted, in spite of whatever aversive conditions that confronts or may befall the parent, and more than likely will befall the child in its development, for lack of adequate resources and planning for its future. However queer or paradoxical this event may seem to you, this is the very beginning of our sense of morality.

Considering that our reasoning are direct results of what has been expressed, impressed, interpreted, and adopted by the human agency used in our thinking before performing an act, commonsense can tell us from the stage of civilization we are at today, that the time-consuming birth and development of a human individual, from fertilized egg to maturity, will never solve a persistent and pressing economic condition. Neither is this event unavoidable in the pursuits and acts of our sexual fulfillment, spiritual worship, and creative output in social life.

In predominantly lower classes of culture, as in pre-industrial times, the reproduction of children represented capital, a natural source of labor, sacrifice, and the perpetuation of the institution of poverty. The compulsion of females from poor families make up the majority of women preoccupied with their reproductive powers. apart from the ritualized behavior of caring for the young, opportunities for gaining satisfaction within the system are governed by individuals' and families' ranking order, where the regulative agencies of social life for development is brute strength and physical prowess, rather than intellectual development.

In this din, the weaker must wait their turn or develop superior undermining skills to secure resources from another, in their common relations, or the formal social system. Where a Social Security System does not exist, such as what has been instituted in the United States since 1935, children are looked upon as labor security for the parents' old age.

PATHOS- THE PERPETUAL CON JOB

Human birth is one basic form of individual cooperative willfulness, and selfish crime against others in society. It is committed by females who make themselves successful as mothers- thus, we have motherfuckers. The first form of authority, ambition, and criminal behavior.

The events of human prenatal care, birth, and subsequent developments to individual control, carry an ingrained human logic that is very seldom denied, or cannot be questioned. This logic carries our deepest feelings of sympathy and compassion-for. It affects that part of our psychic make-up which holds a privileged position in our decision-making. The Greeks long ago discovered this human phenomenon to be unfavorable to the expressions of *truth,* calling it *pathos.*

All our deepest feelings of *mortality* or *moral rightness* and *righteousness* come from the affectations of, or on our pathos from both the human, and non-human environment. Affectations of our *pathos* has always been the main ingredient in all religion, politics, brainwashing, propaganda, and irrational authority. We are literally, and always moved by: pity-for, compassion-for, the sorrows of our own sufferings, and humanity's.

Things are made sacred and holy by pathos, and are cherished with a pre-established preference and faith. It is always thought to be wrong in questioning or trying to verify its grounds of belief or origin. The affect of our individual or collective *Pathos* produces absolute guilt, which is psychic pain; and considers anything which excites or stimulates it as having a privileged position for action.

Pathos' coercive force on individuals' or social groups' conscience comes through the influence of popularity in disapproval of telling the truth. Formal declarations by authorities that are routinely dictated to the masses- even if false, must preclude verification.

Scrutiny from greater publics must be masked, or obscured. Model jocks, manias, illustrious illusions, and attractions of grandeur, selected data, visual aids, and meaningless information or tasks, considered as *important* are the tools of deception used to prevent a circumstance of truth, or to circumvent truth about a matter that a person or a group of persons wish to deny. All assaults are directed to the human pathos to affirm the denial of, or to deny the affirmation of any course of meaningful action, directly addressing an issue.

This pattern of management of our perceptions that largely includes active deception, discontinuity, distortions, crucial omissions, and false hope in all communication systems often drive masses of people to chase the *devil* of vain consumption. It is weaved with, and in the vein of our pathos. Whatever its affects, It is often pursued, and taken to be the *real thing*. These are the Illusions and chimeras of hope, fulfillment, success, and satisfaction- constantly redistributed and remodeled to the masses of people through advertisements, TV shows, and movies-or the great pretenders of Hollywood, living in a vicious place called *hell*.

We know the beginning of hell, which are the myths and mythologies our parents sewed in us, with all their utmost best of intentions. And now we are still sewing them in our own kids. And our kids will more than likely sew it in theirs, ad infinitum.

At the very sight of anything that looks like *gold,* the unaware, ignorant, lesser in rank, and eager seekers of status and ambition, rush to grab a piece of it. To keep the wheels of attractions and illusions of ambition turning, the *fools' gold* or *devil* chased are the endless replenishments of the bombardment of the same vain, banal, empty, and meaningless symbols and images of attraction fostered by producers of audio, visual, digital, and synesthesia effects to consume, or to purchase goods that are masks and impressions of the gold that implies: sacred compatibility, ideal impressions, and dramatic dominance- with explosives, guns, and bombs available on the internet, if necessary.

Again, we believe because it gives us satisfaction, consolation, hope, and significance- even if only for the moment; since it is the necessities of survival which determines human instincts. Instincts in turn determine drives or desires; drives or desires determine thought. Whatever attracts us is what we will choose to notice. Further, the first top grab or hold on our attention is whatever seems advantageous for our own individual survival. Or that which we have become immediately concerned about. Intelligent choice becomes the sole determinant of quality social life.

According to one clear pattern of individual and group behavior observation, *hell* is not timeless everlasting damnation, it is rather "...the unbroken cycle, continuity, and frustration of going round and round in pursuit of something which can never be attained."

Hell is fatuity, or fucking complacent stupidity- "the everlasting impossibility of self-love, self-consciousness, and self-possession." When we are in hell, we feel disconnected from our own humanity. We must always be aware and vigilant of the many forms of con jobs played off on our pathos.

THE STATE

Over and over again, we have seen that whatever we want or desire for ourselves can only be realized and actualized through our relation to the whole state- and mainly industry that provides work, along with the observance of laws or social rules made by government to regulate our behavior towards one another. A simple four-dimensional tier may define our state: the first dimension comprises the real wealth of the nation, which owns and controls all major industries that the majority in the population depend on for mere subsistence or survival. They are also the most powerful influential dictators of the political state, simply because of the concentrations of their influence and real wealth.

All institutional and administrative management positions, salaried or unsalaried, political, industrial, educational, or religious, may now fall into the second category. The third dimension includes quasi or lower level management, and all other lower ranking people with property and income from work, labor, or private enterprise, commonly called middle-class.

Today, the fourth dimension are the vast majority of apartment renters. Not property owners.

Most people within a state will organize their lives around a few ideas, practices, and values which cannot be questioned nor challenged without disruption. Ambitious social positions, power relations, and statuses of preference are credited for the distribution of wealth, proper management of resources, property, capital, profession, and the regulation of social life by direct or indirect force of their communal rules.

Values of ascendant classes and category of people act as a directive for action. They become or serve as an attraction and influence for individual conduct, or to orient and channel group action. It is here, that we as individuals, social grouping, or society feels its sense of unity-subordination, or adherence to common values- values that give us assurance, predictability, hope, certainty, or refuge where we can find transitory or lasting peace. Something we call *real*. For example, virtually everyone will defer to persons of superior competence in any given field of knowledge or expertise, or in cases that they virtually know nothing of, or are incompetent in handling.

Desire for recognition in terms of these values makes it possible to reward or punish behavior. That is, we adapt ourselves to the conditions that holds the prospect of the fulfillment of our basic needs satisfaction. So we habituate and conform ourselves to these rules, conventions, rituals, restrictions, and power relations within a form of the whole social order.

However, the vast majority of the values we adapt from this ascendant class in society today are seriously misleading. Individual and group success in rank and statuses conferred upon ambition that have become a given in society are deliberately skewed or warped, to produce illusions that any who, who has attain such positions, really does have the *right stuff*.

Whether persons are naturally born into the situation, justly attained by merit, attained by deception, hook, or cookery- everything the successful person does, who has attained the visible status of ambition, will now more than likely be advertised, publicized, trivialized with importance, emulated or worshiped by the lesser in rank and status, the uninformed ignorant; and impersonated with idealization of the given status attained or displayed.

The more enlightened we become of such personages, the less

meaningful these devils become. A depreciation in value when they do not serve our purpose. We have already penetrated the mysteries of their commercial value. It is now up to us, looking up to *them*, to continue to adopt to their standards, reject them, or break-away and introduce our own. Dissention is a dynamism inherent in our nation's constitutional make-up. The real fight for betterment of our individual social worlds.

But I must still keep the peace!

We, the innocent, uninformed, ignorant, or hypnotized, are led to the guillotine every time these social models of the state- political, business, religious, scientific, and entertaining men and women, lose their meaningfulness. A new competing dynamo must now be injected into the psyche of the social and industrial economic system of illusions and delusions. This pattern of Americanization has been the very cause and nature of break downs, and the frequent loss of hope, *meaning,* and *values* around which native born and socialized American citizens structure our social lives.

Because most of these meanings and values are acquired from the public which precedes our evolution into society, breakdowns of any magnitude are proportionate, and a direct result of the practices of the ascendant classes of individuals, families, and groups, who enjoy the status of social preeminence, around which majority of the members of the greater population have come to identify with, invest, and organize their lives. Most breakdowns are biologically psychological, and fundamentally economic.

General causes can be readily traced to those who chose to perpetuate and augment their dominance, stay of wealth, or rule of authority, at the expense of others- and at any possible cost. The greatest cost to the general public is deception. A kind of *survival of the fittest* mentality. The very opposite of the supreme values of cooperation, discourse, and comity. If citizens are to recapture their sense of mission which survival demand, then leaders of the nation and state at every level must have the vision and capacity to act and articulate those values.

TOWARD A SYSTEM OF COMPASSION

A monumental example here of not following the patterns set by predecessors and rulers of the state was set by Franklin Delano Roosevelt, a wealthy concerned citizen in 1932, who saw and felt the grueling cries of failure, grief, ruin, want, and fears of *worst things to come* from the general citizenry, about the nation's condition. He led a socio-economic campaign that called for a complete "re-appraisal of values," by the United States government.

Declaring that "the country needs bold persistent experimentation," and that the first duty of the state or government is "to promote the welfare of its citizens." He advocated the implementation of a new American ideology, and system that fostered altruistic behavior. ("Stretching the constitution" just the way Thomas Jefferson did in the *Louisiana Purchase*), this was the new tenet of belief that was to be injected into the veins of the new form of American governance. An expanded sharing of the nation's sovereign authority among its citizens. A concept of active liberty.

In summary of the events that precipitated breaking down of the original form of governance of the American economic system as a direct cause, we see that from its most nascent stages of formation, its owners, captains, and managers of industries before the years of 1935, never gave a hoot, and neither did the working political ideology demand that they should give a hoot, about an individual's or family's fate or welfare, should accidents, injuries, sickness, or death befall them as employees, laborers, or wage earners, throughout its early industrial boom years. The boom years of early American industrialization were the direct outgrowth and developments of predominantly small independent producers, and little cottage industries that blanketed the landscape with early settlers and the slave industry.

In fact, throughout the transition years, when majority of the population were fast becoming factory industrial workers, and laborers, and tried to organize themselves for acquiring the compassion of altruism, adopted and advocated by Roosevelt, for their welfare from private industry, the US government often took an active role in defending industry's rights with led and gunpowder, against the demands of their employees, laborers, or wage-earners.

Steven Swazo

Government's hands off (*laissez faire*) operational policies toward business and industries, up to the last days of Hoover's Presidency, allowed unprecedented individual and corporate accumulation of wealth; while the thwarting of workers' demands for adequate compensation in sharing the wealth they helped generated, allowed too much of it to fall into too few hands. And with the federal government refusing to give direct aid to the unemployed and impoverished, productive capacities of business and industries raced ahead of their buying power, creating a chronic national problem of under-consumption that speeded up a downward spiral in the national economy.

Manufacturers closed plants, suppliers, and middlemen en masse went out of business, millions of workers were laid off or out of work. Small independent farmers and business ventures that were dependent on trade with larger business concerns and industries, as well as the local public consumption of their products, goods, and services in the *free market* system were also left crippled and helpless, as banks closed, and the economic political system cracked under the strain.

The rest of the decade of the mid-nineteen thirties was confined to wrangling with social forces and experimenting with several socio-economic models, to remedy the nation's acute and mass breakdown of its economic political system of *meanings* and *values* in which its citizens had invested their social lives.

Only in light of this historical situation can the monumental impact of the great American Depression on its people, the subsequent frequent loss of hope and courage, being and living in it, can be understood as the fundamental, newly instituted traditional footing for the current political state of the United States we are living in today, commonly called a welfare state.

World is the pattern of meaningful relations in which a person exist, structure social life, and is the design in which he or she participates. To those who were hard-hit at this base by the incidents which precipitated the Great Depression, it was a terrifying breach with reason and sanity, since it had plunged human lives into virtually helpless chaos, nationwide. The New Deal political action that went into effect for the American people, and subsequent changes, became the main content of a new *national hope, meaning,* and *value* for the masses, brought about through the highest level of joint human action, or antagonistic cooperation reaching amicable solutions.

Education and learning have been stressed here as our most basic tool, and most basic value in our self-development. It is the critical faculty we attain by reading, experiencing, probing, experimenting, correcting, inventing, manipulating, and doing; telling us to act by logic, or analytical judgment, experience, training, experiments, and practice. This serves as our only guarantee against deception, delusions, superstitions, blind faith, and false hopes. This is the faculty that protects us from harmful suggestions; holding everything open to unlimited verification and revision. Doing this as a habit is called *science*.

The presence of meanings and values in our awareness prompts us to take or not take action. On the other hand, *truths* or *meanings*, no matter what they are or how they come to us, challenge our social world assumptions and mold them by their forces. While we must continuously yield to truths, their handling, usage, and meanings must be based on intelligent choices.

One man's trash may be another's diamonds. And literally so, since any random individual self-world is always in search of vital missing pieces for wholeness, and for continuous fulfillment of basic needs satisfaction, or the expansion of one's outer self. Whatever these things or usable materials are that we seek or pursue, they are the vitality that make us wholesome, solvent, and creatively virile.

Meanings and values are used and cultivated within wide boundaries. Their boundaries reflect their anchors within a state, which are vast and elastic. They do not occur in a vacuum. They are absorbed every which way, and from every which source. Meanings and values are everything to everyone. And they are all that an individual or collective group of people exist or live for in all walks of social life. Again, when strived for and accomplished, we experience fulfillment and satisfaction.

Besides death of the individual, the political state, which encompass the outer boundaries of our social lives, and which we will be coming to be more familiar with for the remainder of this book, defines our ultimate boundary of growth and development in choice, creation, or the production of artifacts; while the greatest good and meaning of any individual self-development and personality orientation in the political state is when it is in communion with others. This is easier said than done, since change dissolves meaning, violates our roadmaps and plans, bringing about loss and uncertainties.

Local, state, and national administrators, leaders of industry, education, and human health have a significant role in creating our states of mind, since they constitute the ascendant ruling classes of society. They can serve as a moral unity, or as disintegration of it by expressing, or not expressing the core millennial values which holds us or the nationt together. Here, it is the United States Constitution, a sharing of sovereign authority originating in every voter, or member of the community.

3

OUR HOME BASE/INTERPRETATIONS
OF THE ANCESTORS' STAND

O UR HOME BASE REVOLVES AROUND interpretations of the ancestor's constitutional scheme. Fundamental American beliefs in Christianity evolved from the history of Protestantism, confirming beliefs of the Reformation Movement, that free encounter of anybody with the *bible* can create conformity to a social order of mutual respect. Denominational differences, ethnicity, or group membership did not matter. Individuals were not expected to respond to conformity based on biblical revelation. Beliefs and assumptions were expected to be based on the power of individual reason, providing faith, hope, meaning, and lasting values.

Conceptions and blueprints for the republic that was to be formed, when some measure of peaceful settlement was afforded, was in direct contradiction to the tyranny of medieval European and Asian rule that dominated *Old* World civilizations, with the ideal of social relations being *benevolent domination and dutiful submission*. This break was a radical departure in finding new freedoms in the intelligent expressions and use of human energies. The ancestors' clearest ideal model society was to set up a *norm of reciprocity*. Their pre-visions of this new form of political domination were to be realized through the establishment of contracts bound by agreements.

The norm of reciprocity implies that people expect exchanges in all their affairs with others to be just and fair. Recognizing that practically every conceivable law has been passed to safeguard man and woman kind from doing harm to each other, they subscribed to a master body-mind.

This was the coordination of knowledge and effort, in a spirit of harmony, between two or more dissimilar people for the attainment of a definite purpose. The norm of this master body-mind must prevail in all actions of their common interests and relations, with no boundaries to rank or social class ascendance. Their pre-visions preferred this form of justice to forever serve as the basis for the new social order.

With the norm of reciprocity as their ideal, the free exchange of *goods* and *services* will automatically establish bonds of friendship, and create relationships of submission, competition, and domination. This social inequality is favorable and practical in all the transactions of daily social life.

Rewards derived from economic relations and social interactions become important to participants, and may even lead them to sustain such interaction even after they no longer provide concrete rewards in an un-equal relationship. By contrast, that all humans should be equal in social ranking and class, in all the essentials of social life, is contrary to the laws of human nature. It is just the same as saying that no two people are identically alike in their needs and energies, nor equal in social values.

The norm of reciprocity implies an atmosphere or context of cooperation where competition can thrive. It takes into consideration that conflict, or conflicting interests are normal, and are due to the direct outgrowth of our differing individual needs and perceptions in our apprehensions of, and dealing with social reality. So are the activities of exchange and production in goods and services, they automatically lead to inequality in the distribution of rewards such as wealth, money, or property, that results from the eventual competition or quality in talent, and energies invested, or expended for their production or acquisition.

Because every action of every human being springs from a desire which an individual considers being *good,* and to avoid something which is *undesirable,* competition becomes the direct outgrowth of exchange as a result of *choices* we make in the consumption of *goods* and *services* within an economic norm of benign or antagonistic cooperation and competition, owing to diverse and varying interests.

Antagonistic cooperation seems to be the highest value and virtue in any human society. Since it is vested in the organization of the political state and all its other industrial social institutions and organizations; and is based on the free or mutual exchange of goods and services, as well as the redistribution of wealth. *Competition* on the other hand, which is often considered the opposite of *cooperation,* is reconciled in arbitrary transactions between two or more competing parties who can agree or disagree on a set price, standard, or rate of exchange as being just or reasonable. In fact, it is competition that allows for the atmosphere of cooperation.

For example, a potential customer or buyer needs a product, and prefers to pay a modest or low nominal price. A producer or seller of the *good, service,* or product on the other side wants the highest return possible for his or her goods, product, or services, which may give rise to disagreement, arguments, bargaining, or the prospect of another seller or producer of the same kind or type of *good(s)* or *service*(s). To avoid the outcome of argument, conflict, or hostility over pricing, or the qualities of goods or services, makes way for a neutral or friendly relationship with another competing or enterprising person, offering the same product and service at any potential customer's desirable rate or price.

This competition and cooperation is the practical manifestation of human beings with differing interests carrying on their normal business affairs, arriving at a balance in their transactions and social relationships. The political ancestors' pre-visions of this form of New *World* contract and reciprocal norm domination was augmented with a consent to be ruled or governed by *just laws,* that they create in their relations to each other, and to which everyone in the population would eventually be subjected.

These were the property owners, private investors, and others hoping to be property owners and private investors themselves. Laws would be made and administered by representatives directly, or indirectly by the population to protect the interests of all. The nation-state would be a government by law, with clearly defined rules of the game.

The Declaration of Independence penned by Jefferson, and the United States *Constitution* by the Constitutional Convention that ended in 1788, wholeheartedly embraced this spirit of Enlightenment that had already became a part and parcel of the people's free-spiritedness and conquests in their enterprising undertakings. The United States Constitution then became the form and ruling set-up of government, or master body-mind that would now serve as an impersonal restraint upon human beings prone to error.

Representatives must be allowed to use their fragments of authority over the greater masses of free enterprising individuals. And here were summaries of the ancestors plan, according to several sources of historical interpretations: Federal, State, County, City, and Town governments must be set-up as *servants* of the people, rather than *master*, and must be kept that way.[1]

Internalizing the principles of John Locke, that we are ruled by our common consent through our allegiances and submission to the common social order, the state in turn owing each individual citizen justice in same and equal measure, by protecting and safeguarding the rights of life, liberty, and property- from their diverse national origins and ethnic group backgrounds, they agreeably declared in one language:

We are voluntarily giving you- the state representatives- a monopoly of the use of *force* or *power*. This force or power should not be used in a manner that interferes with the constructive activities of the free enterprising citizen that is non-injurious to others. And From their experience and enlightened factual historical knowledge, fears and dangers of dictatorships of any sort must be held in check, or avoided for all times to come.

All up and down the line, it has got to be a government that rules by the *reasons* of *law* enacted by the people, and not by whim or violence. Business must be run according to the rules of the game. No one individual or small group of persons must ever be permitted to get too much power. And the minority, down to the lowest status of an individual citizen, must be protected against oppression or tyranny by the majority of any pressure group.[2]

SELF DISCIPLINE

The ancestors' whole idea of government set-up was to protect freedoms of the individual citizen, not only from outsiders, but also from people in

---

[1] Henry Grady Weaver: The mainspring of Human progress.
[2] Ibid.

public office. Legal restraints that encompass the passing of laws to be administered by government agencies and enforced by its local agents are useful in curbing activities which are clearly injurious and opposed to the best interest of all. Written laws however, are no adequate substitute for individual self-discipline and moral restraints, based on our enlightened self-interest.

Why?

Self-discipline amply demonstrates that without a clear, logical, and workable plan, we are not likely to achieve anything desirable, worthwhile, or meaningful in social life. Self-discipline calls for the control of our anger, frustrations, unfulfilled longings, and rage. To be obedient to the laws of *Nurture,* which are the written and unwritten communal rules of the social order, is to be able to accommodate, sometimes make sacrifices for others, as others have done or pledged for us.

The fundamental purpose that all self-discipline serve is to let adequate reason, calculated risks, awareness, and alternatives, dominate our entire emotional response and reaction to everything that is happening around us- whether we want them to, or don't want them, like, or disgust them with the utmost of fear or repulsion. Self-discipline seeks understanding-to bring every quirk in, and out of human feelings, thoughts, and actions into awareness and existing focus.

Combined with memory and forethought, self-discipline sets in motion a willingness to learn, understand, and respond spontaneously and responsibly. The objective struggle in this understanding is to facilitate growth and adequate response, attain and maintain harmony, or friendly relations with our community or environment. Our individual right to differ or disagree with government, family members, other persons, or social groups is all a part of this understanding and undertaking which comes through self-discipline. Dissent is an inherent dynamism in the United States constitution.

We give our allegiances to trust because we tacitly understand certain processes, in that our expectations will be met, such as in a routine bureaucratic process. On the most common level, *trust* is vested in an organized set of normative values and standards governing individual behavior, common to a social group, institution, or groups of people sharing common economic bonds within the social order in a locale or community.

This social bond exists within contracts and consensus in the structure of our own lives, in the environments that we have become habituated to. It is a result of our interaction with the various elements of necessities and amenities of social life; our personal histories, and the relations we have come to establish, through consumption and exchange with competing and other enterprising families and individuals.

There is a deeper trust which pertains to the universal social feeling, embracing all of humanity. We believe it to be part of, and vested in the United States Constitution, which implies and commands a state of cooperative or mutually tolerable relations, between and among people of similar and dissimilar ethnic groups, customs, habits, tastes, likes and dislikes; hates, and contentions.

The constitution that the average citizen believes in, and subscribe to, are the traditional practice of environment consensus within the person's conscious lifetime, and not so much literally the constitution of the United States' overt behavior interpretations by leaders of the state, such as judges, political representatives, educators, and the most influential people that provide the assumptions, beliefs, and values in which some of us interpret, and make sense out of social life and the social world around us.

Whether the Declarations of Independence and the United States Constitution are original or revised forms of older, unpublished declarations or constitutions, matters not. They are like any other declarations of self-discipline or moral principles guiding human behavior. That is, they are no stronger than the will of the people alive- whom are its individual citizens, to respect, honor, and uphold them.

Each must have goals which in their eyes merits effort and commitment, and they must believe that their efforts will win them self-respect and the respect of others, as voters, consumers, or source of public opinion. This inspires faithfulness and performance from members of society who give their allegiances to the whole constitution.

The *state* is called a government, but it cannot actually govern the individual without his or her own internalized conscience of loyalty and allegiances; also because of the nature and use of individual human energy. Individuals and social groups regulate themselves according to internalized symbolic loyalties to the whole constitutional scheme's environment as they actually see, perceive, and live with it, with radically diverse interpretations, and with absolutely no understanding of its actual wording; In the face of disappointments, losses, or rage, with varying commitments to keep the public peace.

Tacit meanings, or in this sense, *interpretations* are direct causal results of tradition, learning, and habituation, or being accustomed-to. "I feel comfortably at home, and worry-free, with such and such status quo, some law passed, or some state representative such as the President, a Senator, governor, or Congress person," would be the response of some ordinary citizen to any random question about his or her political stand- even if the status quo is non-existent in the perceived form, it ought to be, and is, this or that way.

It is my humble opinion. And I am worried. Or, I ain't worried bout nothing!

No matter how, or in what context each individual may interpret his or her situation, it is still a definition of part of the whole American constitutional condition. How these diverse interpretations of the nation's constitutional scheme are meted out for each person's self- fulfillment and actualization comprise the issues and conflicts of the day.

In all of societies' institutional arrangements and organization of social life, they are taken up in aggregates as *growth issues* by the nation's formal and informal ruling body of official and industrial administrators. These growth issues of *conflict* are often regulated through rules and laws to avoid encroachments, simply because conflicts are the living results of mutual exchange, differing interests, and perceptions in desires, needs, investments, and growth.

The resolutions of our diverse conflicting interests are gains in capital, spiritual, and inspirational lessons of progress that make up the self-correcting refinements of culture. However, the methods and means we individually and collectively use are always subject to scrutiny; and often arouse deep-seated resentments, or a clash with legal laws of local, state, or federal government.

On the other hand, legal laws' encroachment on enlightened

self-interest, or the expression of personal freedoms, (which often give rise to conflict) with concern for the affairs or rights of others, takes emphasis away from personal responsibility; promoting dangerous notions that legalized force can be used as a substitute for self-control, self-discipline, or individual moral restraints.

Encroachments by law enforcement agents of the state, or the irresponsible behavior of industrial enterprise, without adequate redress, now sets the stage for reckless daring, protest, or in criminal parlance, *civil disobedience* by those ensnared or caught-up in such web of basket-weaving, appealing to have their personal rights recognized.

When you get right down to it, any form of government is nothing more than a legal monopoly of the discretionary use of physical force by persons upon persons. And this monopoly is permitted only by common consent, consensus, and economic support of the people.

As individuals and social groups find new ways to define outer limits of their freedoms, boundaries that were originally drawn by rule of law, custom, or tradition are ignored, changed, nullified, or are routinely not enforced.

THE COURTS

The United States *Courts* serves as the voice of the Constitution, establishing ultimate boundaries of its basic structure of government, and comprise written sets of rules on how to control its conduct. In the construction's own wording, the United States' Constitution is "the Supreme Law of the Land."[3]

While the legislative body of government that changes the rules of these fundamental laws by which we must play, (which is the Senate and Congress), represent that combination of groups, industries, and institutions that makes a majority on a rule of law or issue; It is the Supreme

---

[3] Kurland Philip

Courts' Justices who do the *Constitution's* interpretations according to their fairness, integrity, and equity.[4]

These ascendant class positions have been awarded to a discrete minority of justices. While the motions of corporate or industrial interests (which are often concocted emotions well-thought out and mobilized for public acceptance) over legitimate concerns citizen's and the intelligent publics are driven by political interests, must serve for the courts considerations and decisions. Because they are so in the normal state of affairs, they pose an ever-present threat to the *court's* authority and its commitment to render impartial justice. According to Stephen Beyer, "agreement or disagreement about the wisdom of a law has nothing to do with the right of a majority to embody their opinion in law... (*Active Liberty*, Beyer Copy. 2005).

Former Justice Felix Frankfurter who worked diligently with Franklin D. Roosevelt for social reform, was looked upon as a hero and sort of a "a strict constitutionalist" by peers and fellow justices. He had referred to the *Supreme Court* as the symbol of American preference for *law* over *force* as a means, and the ruling mechanism for resolving conflicts that burdens society, basic to our way of individual social life, and fundamental in our nation's constitutional scheme.

Summarizing the inscriptions on Thomas Jefferson's headstone, his voice of dissent and hate for irrational authority, which is literally *emotion* over the *life of reason*, or *force* over law, resonates: despots and legal law encroachment shenanigans by those who wish to empower themselves at the brutal expense of others "should have no place of rest, but a life of torture and restlessness under this grand constitutional scheme."

Frankfurter noted that: the Constitution "...must epitomize *reason* rather than *emotion* in helping seek justice. ...Above all, it must emphasize individual interests against the stamp of governmental paternalism and conformity..." Commenting on our sense of conformity to our own free-spiritedness, he continued: "It is the *faith* that neither principalities nor powers, nor things present, nor things to come, can rightfully suppress that fertility or deny that good. It is the *faith* in the indefectible significance of each one of us." [5]

Reason is the substance by which the human universe develops. And

---

[4] Ibid
[5] Kurland Philip: The Constitution

as humans, we put our faiths and trusts in just about every conceivable goddamn thing! Not only this, we could find damn good reasons anytime, for any course of action we choose or wish to take!

And believe it or go nuts, these are the *real reasons* that give value and meaning to our social lives. These reasons and beliefs are often in the defense and affirmation of our individual selves and beliefs in the face of all obstacles, threats, adversity, perceived danger, or insecurity.

In other words, according to Justice Frankfurter, the life of reason of the sovereign state under the constitution, must base itself according to the principles of science, because the works of science itself contains all trustworthy knowledge. *Science* is logic, and is the art of correct thinking- against anybody's wishes or desires.

The most satisfying and challenging fact is that science does not, and cannot pretend to be true in any absolute sense. It does not, and cannot pretend to be final either. It is something like the tentative organization of a hypothesis stating that for the present, all known relevant facts have been accounted for. So there is no intention to stay satisfied with some final body or sufficient number of facts. It is open end. There is to be only a continuing search for more, as an individual's body-mind that is eager to grow. This growth, as long as it lasts is the true measure of man and womankind.

In our causal thinking our brains make connections with people, places, and things- whether they are there or not there. The beliefs we hold influence our perceptions, thinking, and social feelings. The methods of science were specifically designed to weed them out.

A scientific law describes some action in Nature or Nurture that can be tested. It is the description of a regulatory or repeating action that is open to rejection or conformation. While the description of event or events is in our heads, the repeating action happens in Nature or Nurture itself. The tests we make confirms or rejects them as a law or general rule.

Hard science is based on *good* evidence- meaning, it is observable, precise, and is independent of anyone's wishes, hopes, faiths, wants, desires, meaning, or value system from the context in which it occurs, or meanings attached to the thing or event by the social actors involved.

By contrast, the logic or reason of *common law* is observed custom in sequence and circumstance of events, that always present multiple causal factors which must be brought into consideration where a decision, choice, or conclusion would be reached, based on the preponderance of evidence within generalized boundaries, necessitated by our use of the element *time* in establishing validity of a claim, from *cause* to *effect*.

It is precisely within these generalized boundaries that the life of reason as a scientific enterprise or dictatorship over the masses is reduced to a serviceable moral commodity.

TIME & CLOSURE- THE BOUNDARIES

No human structure, organization, or enterprise in society can exist without the arbitrary use of the element *time* as a base factor or boundary. Our use of time as a necessity or necessary element weighs heavily in everything we do throughout our entire social lives. Our biological body-minds function and respond appropriately because of its dependence on the regulatory (or timely) use of kinetic energy, which is coded information absorbed from the surrounding environment. It is our individual use and conservation of this energy, encoded in a time- release framework, which determines our response and reactions in adaptation. When to work, eat, sleep, fart or shits.

All human energies are organized into an intelligible time-release media form for application in routine living demands. In turn, all societies demand intelligibility of this media-form response from its citizens, which each individual create and produce. This intelligibility is found in our every-day conversations.

Communication is not an individual affair. It is always communal. We are not hermits, but live in a society of other people where we must be understood in whatever it is we say or do, in some recognizable form or pattern, and in the contexts of our communal existence. A six or eight-hour day's work is organized labor, and may also be expected of every adult or child attending school.

These patterns, forms, and contexts are what we refer to as *life concepts.* Concepts are the building blocks of culture. They represent abstract ideas about our physical relations. Concepts are ideas expressed as symbols or words in a particular language. We create them from our individual experiences, induction, creative thoughts, observations, and inferences. The putting together of intelligible concepts is an undertaking and understanding that is always based on *time* and consensus, and is continuous- specifically to guarantee meaningfulness.

I must allot time for work for gainful means. I must allot time for play. I must allot time for re-creation. I must allot time for my child. I must allot time for whatever it is that I take-up to make my social life wholesome. Concepts of *time* are forms and patterns of interaction used within the confines of society's organizations and institutions, beginning with family life. I cannot escape use of the element *time* inside or outside my private or conscious public existence. By this token, we are all constrained by the material tools, cultural contexts, and historical conditions- all organized in a framework of *time* in which we find ourselves.

The very process we employ in the organization of our thoughts involves the conscious use of *time* as a prime factor. How much time are you gonna spend thinking about this crap? Is it worth the time? And therefore, the human focus is always on the intelligent use and conservation of kinetic energy as a *time-release* factor.

In the processes of thought organization and energy conservation, we automatically enter the concept of *closure*, where we are forced to edit, stop, and leave things out. We have considered, and thought about the situation enough. No need to think about that anymore. Our course of action is to do, or not do before the day is over.

The concept of *closure* means that even if we are not satisfied with our status quo, things must settle as they are- at least for the time being. We must forget, or put them aside in order to facilitate something else in the hierarchy of our momentary or pressing needs, which may be much more important, and requires our immediate attention. One undeniable feature and physical definition of *time* is *body-mind fatigue*- felt from thinking, acting, working, or doing. Exhaustion from prolonged use of kinetic energy.

Whatever tentative settlements or conclusions we may reach about anything or anybody; they, or it can be equated with, and may be considered the same thing as a *decision* or *judgment*. Whenever any single one of us reach this state of affairs in closure, in our allotment or use of the element *time*, the basic underlying assumption is that we have allowed or considered sufficient information from all possible and relevant sources (in the use and maintenance of our emotional balance) to enter into our perceptions for evaluation, in order to make a relatively accurate decision, judgment, or irrevocable choice of action.

Our use and need for the abstract elements *time* and *closure* are inescapable. Our understanding and use of the concept *science* emphasize this tentative closure on what must be done, but open to further investigations.

SCIENCE & JUSTICE (IN THE BODY OF TIME)

Just as we can execute a perfect decision based on an accurate relevant body of information; we can also do the same, based on a totally erroneous, inaccurate, and misleading body of information. These decisions, conclusions, or judgments are possible, logical, and scientifically sound in any case- but only, and *only* when these conclusions are based on incidents or events demonstrating *cause* to *effect*, or the *preponderance of evidence* within their generalized time boundaries. All human generalizations presupposes a condensation of time allotted for things.

Objectively, scientifically, and mathematically speaking, 1+1 =2, 0+0 = 0, and we may say that the value of "2" is made of symbols and elements of attachment that belongs to the element "1."

We can also say that the number "2" symbolize a person who definitely committed a crime or violation of law, while the numerical value of "1" may now be conveniently put as *presence, influence, behavior* and *consumption,* or the use of symbols and tools that adds to the actual commission of crime or violation of law. The first number 1, may be interpreted in a criminal equation as presence of person, while the other whole number (1) is usually comprised of twenty or more pieces, such as: .5 for outward behavior, .2 for use of artifacts, .190 for former state of mind, .12 for gender, point yay, yay, yay for ethnic group identity, and so on, as endless pieces of evidence adding up to, or supporting the other part of whole number one. When combined with the other (person in presence), they produce the identity of 2, the criminally accused.

According to our national constitutional Bill of Rights, the constitutional rights of "2" the accused, which is a definite person brought to trial in our justice system, even though presumed *guilty* right away, "2" must be considered innocent by the *courts* until otherwise proven guilty, according to the court's basic logic.

The fundamental task of an ethical justice or ethical system is to provide a standard of means for the resolution of conflicts between individual interests and public welfare, self, and others. Since the interest of one conflicts with the other, without principles superordinate to the conflicting selves, issues would be otherwise settled by violence or brute force.

On account of this widespread potential action by publics, the United States' *Courts* are willing to consider virtually any kind of individual contention, beef, or dispute presented to it in search for fairness or justice, for violation of its written laws, or the constitutional rights of another, as a matter of routine in their duties and function. These contentions, disputes, and violations often involve and pertain to individual civil liberties or environmental security.

Based on the hypothetical example of 1+1 for a decision or ruling to be made on guilt in the commission of a crime, the courts must be persuaded about the whole circumstance and the objective characterization of 2, based on evidence and consensus. On account of this, decisions of justice meted out according to principles of the Constitution and the individual balance of Civil Rights in society can yield the most vexing, paradoxical, and provocative social feelings. For a moment, consider the moral behavior or ethics of an attorney called upon to represent and defend his or her client- even if mister 2 the accused is really guilty:

I must do everything that is legally and ethically permissible to win every case. As a lawyer, I must try to prevent- by lawful and ethical means- the truth, the whole truth from coming out, if that would be harmful to my client.

I must use tactics that are calculated to trick my opponents (who, in this case would be the courts prosecutors, jurist, and victim(s) and their set-ups) for a *not guilty* decision; or I must try to get the best possible results for my client- "even if that's not the best result for society."

The express duty and responsibility of a defense attorney is only to his or her client, the accused. But the government's courts' personnel- the prosecutors, judges, and juries want the truth to come out. And therefore, the courts' only interest is to see that all its citizens-the wrongfully accused-receive impartial justice.

What the sovereign state and federal courts' system, along with the defense attorneys, are saying in unison is that the *science of justice* calls for the ability to ascertain all those qualities that our constitution demands under the Bill of Rights. These constitute our situational, moral, and ethical behavior, with respect to the rights of our fellow citizens.

And yes, rendering justice can be as precisely satisfactory as 1+1 which equals 2, in our conscience of fairness, when our reasoning are based on sufficient evidence, and not on the whims of emotional perceptions and windy indignations, which circumvents the instance of an event or issue brought to the *courts* for a legal ruling.

Should the court's ruling render a *not guilty* decision for mister 2 as a definite person, who is in violation of written laws, or the constitutional rights of another individual, this would free 2 in the eyes of public acceptance, or law by following the jury and justices' reasoning. This case is settled in the eyes of the United States' court system if the individual victim has no resource or recourse for appeal or, if in appealing the victim still loses through legal technicalities and techniques applied by mister 2's attorney.

Philip Kiurland maintains that the Supreme Court has, and must continue to be the strongest force in the vital center of the nation's justice system, maintaining social cohesion that makes for a democratic society in the accomplishment of its missions. The influence, spiritual, and moral philosophy of the nation's constitutional scheme is the understanding of its connection to our individual subjective needs in everyday social life.[6]

The constitution is also called the rational *will* of its people. What is rational to almost all of us, all the time, is a simple mode of logic where we could make connections for reaching common values in understanding. Chapter one clearly shows why *values,* which are carved out of the daily

---

[6] Kurland Philip, Ibid.

concepts and ideas we use in creation, problem-solving, work, and play are the cumulative assets of, or what is significant to each and every one of us.

We accept and look at the Constitution and its Bill of Rights as our national supreme value as: God of *form, reason,* and *logic,* which is the whole background of our Americanization. It is our God of proportion and balance from which an assertive citizen seeks assurance in simple forms. This may be found in an *in-group* or *out-group* sentiment, political party, or social group that is supportive in providing purpose and meaning for the dispossessed or individuals who have lost it.

For the assertive and autonomous, it is found in a wide range of educational pursuits of the nation-states' official values, the universal history of the species, which any of us can visit at will through research, or the creation and production of new consciousness and artifacts in a dynamic balance and relationship to industry, peace, order, law, and government.

The constitution itself is a condensed document, while the details of individual social life are expressions of its generalized and internalized interpretations that have been evident, clear, open actions and practices of other citizens, be they significant or insignificant to us – the diverse configurations of social and economic life citizens have taken up or adopted- irrespective of status, rank, ethnic group membership, or social class. It is here that we learn to revere the acts of all who have contributed to our constitutional whole: heroes and heroines given to us, among many others we can choose at will in the molding our self-images.

Under the constitution, our condition is that form of reality in which each individual has and enjoys his or her own freedoms. These freedoms which we are allowed to live are realized under a wide, and varying range of limits. The limits we face are both individual and group boundaries set by the social realities of the *other's* presence, and their desire or wishes to do or act freely as we would.

Most communal rules are based on this adjunct, or add on to written laws, and are often easily ignored or overridden under the dominance of compelling emotional needs or necessities, leading to many forms of infractions or rule-breaking. One common boundary easily found everywhere and anywhere is in all *in-group* and *out-group* sentiments and their common feelings of associations, superiority, and sense of exclusiveness.

Local administrative courts stay burdened and hamstrung with *interpretations* and *definitions* of these infractions or rule-breaking, because they generally constitute the violations of personal freedoms or their restrictions. This then makes way for changes or alteration of tradition, custom, and law, or the institution of new ones. The boundaries of law or rule-breaking may be definite or arbitrary, while their enforcement are definitely selective.

All humans are dependent on our basic needs fulfillment and satisfaction from the *other*, or other persons. The needs for: justice, sexual fulfillment, self-production, to be a part of the productive process of labor or work; to be appreciated by others for what we do; to be self-supporting, to belong to a greater community of people with similar ways and pursuits in social life, and to have some measure of control over our individual destinies, comprise our basic needs fulfillment from the *other* or other persons in society.

These essentials of quality social life are what makes the human social grouping deathless, and an absolute necessary support for individual social life. It should be firm and fixed in the readers' body-mind by now, that the struggle for existence, and to maintain existence is never carried on individually. Each of us profit by the others' experience. And in this correspondence we agree on that which we consider to be good, worthwhile, or expedient, bringing about cooperative action under the supreme law of the land. These are the real meanings and values that give us understanding of the *other*. We are thus parties of compromise to a common set of social and economic values and meanings.

With agreement- even to agree to disagree, is the key element in the genius of human sociability; showing how simple and easy alliances and loyalties are formed, broken, and reconstituted with strong emotional bonds, logical appeal to rules of order, and a just norm of reciprocal exchange.

With the rule of law or the constitution hovering over their heads, our leading founders of our current-day American freedoms were clear on this. Because of this basic recognition of interdependence for individual self-fulfillment or goal pursuits, we are not dammed, destined, nor cursed to be confined to any one single group membership, alliance, allegiance, or loyalties, other than the general will or Constitution, unless we choose to do otherwise.

This social world we live in limits our options, shape our beliefs, and behavior, and can be changed in innumerable ways according to our individual free-will. Therefore, we are not locked into an inevitable set of rules, laws, structures, and relationships on account of our social location at birth, our ethnic group backgrounds, current status, inequalities in accommodations, education, and learning; work, job, profession, or craft rewards under the United States' constitution.

This is the intended impartiality of instituted laws that actually makes way for the prevailing peace, allowing us to continue our affairs and relationship in an ongoing, negotiative processes with our common adversities, likes, dislikes, hatreds, and contentions.

The freedoms we live within the Constitution and its Bill of Rights are actualized under the set national constitutional limits and the dependences which originate within an individual's personality or character structure formation itself.

This *me,* or *I* is fundamentally formed through beliefs and choices. Ideas which are not believed or inconsistent with individuals' ideal self-image formation are rejected, or simply not acted upon. While those that seems consistent with his or her chosen system of self-image formation are accepted. At this very center of our system of ideas or self-image formation lays the keystone and base upon which all else is built in the organization of our social lives. This is where our individual motivation and aptitude for learning, discernment, acceptance, or rejection of *facts,* according to our concepts of supreme good, in which it is experienced as *more-life!*

Without any reflection, the wide range of behavior fostered within limits of the United States Constitution often appear limitless- just as any other nation's constitutional scheme to their disparate citizens, whether they know it or not. What generally keep us in bounds are the two primordial laws, so-called *golden rule,* because they are the most simplest, and most universal to accept or recognize.

In the observation and enlightened awareness of these two primordial laws, love thy neighbor as you love yourself; and do unto others (before you are being done in), or as you would have others do unto you, it is hardly ever conceivable to consciously violate the boundaries of another human self in the struggle for existence, other than through sheer innocence or the ignorance of not knowing.

What is actually internalized, and virtually automatic in the head of the individual is that the cultural institution of positive written laws of the nation's or state's boundaries, impose something like a universal limitation, and mutual constraint on all members' behavior in their relations to each other. The practical pursuits of our goals and duties thus reflect our moral obligations to these boundaries or mode of interactions in all our affairs, contracts, agreements, or exchange.

Consequent laws or rules which originate from these human transactions are thus considered essentially rational, moral, and not accidental. This was the very object of our settling ancestors' pre-visions of a norm of reciprocal exchange- what we now call *Americanization*; or the true intention of the New *world order* and state of affairs that they had in mind- that which was, and still is practical, and essential in the activity of its members, and our individual dispositions duly recognized.

It is this absolute moral whole, social feeling, and interest of country and town-folks' reasoning, that *ought* to exist throughout the affairs of their chosen forms of government. Further, it must also be understood that all our individual self-worth can only be attained or realized through this prevailing state of affairs of justice.

To our settling and conquering American ancestors, their pre-visions of the nation were like a divine idea that *must* exist on *earth*. This was an ideal that must be consciously lived out. Positive laws which all will be eventually subjected to observe, would become the objectivity of spirit and the state. Foremost in their enlightened scheme was individual responsibility.

In spite of existing radical disagreements, others that were inevitable, or are likely to occur over time, the social compact must remain the ultimate arbiter, catalyst, and central facilitator to goodwill and maintenance of the social order, which is only possible through its defense, the meting out of divisions, contentions, and other differences through its tribunals, and the peaceful exchange of goods and services recognized in mutual contracts.

Philosophers Georg Hegel and Paul Tillich observe that "It is only that human will which obey laws which is free, for it obeys itself."[7] The national compact calls for a subjection of this *self* to the moral whole and common good.

Truly, an obedient *self* is one which commands itself, and by so doing, it risks itself. Through this act, it also becomes its own judge, and its own victim. It may command itself according to the rules of commonsense communal laws of survival in everyday social life. But the individual human *self-will* always commands itself more according to *laws of transcendence* of all limitations imposed on it- be they real, possible, probable, or impossible. Possibilities always exist in the human will of transcendence. The real dilemma and difficulty lays in our ability or inability to successfully ground or experience the possibilities.

All possibilities fall under the laws of *human perception*. They are highly subjective, and are driven by our imaginations to rational and irrational extremes. They are real to the experiencer, no matter how bizarre or quirky. They are human, and the real stuff science is made of. Make no mistake!

The real dilemma is that they are hard to pin down to our ever-changing surrounding social realities. More so, because they are yet to be organized and formed, physically created, and applied, which are the very state of *positive laws*. The scope and roots from which our emotional states expresses itself in *form*, yields the product of positive laws.

The laws of human perception confer upon this self-will for all transcendence as the creative will, sometimes called *creative Eros,* or the *creative-erotic*. Our creative will makes a whole out of the sensations we feel, the fragments of memory or history, puzzles, frustrations, and everything else we encounter from the social world around us.

A whole concept or form is made from our efforts in the organization of sensations we feel in order to accomplish something important to us; to rid ourselves of temporary discomforts, failures, and difficulties that social life is posing for us. The creative erotic in us always stands beyond the state of a *bad* conscience. It is the elusive God in us; that cannot create and build intelligibly or relatively accurately for our survival, unless some measure or degree of understanding and awareness about the *true* nature of the environment outside our individual body-minds is learned or absorbed.

---

[7] Hegel Georg, Tillich Paul

Ideas of our ideal selves, and theories concerning the social world around us begin in the realm of human thought that contain illusions, imaginations, speculations, and gross misconceptions, sliding into dreams and fiction. If these concepts are not grounded in some form, or forms of *truth* about the environment, God will never show his or her face benignly.

Conversely, when the organization of our thoughts are grounded in *truth* about whatever it is we have to handle or create in this world of forms, our response or reactions will more than likely be successful. God will definitely show up! Concepts represent abstract ideas about physical relations; and are generally expressed as symbols or words in everyday communication or some form of physical reality.

Destruction, violence done to the other, actions labeled *evil, bad,* or *heinous* are all attempts and efforts by the creative human will to surmount or transcend obstacles in the path and direction of individual freedoms pursued, desired, or wanted to be lived-out. "When people are deprived of due credit, or are served the brunt of condemnation, they respond in appropriate ways. They escape from those who attack or deprive them in order to weaken their effectiveness. It identifies those who infringe on a person's worth, and the practices they use. Personal freedom thus concentrates on weakening those who deprive others of due credit. We react or respond to the controllers by protesting, opposing, or condemning them in return," says distinguished Psychologist B. F. Skinner.

GENERALIZATION (OF CONSTITUTIONAL WILL)

When our internalized, individually subjective wills submit to the true intentions of laws made in the spirit, morality, or philosophy of our nation's constitutional scheme as stated here in its widest possible breadth of interpretations, together with their administration and enforcements by personnel and citizens, no contradiction can exist between freedoms sought, with respect to others' individuals' rights, necessities, and responsibility. Thus, laws passed are then considered rational and necessary for existence of the social order, and being the true substance and reality of things in a changing world.

However, when we say that we are free in recognizing them laws, and following them as guides to our behavior, or being in society- only insofar as they make and keep us whole, the reasoning of our justice system holds or states that when our attitudes toward its written laws are this or that way- our gut social feelings about anything, (which may be the conscious refusal to obey or comply with them, when we believe them to be unjust, immoral, encroaching, and unconstitutional), we are all guilty of *civil disobedience.*

In matching our own individual deviant action of fulfilment to a rule of law, Justice Benjamin Cardozo noted that "we seek to find peace of mind in the word, formula, and the ritual. The hope is an illusion.... In the long run there is no guaranty of justice, except the personality of the judge."

Well fuck! What about mine?

Our inclinations to the commission of civil disobedience may be, and often times are the result of deprivation of deeply felt primary needs to be satisfied; being rest assured that the goal of every human being is to become a self-fulfilled person. Since Self-fulfillment is a natural drive and compulsion which every living human being *must* achieve from moment to moment. Because we are not born with it, neither is it a given. Fulfillment is a status that must be achieved over, and over again- or maintained at whatever cost.

The cry, concern, and worry about our system of justice becomes acute when the nation's political administrative processes are not carried out in accordance with guarantees of the nation's constitutional scheme, or the general will of the people within a state, county, city, small town, or community.

This authority, as we have seen, generally installs itself in some measure, in the conscience of each individual citizen, making all of us potential criminals, if not real honest criminals. We actually do not choose to become criminals, simply because this social authority that operates within us is the one which we have absorbed from dominant formal culture. However, as this authority, embodied in justices of the courts, political leaders in government, heads of industries, the popular and influential, religious organizations, and other social institutions diminish, the balance within us- we the people subjected, who give them our allegiances and loyalties, wanes, and is also upset.

A pervasive sentiment and generalized social feeling is developed, which then becomes the actual state of affairs that makes way for many forms of alternative adaptations and variation, in shouldering the burdens of social life. Radical departures and an independent adjunct justification system of the willful violation of laws or communal rules, different from the formal ones intended or decreed by the courts for the good and safety of society are common modalities of adaptation.

Again, these justifications are clearly seen and expressed in the dimensions of our basic fulfillment needs- freedoms that none of us would never want to deprive our individual selves of. Consequently, there is often great public outcry when some laws and rules are enforced or not enforced- and against whom.

An individual's social world of basic needs satisfaction provides his or her absolute reference point or base of assertion, without which time, place, participation, or motion in society makes no fucking sense. Freedom is a possession. It is something we express spontaneously or as a plan of action against the resistance and persistence of forces against our will to do, or action to take. However, the most primary expressions of individual freedoms rests on responsibility and the application of knowledge reduced to a serviceable commodity.

These conditions are superseded and superimposed by the political state, ultimately dictated by the courts and its justices' actual interpretations of the Constitution or common laws passed. Thus, the freedoms we are allowed can be broadly or narrowly defined under what circumscribe our *Bill of Rights*. "We are under a constitution, but the constitution is what the judge say it is," according to former United States Justice Charles Evans Hughes.[8]

The United States constitution created a government dedicated to equal justice under the law. The attached *Bill of Rights* and Fourteenth Amendment emphasize and embodies this ideal. Conflict and complications arise with the *means* or *methods* each individual and social group, or organization use in our objective interpretations of it. It is the

---

[8] Kurland Philip, *The Constitution*

status we achieve, and adjustments made in shouldering the burdens in the maintenance of social life under actual conditions.

In real broad terms, these adjustments of individual and group actions in the community act as a feed and fodder for the *court's* raw material to process, mediate, and enforce as rules or laws by administrators of the political state for the people or a community. To this natural cycle of the structure of our justice systems' behavior response, Former Justice Learned Hand made the observation that, "....among multitudes, relations must become standardized; to *standardize* is to *generalize*, and to generalize is to ignore all those authentic features which mark, and which indeed creates an individual."[9]

Earlier references were made concerning the standards of *science*, which seeks to demystify, unravel our deepest experiences of social reality, and arrive at absolute or relative truth, independent of anyone's wishes or desires. Further, the destination or goal we wish to attain, arrive at, or fulfill is bounded by our use of the element *time*, and the concept of *closure* in the organization of our thoughts and lives. Both *time* and *closure* necessitates generalizations in all our reasoning and understandings.

In all our ongoing social relations in Americanization, the process of individuation has become a necessity in which attempts are made to render true justice to anyone and everyone we encounter and interact with. This is no easy give-and-take for most people; since our individual sense of justice arise from states of freedoms that we have become accustomed to, and what we faithfully believe to be right. Justice represents the deepest meaning of individual freedoms which must be acquired and fulfilled. It may be said to be a base, or the bare state operational that an individual needs to carry-on any transaction between and among others.

If balance is Justice in this generalized sense, then the practice of science indeed creates the upright individual character, personality, or self-formation. It is also the same in saying that, with consideration for the rights of others within reasonable boundaries, persons who adhere to scientific principles are the most ethical citizens of society. Although perfection in execution is not always required by any one member of society, approximations are good enough for all practical purposes for carrying on the business of social life.

[9] Kurland, Ibid

Thus, generally speaking, adaptation and survival strategies that individuals and social groups take up, in relation to each other, industry, and the political state, are by their very nature conflicts, and are the days' basic issues which the courts or United States justice system address. But not all individual cases are taken up. All are not given consideration, equal time, or any time at all for due justice.

So, what do we do? The vast majority of citizens are stuck with their wits, wisdom, physical and intellectual abilities to work out for themselves a just and balanced mode of coexistence- their own godamn salvation!

Today we bear witness to see how so many organized interests and industrial groups reinforce religious beliefs, social inequality, harm public welfare, and embark with their own enterprise and agenda without any regard for individuals, family, or social groups' rights, by promoting their own interests, distorting public agendas, feeding meaningless information, and by defining what public issues of concern are to be considered *urgent, important,* or *meaningless.*

These Closures and generalizations, bounded by the element *time,* can be created and manipulated at will in our imaginations, or in actual physical forms. In fact, any object form that we create or produce is a generalization of feelings, thoughts, and actions, put into form that can be accepted, rejected, re-constituted, or improved. It is thus absolutely necessary for each and every one of us to increase our awareness about these applied and generalized concepts which dominate our conscience as laws or social rules by which to play.

But we must first increase our awareness about the applied concepts in which our values, meanings, and hopes are sought, such as work or labor, and our relation to each other under the United States Constitution.

4

EXPANSION & THE SLAVERY BUSINESS

L OOKING BACK TO EVOLUTION OF the nation's original consolidated or generalized will, and the debates held over its ratification as a working national consensus, we find the purpose of its government, political parties, and system of justice. From its inception, the new nation was to be a republic, emphasizing representative democracy. Its leaders elected to speak for, and represent the people. The body of individuals chosen- then make binding authoritative decisions for society, by resolving conflicts of interest among free enterprising individuals and groups; as well as allocating the nation's resources and surplus; that amounts to *who gets what,* and *how much.*

The most basic vehicle to this reciprocal system of representative democracy are political parties, whose leaders must depend on the attitudes, sentiments, and opinions of their voters or citizens. Representatives then wrangle with contentious issues of freedoms that needs legitimacy or to be outlawed. The quest for ratification of the Constitution in 1787, which was to be the current working framework of our government, concerned itself mostly with personal freedoms that provided the most contentious issues of the day.

These were the Bill of Rights. Further, during this odyssey of expansion, all were not free to be enumerated in the population. The status of an American citizen was still not clearly defined. There were still "one-half", and "three-fifths" persons. This was the black industrial slave population. Heated debate over these issues forced representatives to split into irreconcilable differences and factions of Federalists and Anti-Federalist parties; marking the actual beginning of the now dominant two-party system. Moderates, or cooler heads of both factions hammered out a compromise that led to the Constitution's ratification in 1791, with the Bill of Rights and first Ten Amendments.

Compromise was reached on the contentious issue of *slavery* that had reduced the human biological status of a black person. Tampering with it as a free-trading enterprise was forbidden until 1808. After this compromise, slave trading aroused very little conflict. But as the country was expanding westward, conflicting ideas of the manufacturing North and slave-holding South now became more and more pronounced and volatile.

The term *sectionalism* was soon to be employed in usage on account of demands from new agricultural settlements emerging westward. But the word itself was soon to be confined wholeheartedly in everyday jargon of the slave-holding South, which was diametrically opposed to the free-enterprising industrial Northeast. On account of this division, each developing section of the emerging nation's states demanded legislation that would benefit their economy.

The North invested heavily in building home markets, internal improvements, and high tariffs. The expanding agricultural West needed low-priced public lands to encourage settlements, Federally-built internal improvements, and protective tariffs. The slave-industrial cotton-picking South favored low tariffs, and constant expansion of the *slave market* to facilitate commercial exchange with Britain. Mirrored in, basic to, and throughout the whole political process were featured antagonisms of *sectional* conflicts revolving around the particular issue of slavery itself.

At the time when eleven *free,* and eleven *slave* states constituted the Union, there were twenty-two Senators representing each side. But owing to the shifting balance in the nation's population of the North by a little under a million people, the Lower House of Representatives had amassed 123 Congressional members against 89 for the *slave* states.' Sectional concerns eventually became the binding link to political action and economic demands repeatedly; while the consensus of *compromise* was the bridge that held the Union of newly-formed states under the Constitution together.

As a general rule, northerners habitually objected to adding new slave states, and their fears had centered on the vast lands that lay beyond the Mississippi becoming slave-holding territory. Under the *three-fifths* persons head count of slaves in the compromise for passage of the Constitution, states formed in the west would be overrepresented in Congress.

The first and most critical concern of sectional politics surfaced in December 1819 in a meeting with Congress. When Louisiana entered the Union in 1812, the rest of the *Louisiana Purchase* was organized as the Missouri Territory. Now that Missouri is about to enter the Union. Northern debates did not center on the morality of slavery, nor the status of a black person. The real questions of discourse were the balance of political influence.

Article IV, Section 2 of the United States Constitution states that "the citizen of each state shall be entitled to all privileges and immunities of citizens in several states." When Missouri submitted its constitution for approval by Congress, the document, besides authorizing slavery and prohibiting the emancipation of slaves without consent of their owners, required the state to pass a law barring freed blacks from other parts of the union from entering the state "under any pretext whatsoever."

Every right- thinking political representative of the day had realized the extreme potential horror inherent in Missouri entering the Union as a slave state. To preserve the balance in the Senate, Maine was admitted as a free state after its separation from Massachusetts. In order to prevent further conflict, Congress adopted a proposal that "forever prohibited slavery in the westward extension of Missouri's southern boundary." This settlement that brought on a new national status quo, and continued to hold the expanding Union together was now known as the *Missouri Compromise of 1820.*

In search for its identity, establishment, balance, and distribution of equal justice, interpretations and broader definitions of the nation's constitution did not come into sharp focus until John Marshall became Chief Justice. During his tenure between 1801 and 1835, a number of important decisions were meted out, and rules laid down that expanded authority of the nation's Supreme Court. This was known as *Judicial Review.*

Powers of the national government were defined in the doctrine of *Implied Powers*; and Marshall diminished the powers of some states by making laws enacted by them unconstitutional when they are in conflict with the nation's constitutional scheme. The *Marshall courts* concerned itself mostly with interstate commerce and property, which took precedence and representation of individual freedoms.

Roger B. Taney, this marsupial, succeeded John Marshall as chief justice and followed his predecessor's patterns of decision-making in his court rulings, which were usually made in favor of industry and expansions. Underlying these court issues and court decisions were the fundamental moral issue of *slavery* and the definition of an American *citizen*. These decisive and divisive issues will now silence the courts national influence and leverage in the defense of Human Rights, through sectional, industrial, and entrepreneurial demands in the body politic of *compromises*; but only to re-surface, with more and more convictions in the precipitating, acrimonious moments of deliberations, leading to the Great Civil War that was in the making.

Although sectional emotions had cooled down after the Missouri Compromise of 1820, misunderstanding and distrust of the Union by several states remained, and was the order of the day. Relations between North and South did not improve anything, owing to the sheer inability of both sections to live up to its terms. The South was always threatened by the North, who were no abolitionists themselves, but preferred a dissolution of the institution of *slavery* altogether; and therefore were always in favor of *Free* states. So, as soon as conquered territories got settled, populous, and applied for statehood and admission to the Union, since the nation's boundaries had not yet been finalized, the vexing and divisive *slave-holding* or *free-state* issue balancing act in Congress would assert itself again.

Pus continued to gather around the nation's moral wound of slavery as emotions festered and fermented for the next twenty-eight years. Upon his election to the presidency, without even drafting a platform, and without consulting or the consent of Congress, President Zachary Taylor advised both the new settled territories of California in1849, and New Mexico in1850, to draft anti-slavery constitutions, and ask admission to the Union. This action placed Southerners in punk mood when Congress assembled in December.

Taylor, who is said to have scorned compromise, threatened to veto any kind of compromise measures on the issue. But he took sick instead, and his unexpected death in July of 1850 caused the ascendance of Millard Fillmore to the Presidency. A spirit of concession which espoused the concept of a sectional balance was then engineered by Senator Henry Clay of Kentucky. Fillmore fully agreed with, and facilitated adoption of the compromise Bill. This Bill was a set of "compromise measures" that sought to please demands of the South, and are referred to as the *Compromise of 1850*.

Northern sectional anger and outrage on this occasion were openly expressed by Senator William Seaward of New York: how could there be compromise on a subject as morally reprehensible and outrageous as human slavery? He questioned. Then stated, "I think all legislative compromises radically wrong and essentially vicious," on this issue.

Franklin Pierce, the next succeeding President fully endorsed the compromise as being constitutional. He also exerted great effort to push through a pro-slavery Bill called the Kansas-Nebraska Act of 1854. The passage of this Act then repealed, or nullified the Missouri Compromise of 1820, which was enacted to keep unincorporated territories "*free* 'forever." However, this nullification enabled Kansas to become a *slave* state if settlers voted for it. Essentials of the *Kansas-Nebraska Act* were also known as *Popular Sovereignty*.

With Pierce upholding their right to do so, Kansas was promptly infiltrated with a pro-slavery government, despite outcries of anti-slavery sentiments from the people of Kansas and Northerners everywhere. Kansas quickly turned into a bloody battleground with the senseless slaughter of Abolitionists who were swearing to keep Kansas free, while four months of irregular fighting that amounted to a civil war, took a toll of more than 200 lives by the end of 1856.

Northerners, specifically New Englanders, took a heavy hand in trying to keep Kansas free. Meanwhile, for some time now since 1846, Abolitionists have been busy in the state courts of Missouri where Dred Scott, their black slave defendant was born, but was now residing in the free states of Illinois and Minnesota. When the Missouri Supreme Court ruled against his plea to be a free person, Scott was sold to a J.F. A. Sanford And Son in New York. This was a legitimate business transaction for those days. But it was done specifically to get the case into the Federal courts, which were authorized to settle dispute between citizens of different states. The United States Supreme Court agreed to take up the case in 1856.

This year marked the beginning of another pro-slavery President elect- James Buchanan. Buchanan firmly believed that *Popular Sovereignty*, the concept coined by Senator Stephen Douglas of Illinois, was the only practical means of settling the *slavery* issue. Two days before his inauguration in March of 1857, United States' Supreme Court Justice Roger B. Taney informed Buchanan that he was about to hand down a pro-slavery decision.

Discussing the bitter dispute in Kansas during his inauguration, the President called upon the nation to regard the flaring issue of *slavery* in the territories as a judicial question to be settled by the Supreme Court. "...to their decisions, in common with all good citizens, I would cheerfully submit..." Buchanan stated confidently through the foretelling of Justice Roger B. Taney's anticipated court ruling. Northerners were angry, since the President was trying to make the country accept in advance a decision that could decisively extend slavery.

On March 6, 1857 Taney and the Supreme Courts Justices ruled that: black Americans are not included, and were not intended to be included under the word *citizens* in the constitution. Dred Scott was not a citizen because he was black. "Framers of the constitution did not consider black people citizens." He was still a *slave*, and the laws in any state he visits or reside does not affect this status.

Our nation's judicial history is filled with cases to bring justice to an individual, social group, or economic enterprise. Most of these cases were meant to settle a point of law. Dred Scott was a frail, and dying, old black man destined to die within a year. However, for the divided nation, slavery could never more be contained by compromise. The court's ruling on Scott's case amounted to a decision against *Popular Sovereignty*, the very membrane that had held sectional politics together.

Southerners were delighted with the Court's ruling. It confirmed their belief that slavery should be transportable to any territory. Northerners, on the other hand contended that all parts of Chief Justice Taney's decision were based on "gratuitous judicial opinion" that were too partisan to be impartial; since seven of the nine justices on the court's bench were Democrats and five of them were from the South.

Prior to the court's decision, the South had exercised an influence in the national government far out of proportion to its productivity and population. They dominated the Presidency, Cabinet, and the Supreme

Court. That influence should have peaked in the 1830's. But simply because Northern political advocates benefited from the prosperity *slavery* evoked in frontier expansions, *they* helped to sustain the Southern power beyond its time. And as it flourished in this atmosphere, questions of the many implications of slavery, the unsettled business of *status, citizenship,* and *personal freedoms* were debated, and re-debated vigorously, until the peoples' nerves were rattled and wore thin.

With the Democrats now holding a majority in both houses, Buchanan tried to put an end to the agitation that was going on in Kansas, by asking its admission to the Union as a *slave* state, under the *Lecompton Constitution* as its frame of government. Stephen Douglas, a Northern Democrat like Buchanan, revolted; joining Republicans in the House of Representatives to defeat the Bill. The Bill was overwhelmingly rejected by Congress in January of 1858. This act then drove a wedge between Northern and Southern Democrats, who were now hopelessly divided.

The sectional gulf grew even wider between 1858 and 1860, when the Illinois Senatorial seat held by Stephen Douglas was contested by Abraham Lincoln on behalf of the Republican Party. Although Douglas was re-elected to his Senate seat, the debates held with Lincoln, called *The Freeport Doctrine,* were totally rejected by Southern Democrats. Laws desired by Northern business leaders were routinely defeated in Congress. Sectional feelings then became more inflamed as Northern Democrats defected to the Republican Party fold to elect Abraham Lincoln as President, and as a solution to their disproportionate share of the irrepressible conflict and impending crisis.

The sore festered, as poison ran through the nation's body politic. The disease had become obviously incurable through the soluble spirit of compromise. The South, which held its own presidential election, immediately seceded from the North when Lincoln became President, and five long years of an ugly, grueling Civil War ensued.

Depending on his audience, in Chicago, where anti-slavery sentiments were ebbing and strongest, Lincoln resonated in the people's ears the Declaration of Independence: "...Let us discard all this quibbling about.... this *race* and that race and the other *race* being inferior..." Two months later in a town where many Southerners had settled in Charleston, Lincoln explained the deep sentiment he also share with some of his less fortunate fellowmen: "I will say...that I am not, nor ever been in favor of bringing about in any way the social and political equality of the black and white races... making voters or jurors... nor of qualifying them to hold office... Nor..." on, and on with a rant that descended all the way down to sexual bondage.

Incidentally, the entrenched, immature national belief in *white ethnic group* superiority in comparison to, and with the black ethnic group population, commonly used as slaves during this period of our American history was a given, and also a taken-for-granted mode of adaptation for most Americans who considered themselves *white*. The enlightened were the exceptional.

They became the most vocal, and most radical elements that were to challenge this ideology head-on, and push for its transformation or overthrow. Because the unitary give-and-take spirit of compromise had dissolved between the Northern and Southern extremists at this point of no return, an overthrow of either ideology was inevitable.

Mass armed rebellion of punishing, prolonged warfare was waged by the seceding south, who were now a confederacy. For two painful aching years the war dragged on as the Union Army incurred heavy loses, prompting Lincoln to put forth a conditional proposition for the South to come back to the Union. This was the *Emancipation Proclamation Act* issued in September of 1862, stating that *slaves* in all states still in rebellion were to become free on January 1, 1863.

The Confederate states would not have any of it. And the South waged on with the Civil War until their supplies were dwindled and exhausted. This lead to their surrender to Union forces on April 9, 1865. Five days later, Lincoln was shot by a determined, brooding, assassin and sympathizer of the Southern cause. He died on April 15th.

Vice President Andrew Johnson was sworn in as President, pledging to continue Lincoln's Post-war Reconstruction plans. The President wanted a soft peace for the rebelling Southern states. And in vain, he labored in the grooves of the Constitution to be just and fair as President of the Union, only to be annihilated by an impatient and intolerant committee of Senators and Congressmen called the *Radical Republicans*, ready to impose their own will and ideals to bring the nation aligned with a new moral order.

Lead by Charles Sumner and Ben Wade in the Senate, and Thaddeus Stevens in the Lower House of Representatives, *The Radical Republicans* overrode vetoes of the President, and denied the nation's Supreme Court's authority over its plans. As results of their determination, individual status and American Citizenship was now clearly defined and added to the Constitution in 1865. *Civil Rights Act,* emphasizing the rights of citizens was passed, and later incorporated into the Constitution in 1868 as the Fourteenth Amendment. The Fifteenth Amendment which established the right to vote was later added in 1870.

The Radical Republicans taking charge and effecting the social feeling as representatives of dramatic change drove on to accomplish what was badly needed for economic reform and the nation's social transformation. Although President Johnson had vetoed their will on solid constitutional grounds, overriding sentiments with determined leadership would no longer tolerate Constitutional arguments against the status of a black person or any other persons in society, equally protecting their rights and civil liberties under the Constitution's definition of *Citizenship* and *Naturalization.*

The Radical Republicans accomplished what has profoundly influenced the development of the truly progressive and enlightened spirit of American dissention and freedoms from the tyranny of ignorance and arrogance, based on a false ideology of superiority or *white supremacy,* and also defined the courses that our constitutional justice system should pursue.

For clarity on our national condition during this period and subsequent developing periods of human history, we should not forget that also present and inherent in this process and struggle for Americanization was the all absorption or elimination of indigenous tribes, so-called *Indians,* who were the original or host inhabitors before invasion and subsequent conquest.

It is also absolutely noteworthy here to make a declaration that ever since the beginning of recorded time, the civilization of humans, that is, how we become civilized by a particular culture- worldwide, has always been based on four core universal values prevalent in any human society or grouping of people at any given time:

The first is superior force, with tools of domination, or a military conquest that enables the victor to establish political and economic domination over an indigenous people within their territorial boundary. The second, involves frontier expansions, with the dominant group pushing the vanquished from their territory, killing off resistors, making them slaves, isolating and imprisoning them, or making them subservient to their rules of order.

The third condition, to a lesser extent is involuntary migration, with the dominant group importing captives for use as servants or slaves. The fourth condition involves the voluntary migration of foreign ethnic national groups, or individuals seeking economic opportunities, or political refuge. However these four conditions are accomplished in the conquest and formation of a territory, nation, or state, stable institutions must be created for their continued existence and perpetuation as a territory or society by their conquerors.

Once more, these institutions are the human family, the patterns of status, values, roles, and norms that are common to any human tribe or society; and are the first form of government we are exposed to, or experience in our childhood years. Meanwhile, the institution of education imparts knowledge, skills, values, and norms that the evolving dominant culture imposes. Institutions of religious or personal philosophical beliefs serve to meet people's need for answers to the meaning of social life's complexities. Also, humanitarian or altruistic support such as caring for the sick, elderly, disabled, and disadvantaged are core offshoots of this institution.

By setting goals and creating policies to reach or meet these goals, the political institution of government is designed and instituted to maintain unity of its people, inculcated in their moral responsibilities as citizens. The most pronounced institution of concern in all governments, and having the most dramatic effect on all citizens and adult members of society is their *legal system* of laws, which try to insure order through the application and enforcement of formal rules and procedures. This concept of subordination is established in the United States' Constitution being the "supreme law of the land."

The final and chief institution of concern in our everyday social lives is the economic institution, which is based on what we do for a living, and how we go about doing it. Human industry is primarily concerned with the ways and means of production, distribution, and consumption of gods and services. In all societies, primitive and modern, these institutions fit together as an integral whole. And because of their characteristics being attached to humans, and humans being attached to one another in the fulfillment of our basic needs satisfaction, it is virtually impossible to change one institution without structurally changing the others. Also, our sense of individuality and consciousness are derived from the same institutions, simply because these conditions envelopes our evolution and roles into society.

National conquests world-wide continued unabated, both for the United States, European, African, and Asian nations, with a virtual deceleration after World War II. The living anomalies of wounds, scars, loss, pain, hatred, and racism, suffering from wars inflicted by both conquered and conquerors are of the most heinous, hideous, and nerve-wrecking consequence humanity can bear. I sure don't need to explain nor weep for any here. Given such awareness on the human condition, the argument for justice sits in the human soil of our potential capacity for just about any form of aggression.

Here, we must pay homage to Edward O. Wilson's research analysis on our socio-biological condition, concerning human aggression. In the final analysis, and to its most irreducible level, Wilson noted that *human aggression* cannot be explained as a "dark-angelic flaw or a bestial instinct. Nor is it caused by the pathological system of upbringing in a cruel environment. Human beings are strongly predisposed to respond with unreasoning hatred to external threats, and to escalate their hostility sufficiently to overwhelm the source of the threat by a respectably wide margin of safety." [10]

Meaning that, we must all embrace human aggression as an all pervasive condition of human existence. We must not only embrace it, we must also create systems of meaning to channel its proper dispensation, which is neither detrimental to self or society.

Human aggression in the quest of problem-solving have developed useful knowledge and efficient organization that has produced tools of domination, superior weaponry, Industries, institutions, and relatively stable values that have accounted for the ascendant ruling and living classes of conquerors, occupying the highest status positions in all societies. This

---

[10] Wilson, Edward O., *On Human Nature*

class has the ways, means, and resources of material production at its disposal. And as such, it also has the means of *mental* production, which is the desire to keep, preserve, and maintain its profitable forms.

The inhuman antagonistic ideology of the Southern states in the Union, versus the humanistic ideology of Northern states, cultivated natural human tensions of precipitating aggression that overburdened the instituted ethical system of values that had evolved in maintaining and preserving the Union together, leading to the undesirable consequence of the grueling Civil War.

Since all are not equal in social values and treatment in society, all adults must strive or struggle to acquire, maintain, or aggrandize their rank or social status relative to the other. This satisfies the compact's ideology of *no limit to class ascendance*. Besides personal health, the most stable values in any society is money, negotiable property, or wealth. Anything else and everything else is in second place. Those of us who are not born into wealth must persevere to attain it, since it is the chief dictator of the status we all occupy, enjoy, or would like to enjoy in social life, and in any society. Here is where the vast majority of man and woman kind struggle, irrespective of ethnic group membership or identity.

Effects of the Civil War and a whole series of subsequent developments in this historical background displaced the once prevalent allegiances held to provincial patriotism in favor of a national social feeling. Our emergent forefathers of this new day, the Radical Republicans, insisted that this cornerstone of sentiment must now rest on the true intentions of *rationalism*, even though most lower classes of Americans' primary faiths and core value operational in daily social life are religious-God based, rooted in Judeo-Christian beliefs, or traditions and translations through the King James Bible, and other versions.

The enlightened and progressive on the other hand, often embrace a quasi-religious one based on the values of Enlightenment- that is, their own individual will, ideas, or concepts of a supreme being. Others may only worry about bible and religion only a couple years before they croak. In fact, widespread currency was given to religious and intellectual elaborations on the institution of slavery, based on them Judeo-Christian bibles. Giving rise to an explicit system of thought in the assumptions of human biological superiority, in order to buttress the existing system of property, power, and privileges in Southern states.

We claim our national Constitution's concepts core operational to be morally based, by embracing both religious and quasi-religious sentiments,' believers and non-believers base assumptions. However, in the spirit of rendering true justice- we the citizens of the United States expect it to be partial to none. This form of democratic rule when properly applied, basically rests upon the principle of Natural Law- which is the outgrowth of many, as opposed to personal rule and the questionable autonomy of an individual member of the lay or justice system.

All humans are religious by nature. American democracy is intimately tied or connected to religious freedom. Perhaps the deepest sentiment of man and woman kind is to express ourselves in whatever forms of worship we choose, and bear the responsibilities of its consequence. Our forefather's theory of government is categorized by this direction of reasoning level of social reality. Their all-consuming activities in the clarification of this form of Enlightenment they left behind, explain the overall framework of assumptions in which their concepts of democracy were rooted and embedded.

5

SCIENCE

THE STRUGGLE FOR RECOGNITION OF an individual's *Inalienable Right*, forcefully put forth by Thomas Jefferson, reflects the position that human freedom is compatible with causality. Meaning, human behavior was not subject to restraint by some arbitrary, mysterious God; but is caused, determined, influenced, and conditioned by something that is definite and verifiable by any other person. This concept of freedom came mostly from a value system of faith in the rule of impersonal law, and optimistic rationalism, backed by ethical individualism that characterized the Enlightenment Movement. Its emphasis on science incorporated a rational individualistic tradition because it is disciplined, functional, active, and open-end.

A scientific enterprise requires systematic diligence and honesty, and it is agreeable with all the necessary means for human progress. Science is the orderly gathering of knowledge or information by methodical inquiry and experiments, to build or remedy with economy and maximum efficiency. The ways of science are replicable methods that produce the same results, under the same conditions, with due margin of error admitted. It is a social institution, and the most rigorous and efficient means to produce solutions, useful tools, invent, or build artifacts.

The body of science grows as an ongoing process of eroding ignorance and enlarging human freedoms through meaningful action. In this light. Thomas Jefferson had approved of the Constitution in its original structure of government, but adamantly insisted, along with many other like-minded people, that certain fundamental *inalienable rights*- Rights considered to be natural and innate, and incapable of being denied, such as the right to protect one's life or property, freedom of worship, speech, and so on, be added to the document.

The source of this inviolability must be considered beyond civil, legal, or other forms of constitutional interpretations, for they are universally possessed by all humans. In the final analysis, freedom ultimately rests within the autonomous, morally responsible, and enterprising individual. And in all sense of human freedoms, these *inalienable Rights* may be said to guarantee each individual leeway and openness in the pursuits of his or her own interests.

One common interest we all develop is a fundamental belief about social life and the world we consciously inhabit. It is our philosophy, or deepest belief about humanity. It grows with us and is modified according to our individual satisfaction. It is commonly called "religion".

Jefferson's defense of this state of affairs was enacted into a Virginia law against the Church of England, between 1776 and 1779 which stated in part:"...No man shall be compelled to frequent or support any religious worship place or ministry whatsoever, nor shall be enforced, restrained, molested, or burdened in his body or goods, nor shall otherwise suffer on account of his religious opinions or beliefs; but that all men shall be free to profess, and by arguments to maintain their opinions in religion, and that the same shall in no wise diminish, enlarge or affect their civil capacities."

This statute later became the basis for the First Amendment to the Constitution. To the enlightened American of the day, this was a welcome release from the restraints of religious dogmas, moral, and social dictatorships that plagued the Old World, with its shadows constantly threatening the free-spiritedness of the New World of America that they were trying to build.

One of the most difficult thing to lose or get rid of, if ever, in the human psyche are the imprints of tradition. They are so reassuring. Even when they are no longer functional.

Faith, the unreserved opening of the human body-mind to truth, whatever it may turn out to be, is the essential virtue of science and human freedoms. We trust and believe in its principles, methods, and inquiries. It is just like any kind of religion that is not based on self-deception, or self-denial. In this sense, religion is an attempt to construct ideals and values toward which an individual can devotedly strive to regulate his or her own conduct. However, all organized religions or their religious practices by nature are not progressive. While the scientific method is constructed to be just that way. To move on. Not to go around in fucking circles.

Logic is the primary tool of science. As such, it is used as *the* instrument for unlocking all the mysteries of the universe, the intelligible connections found in human concepts, meanings, and all the things we must use, do, or invent. Summarizing the epitome of his pursuits, dedication, and life philosophy to the nation and state, an inscription on Thomas Jefferson's headstone reads: "I have sworn upon the altar of God eternal hostility against every form of tyranny over the mind of man." [11] Organized religion is one of these primary institutions.

The practice of science is the practice of justice. No tyranny exists when justice prevails in our day-to-day affairs. But there are many bitter days, confounding situations, and loony moons when we must live with the agony and anguish of injustice, simply because it is intimately tied to obtaining many of our basic and most intimate needs.

Injustice must be treated as sort of a bureaucratic process to be resolved later on. It is a bad take from others that we may not be properly equipped to deal with momentarily, and must be set aside for our own convenience or mere survival. If not, until sufficient resources are available to confront its source overwhelmingly. These are the conditions of human existence that summons an aptitude for the organization and reorganization of our value concepts, learning new ones, or their creation, in order to confront the ever-flowing conflicting interests by which we are implicated, through no fault of our own, by being parties of/to something within a given transaction or situation, or, simply by being an individual or ethnic group member, and so on.

Knowing this, is the real reason why most people maintain their ground or rule, or impose their will on others through the sheer manipulation of needed satisfaction, or the privation of basic needs, and more so when our existence is marginalized. We feel intimidated. We are wounded. Weak, have meager or insufficient resources, or in need of one or more of our basic fulfillment needs.

This is done routinely, both overtly and covertly by those who pursue

---

[11] Lorant Stefan, *Pesidency*: Thomas Jefferson

us. One method is by appealing and conforming to the ranks of authority, or others considered more powerful than the individual or group. These are society's honored vicars who are visibly and audibly displayed as symbols of God, virtue, goodness, power, and adoration. We are then conned, cajoled, tripped, and tricked to look upon them as the proper model in the hierarchical dispensation of privileges and empowerment.

Can a person's wife or husband really do this?

Yes.

Can a person's own biological son or daughter do this?

Yes.

Can a person's biological mother or father do this? Yes. Can a person's most trusted friend (s) do this?

Yes. Can decent societal people do this? Yes. Can God's loving people do this? Yes.

They do it all the time.

We do it all the time.

The impact of science on any myth or body of myths results inevitably in moral disequilibrium.

6

THE PLIGHT OF LABOR

F OUR SUCCESSIVE PRESIDENTS AFTER THE Civil War, both Republicans and Democrats subscribed to lip service about furthering equality of opportunity and constitutional Rights for the many who were now implicated on a new kind of economic landscape that emerged through the Radical Republicans' agenda, during, and after the period of Reconstruction, but neither Party did anything to implement them.

In fact, political action was more overwhelmed by its own new organizational form and direction. Unfettered by outmoded ideas about the proper limits of government authority, Justice Wendell Holmes set out to publish *The Common Law* in 1881, arguing that felt necessities rather than precedent should determine the rules by which people are governed; repeatedly stressing the rights of the people through their elected representatives.

This suggestive approach by a notable justice of the bench did little or nothing to influence the physical enlargement of individual civil liberties and the necessary human solidarity that was needed to be cultivated for the new, rapidly- changing society. Neither did it implicate a stable set of standards and values by which the emergent population, with lesser in resources, were now compelled to move in. While demands of new plants, factories, and industries continued to prevail.

The nation's vast natural resource and growing technological innovations fed an unsurpassed industrial boom, as traditional power is now conferred upon industrialists, who were now bankers, manufacturers, and builders, rather than little cottage industries, scattered small farmers, indentured servants, and Southern slave-fed industries.

Spurned by a free reign granted by the Courts and wheedled by political influence, unparalleled business growth consolidated to reap the benefits of mass production and the national marketing system, while the masses of once scattered independent producers were now fast becoming dependent wage-earners, and unable to bargain for a fair share of the escalating wealth.

Wages remained fairly stable through the end of century, and the cost of living fell, but the average worker did not prosper. When business and industrial concerns could not keep their plants and equipment working in full operation during slow periods in business cycles, a worker was temporarily discharged without compensation. If a worker was sick or got injured on a job, this matter would fall under his or her total responsibility, also with no compensation expected from the employer.

When demands for products were high, a wage earner would be forced to work seventy to eighty hours a week. (In fact, that little guy out there right now from a poor family, working for any small private employer, still relatively suffer the same fate in modern day). Still believing in the ability to rise above the average according to his or her own talents, the new American wage-earners were extremely reluctant to join Unions. But later, the immensity of exploitation and consensus over economic imperatives will force them to do so.

During this period somewhere around 1881, governmental agencies on both national and state levels were in their nascent stages collecting data regarding labor. Its social implications on hours worked, wages paid, classification on types of employment, and so on. As organized labor movements struggled to gain recognition, the need for professional administration in society grew larger and more complex, and government began to take on more functions.

Passing the Pendleton Act in 1883 began the classification of about 10% of government jobs, and the creation of competitive examinations for these positions. The most significant element of administrative concern were the first big business in American development, which were railroad-building, followed by the iron, and steel industry, oil, and electricity.

Besides using violence and murders as their bargaining weapons in the assertion of their labor Rights, strikes were the only effective ones organized labor developed in contesting conditions with the big industrialists of the day. However, since strikes often accompany the former conditions, Federal Troops must often intervene to maintain the social order.

As a matter of fact, it was on account of the rampant restive labor unrest and strikes that had been going on in previous years. One featured the Haymarket bombing that centered the government's attention on labor problems throughout the 1880's. In 1892 a violent strike broke out among silver miners in Idaho, and a far more expansive clash at Homestead Steel Plant of Carnegie, near Pittsburgh took place against the organized labor group of Amalgamated Steel Workers a few months later. Strikers attacked 300 private guards who were hired by the plant to protect strike-breakers. Seven of the guards were killed, and the rest forced to surrender.

The strike was precipitated by decisions of company official to crush the Union at all costs. Owing to the brutal violence that prevailed during the strike, public sentiments that had favored the workers' plight turned against them. Federal Troops were called upon as a result to restore order.

All said and done, management had its way and was able to hold out for at least five months against the striking workers. This was more than enough time to drain the striking worker's reserves, financially starving them into going back to work "on company terms." As an effective bargaining force, the violence done by the Amalgamated Association of Iron and Steelworkers destroyed unionism in the steel industry, and organized labor all over the country.

During 1894 and 1895 a really important strike with the railroads took place with a walkout by workers at George Pullman's Palace Car factory outside Chicago, protesting wage cuts. For weeks strikers refused to handle trains with Pullman cars, which resulted in tying up trunk lines running in and out of Chicago. Wage workers' and unemployment unrest grew, as the nation was wallowing in the worst depression the new economy had ever experienced.

In an effort to win support for their plight, an employment scheme prepared by Jacob Coxey, who represented the unemployed, staged a protest with a march to Washington presenting their plea to Congress. But the new wage-workers' and jobless demands were completely ignored.

. Meanwhile, the strike in Illinois had prompted railroad owners to bypass the state's governor's office and appeal to President Grover Cleveland to send troops to preserve the order there, on the pretext that soldiers were needed to ensure movement of the mail. The President agreed. Followers of the strikers were rudely dispersed by club-wielding policemen, while leaders of the American Railway Union workers were locked up for defying a federal injunction.

7

BRAINWASHED/PROGRAMMED

SOCIAL INEQUALITY

The callous treatment of the new wage-earner and laborer by government convinced many that American government had little interest in the people's suffering. Reconstruction governments in the South could stand only as long as the Army remained there, while Congress continued to be controlled by the Radical Republicans. Two of the most insistent demands of the newly freed black people were education and political power. Laws that were passed by the Radical Republicans in 1875 that guaranteed equal accommodation for the newly-freed black slave population were nullified by Civil Rights cases brought to the courts in 1883. The rights of workers, and the newly-freed were of no importance.

Still demanding to uphold their false assumptions and ideological beliefs concerning their superiority- led by Mississippi and Louisiana, Southern states began their customary trek back to their basic instituted concepts and perceptions about black people being a distinct *race,* other than members of their own human *species.*

Practically every Supreme Court decision after 1877 was focused on the persecution, containment, or nullification of black persons Civil Liberties. Southern States' disdain and derision argued that the Fourteenth Amendment guaranteed their rights against invasion by the States, but not by individuals.

A Supreme Court decision in 1896, elevated to the national status of Dred Scott, (this time it was a *Plessey v Ferguson*), ruled that the segregation of black colored people from white colored people was legal in both public and private ownership for public accommodation, so long as "separate but equal" facilities were provided.

Justice John Marshall Harlan, a dissenting justice of the bench stood up to defend the breadth of the Constitution, proclaiming that if one ethnic group "be inferior to the other socially, the Constitution of the United States cannot put them upon the same plane. Our Constitution is color blind. The arbitrary separation of citizens on the basis of *race*...is a badge of servitude wholly inconsistent with civil freedom and equality before the law established by the Constitution."[12]

It took more than fifty-eighth years of terrible brain-fucking, before the United States Supreme Court came around to Justice Harlan's reasoning. Meanwhile, total segregation of people according to *black and white race schemes* were imposed throughout the South's social, economic, private, and public institutions. In fact, the doctrine of *separate but equal,* remained law of the land until 1954. Apartheid was the state of affairs.

Historical records claim "nearly all Biologists, Physicians, and other supposed experts on the human Race were convinced that black persons were inferior beings..." This was a natural scourge to the educated and enlightened American of the day. While little was being done to dispel the gross human assumption and subjugation, justified in the name of our Judeo- Christian god.

Wheeler-dealers of the economic North supported both the government's and Courts' decisions. Nearly all communication mediums commented favorably on decisions handed down in subsequent Civil Rights cases, backed by derogatory pictures; stereotype reporting, and other technical props of reinforcements, used for mass media coverage to validate black subjugation.

Our fundamental American identity orientation is based on definitions of freedom, equality, responsibility, and justice under the law or Constitution. If all are equal under the law, then all have equal rights to judge their fellow men and women, and to regulate their conduct according to commonly accepted standards of group, community consensus, or customs of reciprocal rights.

---

[12] Garranty, John/MC Caughy, Robert A. :*A Short History of The American Nation, Fifth Edition,* Harper&Row, New York, Copy 1987

It was the insistence of the average citizen upon the equality of political Rights that actually forced the *Bill of Rights* into the Constitution. Themes in its crystallization continuously arise from real problems which overburdens those most productive elements in the population who give their allegiances to this whole form.

Seeing the world in scientific or moral terms does not mean conformity to a state of detailed prescriptions of a particular political or moral code, it is rather a systematic orientation towards the moral whole by which human conduct is judged. This conduct is made up of a core belief system, attitude, and habitual dispositions within a given territory. The strain towards equality of legal rights for all citizens is, and has been the strongest value, and continuing urge for all Americans.

From its inception, any so-called white American could have said "no" to black people's subjugation, and lived a relatively happy fulfilling life in these frontier days, as a community of people. The same could be said of an indigenous tribe member. How many did? We will never know. An accurate statistical assumption would conform that very few did in some parts of the unsettled territory.

But I would not waste a single second elaborating nor speculating on any of this. Because virtually any black or white historian can cook-up a Black & white Garden of Eden in America, before, and during frontier days, and make it believable.

Any knowledgeable historian will agree, that from its most nascent conception and early formation, the Nation-state has always been a harbor for diffused constellations of beliefs and attitudes, that musts an attitude that would be reconciled by its judicial set-up, in deciding burdening claims of legitimacy or illegitimacy.

These formal legal Rights sought are what guarantee the individual leeway and openness in conducting his or her own affairs, without undue hardship or encroachment on other citizens. The case of civil liberties' containment or denial, while available to the others having the same, or equal status by existence, stands as a real emotional power keg to the intended principle of the Constitution, as the supreme regulator of human behavior towards one another. During this period in U S history, judicial activism in the interests of mass publics was virtually silent.

It is not that all people or majority of the people in a community or population will often agree with, and follow through the Courts' decisions. In fact, *dissention* is what prepares and provides the very ground for the *new* all-pervasive social feelings that will once again enter the Courts at a later date, for a broader or more comprehensive definition of individual or group freedoms, sought or demanded, as *equality* in treatment and *due justice* under the Constitution.

In, and throughout the Civil War era, the stronger elements and proponents of American freedoms rebelled and championed the Dred Scott Court decisions. After the Civil War ended, the Radical Republicans overrode the Courts' and Presidential rulings that were profound obstacles to constitutional freedoms, in order to obtain a definition of human status by existence in American society.

This determined effort established the grounds of hard-fought freedoms that some of our concerned American leaders speak of today- if, and when it registers or resonate in us. Majorities are still led today to believe historically, that Democrats have always been the champions of Black Civil Liberties. HA!

As stated earlier, the basic needs for: Justice, acceptance, recognition, or appreciation for what we do, are a universally sought commodity in all societies. In order to obtain these, we must conform to certain communal consensus and expectations. These are fundamentally economic, and pertain to the ways and means of making a living, or carrying on the business of individual or familial social life.

The justifications for any ethnic group's subjugation, by whatever features of distinction, rather than merit or aptitude, for whatever their capabilities and capacities are, is contrary to all practices under the supreme law of the land. In spite of this principle, conditions of the South's false ideology festers with its technical props, well supported by Jesus. This permissiveness is relatively stable and conservative.

After the Reconstruction Period had ended, industrial values were to forever dictate the course of American society. They were: controls over profit-making property, Individual, or corporate capital investments in industries, and the organization of production and distribution of goods and services, which involves the management, coordination, and placements of human labor.

The social class of workers at the bottom, during this period of Americanization had no say over investments, nor were they educated enough, or had the ability to organize and coordinate production. The vast majority of these people at the lower rung of the economic ladder were once slaves, indentured servants, free independent farmers, and small cottage industry owners. Now, newly implicated, they lacked the ability to assert authority over others, and therefore must follow orders to keep their jobs.

Meanwhile, formal education of this new world order, ushered in by practical inventions and rapid technological advancements, began to assert itself more as a social selection process in the labor market.

Since the deepest of human values relates to the ongoing economic structure of the society in which we find ourselves, our values are so naturally influenced with its changing feature over time, or with the onset of new technologies. From the date of its establishment to this point in our historical analysis, we bear witness to a changing body of constitutional rulings by which society is compelled to play. We also participate and learn about key players.

In its processes of change, the Supreme Courts' attitudes and dictatorships over the population are partially summarized this way: The fate of a public policy hangs on the validity of an act. An issue awaits judgment in a lawsuit. A new case or lawsuit may now turn upon the boundaries of a phrase or wording in the Constitution for the exercises of an individual's or corporate group's freedom or encroachment on it. Whatever is meted out from the rulings on these events or issues will now become the formal norm by which society ought to play.

Once we have categorized anything, we have classified, arranged, labeled, and described it to its most irreducible level of use or purpose. This chapter and book section has been spent on the clarification of our home base; why each citizen must come to the awareness of his or her evolution into society, and the national historical background that formed the territory, nation, and society- the place called *home* and *country,* as a simplified common generalized frame of reference. As Americans, It is a way to consult our integrity and structure our thinking when familiar patterns break down, are in dissolution, or things are in disarray.

BIBLIOGRAPHY

INFORMATION SOURCE AND AUTHOR'S WORKS CONSULTED

Chapter 1, & 2

B. F. Skinner: Beyond Freedom And Dignity. Topics on Aversive Conditioning, Reinforcements, Controllers and the Controlled individual.

Rollo May,: The Courage To Create. Issues of fulfillment and purpose in existence.

Maxwell maltz: Psycho-cybernetics And Self-fulfillment. Principles of self-fulfillment

Bandler/Leslie Cameron: Neuro-linguistic Programming.

Chapter 3

Henry Grady Weaver: The meaning of Human Progress. Copy 1947, Foundation For Economic Education Inc. 1, 2, The ancestors' stand on what American government should be like under the Constitution.

Paul Tillich: The Courage To Be, Copy. 1952 Yale University Press: footnote 7

Eric Hoffer: The True Believer. Copy. 1951. Time Inc. Book Division. Topics on belief systems and the vicious cycle of poverty

Kurland Philip: Politics The Constitution And The Warren Court. Copy. 1970 University of Chicago. Explains the U.S. Constitution as interpreted by the court's justices. Footnote 3, 4, 6

Stefan Lorant: Presidency. Copy 1951, The Macmillan Company. Thomas Jefferson's contributions and formation of U. S. political culture.

John A. Garranty/Robert A. Mc Caughey: A Short History of The American Nation, 5th edition, Copy1989, Columbia University. Topic on Jeffersonian Democracy.

PART II

1896 THROUGH 1932

8

THE PROGRESSIVE MOVEMENT

O UT OF THE DISCONTENT AND travails of American farmers of Western and Southern states, the frustrations of organized labor, and new wage earners, gave rise to a Populist Movement that now sought political action. By mid-term elections of 1894 they had already accounted for at least 42% of the popular votes. William Jennings Bryan embraced and represented the Populists' movement sentiments, and was nominated as the Democratic Party's Presidential candidate for 1896. Bryan conducted a vigorous grass- roots, agrarian-based, parochial campaign, grounded in the issue of *silver mining*. He wanted silver to restore the nations' acute money base, which was then on a gold standard.

Meanwhile, the industrial North was gripped with a wave of fear from these "social revolutionaries," (as the Populists' Movement was often referred to), and what Bryan was generating in his audience during his fiery campaign speeches. He was only thirty-six years old. In direct opposition to Bryan's quest for the Presidency, working men were told that factories would be closed if the thirty-six-year-old became President. Banks also informed farmers that if his Republican rival William McKinley is elected, their loan payments would be extended at lower rates of interests.

Backed solidly by business and financial interest, a preponderance of labor votes, and thousands of farmers,' William McKinley was elected President over William Jennings Bryan, with a little over half a million popular votes, and 271 to176 electoral votes; ushering in a sigh of relief and wave of confidence for commerce. The new session of Congress that the President called in March of 1897 completed its work by July, passing legislation that built a high protective tariff around the country, and the currency being set on gold standard instead of silver.

Recovery set in with an upturn in economic activities, and the nation's attention now turned in a new direction- Cuba. Spanish rule exercised sovereignty over Cuba, which was crucial in controlling the Caribbean. Cuban natives had sporadically rebelled against Spanish monarchial rule, while American businessmen had made substantial investments in Cuba's sugar industry. A serious uprising began in 1895 and was crushed by the Spaniards. This was to be followed by some harsh repressive treatments against the Cuban people.

Now goaded by the spectacle of European powers establishing spheres of influence abroad, expanding into Asia and Africa, and further driven by the arguments of merchants and traders in political speeches, newspaper editorials, academicians, and religious ministers, the nation developed a compulsion to establish an overseas empire to secure raw materials for industry. Also, American industries and agricultural products required new markets, since their surplus-capital always led them in search of higher returns outside the boundaries of the country.

Former President Grover Cleveland had avoided any serious American involvement in Cuba. But as the Spanish conflict precipitated with threats to American business Interests, in May of 1897, McKinley asked Congress to appropriate money for the relief of United States Citizens stranded on the island, while other events contributed to the making of war.

Following an ultimatum for arbitration demanded by Britain, the United States government required the peaceful settlement of a boundary dispute between Britain and Venezuela in British Guiana, while Spain remained the only European power to challenge the United States in Latin America.

On February 15, 1898, the U.S. battleship Maine was mysteriously blown-up and sank in the Harbor of Havana, killing most of its crew members. This event immediately set off a storm of popular reaction across the nation, now calling for war. Forbidding its annexation, but yielding to the demands of war, Congress empowered the President to declare war on Spain on April 25. The Spanish-American War itself lasted no longer than four months.

On May1, the U.S. Navy destroyed a Spanish fleet in Manila Harbor.

U.S. Marines landed in force at Guantanamo Bay; and on July 3, the Spanish Caribbean fleet was destroyed at Santiago, Cuba. On July 7, McKinley signed a congressional resolution approving the annexation of Hawaii. U.S. troops landed in Puerto Rico on July 25; and the war ended with the unconditional surrender of the Philippines on August 15th.

The nation's attention that was focused on conquest, expansion, and the protection of its frontiers then came to a quick close. All interests were not in the development of an empire, but rather the expansion and growth of industrial and economic wealth, driven by superior technology that was constantly in the making.

Vice President Garret Hobart had died in his first term in office, and Theodore Roosevelt, who was then Governor of New York was chosen to replace him as McKinley's running mate for the election of 1900. McKinley easily won re-election against his former opponent, William Jennings Bryan who ran for a second time. Roosevelt was inaugurated as Vice President on March 4, 1901, and presided over the Senate for five days in a special session called to approve presidential appointments.

In September of the same year, President McKinley set out to address a gathering at a Pan-American Exposition in Buffalo, New York, when he was shot while shaking hands with a would-be assassin. He died on September 14, and Theodore Roosevelt succeeded him to the Presidency. Roosevelt repeatedly stated his intentions of carrying out McKinley's policies. According to one political analyst of the era, McKinley's Presidency, coupled with the ascendency of Teddy Roosevelt, marked "the first great protest of the American People against monopoly- the first great struggles of the masses in our country against the privileged class." [13]

The economy was robust. Many, especially the educated, had achieved a comfortable life of complacency and self-reliance as owners, leaders, and managers of institutions and industries, and had become the dominant social class throughout the nation. Riding high above this pervasive social class of the modestly prosperous in business, trade, and professions were "the worrisome, extravagant, and domineering class of corporate tycoons who accounted for no more than 8% of the population, but owning and controlling at least 70% of the nation's wealth."

Struggling below both strata were the new wage-earners and laborers

---

[13] Lorant Stefan,Presidency: Macmillan Company, New York

of industry. Their discontents were well articulated and pronounced in the violent confrontations with business ownership and management throughout the1890's; while substantial support of political representation from different states in the Union were continually being elected to Congress.

The pursuit of education became synonymous with progress in every aspect of economic social life. New inventions required and demanded more efficient means to deal with a more urban, industrial, mechanized, centralized, growing, and complex society. Meanwhile, the good times that emerged after the Spanish-American War suffused the nation cities and states with the vulgar antics of "machine politicians," who were now making a mockery of tradition, duty, service, and patriotism.

Meanwhile, the formidable, quality-life seeking middle-class population became restive, and proactive in government affairs. They were now able to support reform measures that would improve the quality of social life surrounding them. Both the physical and intellectual currents of the time harmonized with this dominant social feeling for reform, or a new ordering of government business. This concerned lot of Americans were now called *Progressives.*

The number of laborers had grown, aided by unions and local political machines. Their influence had increased to a point that was becoming frightening to professional people. Blue-collar radicalism, the middle-class argued, could prove as disruptive to American civilization as the current state of unprincipled wealth. Indeed, a new order of government business and mediation was needed for the ambiguous state of "boss-ridden" city and state administrators. They were carry-over residues of the Reconstruction period after the Civil War.

The new form that American government will now take was charged with a venerable leader who would clarify, define, enlarge, and influence the direction of core American values and structure of social life. The ideological framework and foundation incorporated into the nation's Constitution was not the kind of change the new order sought.

Rather, it was an awakening to make government more responsive and representative of the will of decent citizens, now requiring better institutions to meet the changing demands of quality social life- that which innovation and technology had evoked and afforded through applied science, discoveries, new inventions, as well as tools they now had at their disposal.

Whatever its virtues were, the government and its Courts' hands-off off/ *laissez faire* ways of conducting business with industries was obsolete. The eight or nine percent of people who owned more than seventy percent of the country's wealth must now be compelled to behave fairly; and their acquisitive drives curbed in the interest of justice and equality for all. Other elements of society that needed more attention included lower classes of the poor, disadvantaged, sick, aged, and disabled, who must be protected against the unscrupulous.

All notable progressives who have now become the formidable middle-classes, felt that it was their duty to assume new responsibilities toward the unfortunate. Many of those who wanted to improve the living standards of the new industrial and factory workers rejected the notion that workers could best help themselves by organizing powerful unions. In spite of this dread with labor, aspirations of the American people were elevated with the tone of politics as the means of resolution.

Authors, journalists, other professions, and periodicals of the communication industry had begun their blitz and assault on various forms of social injustice, by exposing the harsher aspects of American social life- thereby throwing off romantic illusions of status the nation had achieved as an oligopolistic state. These were the voices that are said to have been the loudest, most vocal, and were on the angry fringe of progressivism.

Consistently, in nearly all subsequent dramatic socio-economic change, or social upheaval that will occur in American character- to this day is often generated by them. This growing lot of middle-class Americans and their attitudes toward progress, always provide the vital catalyst that stimulates the rest of the population to take political action. Through their influence in science and education, published facts, propaganda, leadership in business, private organizations, and governmental affairs. Recently, most of their demands, at best are trivial, and driven purely by self-interests. While the intelligent public bear their challenges and unreasonable demands.

Philosophical tenets and assumptions of progressives' ideas for unraveling or disentangling entrenched political power that flaunted public interest during these early industrial years included: the affirmation of the facts that progress depends on human effort; that master and control of the environment must be effected through intelligent planning- meaning, the future will not take care of itself. Humans are not confined, nor bound by traditional values or forms; and they demanded that past theories and institutions prove themselves in light of current needs for justice in social relations, democracy in politics, and equal opportunity in business. Their pragmatic approach argued for the fact that the consequence of a policy determines its worth. These were the progressive's main agenda.[14]

The new political leader taking the challenge was the descendant of an old stock of wealthy Americans; well educated, had amassed a string of heroics at the age of forty-three, but also had many more daunting, far-reaching goals that were to be accomplished for the nation-state, as he saw it. The dynamic, vigorous, and energetic Teddy Roosevelt was described as a hero in the Spanish-American War with Cuba, served as a New York assemblyman, Police Commissioner of New York City, Assistant Secretary of the Navy, and Governor of the state of New York. Another medley of his repute was captured by many:

In dem there days, it was one thing to have operated a cattle ranch, another to have captured a gang of rustlers at gunpoint. One thing to have run a metropolitan police force, another to have roamed New York slums in the wee, wee hours of the night in order to catch policemen on their beat fraternizing with thieves and whores; and yet another to have commanded a regiment and personally killed an enemy.[15]

A president with such thorough ruggedness was seen as a person who did emulate and embrace the entire philosophy and spirit that progressivism demanded. The people's plea for responsive representative democracy to the common problems of the time subsided and resided in actions that were to be effected by Roosevelt in line with the will of the majority, as they saw it.

In vein of the day's politics, this had meant less regard for special interest groups that maintained the continuing power of corrupt big-city

[14] *The American Profile*
[15] Ibid

political machines. In industry, his actions was to curb the acquisitive drive of companies, trusts, or corporations in the interests of small business owners who were generally put out of business due to steep transportation rates, grain costs, or tariff's. Rising tensions between industry and labor also demanded government intervention.

Shortly after taking the oath of office, Roosevelt immediately went to work asking his Attorney General to prepare an anti-trust suit against Northern Railroad Securities Company, a giant railroad trust of the time. Labor discontent rose to a fever pitch high in May of 1902 when 140,000 members of the United Mine Workers Union went on strike demanding a 10% increase in higher wages and better working conditions in the anthracite coal mines of Pennsylvania. Coal mine owners refused to negotiate with the union, and the strike dragged on through fall and late into the oncoming winter, while the prices of coal kept rising and stocks of coal disappearing. Many schools and hospitals had been forced to close by October for lack of fuel.

Incensed by the occasion, and his determination to get the mines back into operation before the winter got worse, Roosevelt "privately threatened the owners…" telling them, should they fail to comply or agree to arbitration, he would go ahead and take over the mines, even though no legal power is mandated through the Constitution for him to do so.

Nonetheless, in the face of this daunting, the owners agreed, and ended the strike. Coal miners won their ten percent increase in wages sought. Concessions made to the mine owners through arbitrations granted them ample compensation too. They got a ten percent increase in the price of coal; and the companies were not required to recognize the workers' unions as legal arbiters. Although the companies lost very little through the labor strike, workers were relatively pleased with the President's action and the *Square Deal* they got.[16] But the price of fuel they had to burn in their homes did go up.

Far beyond the domestic front of efforts toward improving the conservation of natural resources, Roosevelt had called upon a stronger Navy, urging that a canal be built at once to connect the Atlantic and Pacific Oceans. Six months after he had pressed for the project in his first

[16] Ibid

message to Congress, He signed the *Spooner Act*, authorizing government to negotiate for the canal's construction.

During this period in history, Panama was a province of Colombia, and in subsequent negotiations, Colombia's government resisted giving up some of its sovereign rights in Panama unless the United States was willing to pay more than what Roosevelt was willing to offer.

With his encouragement, a revolt was organized in Panama on November 3, 1903. Assured by the muscle of U.S. warships that were on stand-by off the coast, the Panamanian rebels were successful. Panama then declared its independence from Colombia. Roosevelt immediately recognized the new government. A treaty was concluded with the Panama government without much delay, and construction of the canal got underway.

According to Roosevelt, the building of the Panama Canal is regarded as his most important contribution as President of the United States. "I took Panama without consulting the cabinet." [17]

By acclamation, Roosevelt was nominated and elected President in his own right in 1904. He began to act even bolder on domestic affairs for reform legislation, demanding federal regulation of railroad industries. Progressive state governors also demanded federal action; farmers, and manufacturers, especially in mid-western states, who clamored for relief against arbitrary discriminatory rates, fared no better. The unified consensus of the times prompted Roosevelt to put teeth in the Interstate Commerce Commission (ICC), not merely to challenge the railroads, but also empowering it to fix rates.

Thoroughness of the ICC demands struck at the heart of rights that most businessmen of the time considered sacred, while many of the non-progressive congressional representatives were not too pleased with the action. But the President, combined with a broad unanimous public base support, pressed on for stiffer regulations, causing a majority of big concessions to fall in line.

The mounting awareness made through newspapers' opinions, magazine articles, and scientific data published by concerned and assertive academicians; the works of columnists, journalists, and book authors directing attention to the evils of industry and the deteriorating quality of

---

[17] Ibid

American social life, irked Roosevelt to the point of dubbing the American progressive intelligentsias as a bunch of "muckrakers." Nonetheless, with strong evidence and good reasoning, he did respond to Upton Sinclair's novel titled *The Jungle*, a book that exposed the sordid conditions of the meat-packing industry.[18]

---

[18] Ibid

9

WHAT IS MEANT BY THE TERM PROGRESSIVISM? ACTION!

WITH YET ANOTHER DARING TO the recalcitrant congress he was working with, Roosevelt threatened to go public with the issues himself. Without any more pussyfooting and whining, Congress passed the Pure Food and Drug Act, forbidding the manufacture and sale of adulterated and fraudulently labeled products.

Progressive thinking Americans have always been around ever since inception of the nation's ruling Constitution. The most accurate definition of progressivism is that it is a realistic and scientific attitude toward the present conditions of our physical and intellectual surrounding world, coupled with a real spirit, fervor or zest for changing it toward a better quality of present-future existence.

Progressivism as lived, is the path of authentic human struggle for comity, vision, ideas, speech, and sharing among our fellow men and women. Action which confers upon variety in the many forms of social life. Resolve- which means to build, fix, remedy, or settle issues and things by deliberate choice or will. Progressivism is a way or practice of focused awareness and mindfulness of others. Progressivism is comity.

As progressive individuals, families, and social groups accumulate more knowledge and truth about the nature of the environment in which they live or move about, they automatically change or reorganize the structure of their thinking. In some instances and extremes, it may be the entire foundation upon which their current individual basic life assumptions and beliefs rest. And it must be scrapped at all cost once truth is ascertained about our real human condition.

Any resistance against change of any form or magnitude is proportionate to the proof of social reality individuals can experience. In all its essence, a Progressive attitude are the words, acts, and images of what we call an *individual* in his or her communal confines of experience, self-production, and self-expressions.

Contagion of the new forms of Progressivism that emerged helped to remove antiquated and disgraceful political *boss-ridden* city *machines* that were no more than tyrants. The rapid and disordered growth of the nation's urban areas after the Civil War had encouraged the *Boss* system, which was in reality, the strong man and his *machine* that would rule and exploit the city. Their disappearance was replaced by new urban political institutions that gave the people more representative forms of government.

But the public had only its indifference to blame for the decadent mismanagement of their government. Since all municipal governments must depend on the authority of a sovereign state, the support of legislators is necessary to carry out needed reforms. But the local *bosses* were also entrenched in the more powerful state *machines*, while most legislatures were controlled by rural majorities insensitive to the growing urban needs.

One of the most remarkable figures and representative of the new forms of Progressivism was Robert M. La Follett, a three-term Republican Congressman (1885-1891) who transformed the state of Wisconsin when he was elected governor in 1900. The fundamental tenet and article of La Follett's political faith was plain and simple "...People will do the right thing in any situation if properly informed or inspired."

Over the opposition of conservative Republicans subservient to the railroad and lumbering interests in Wisconsin, he obtained a direct primary system in nominating candidates- a practice which was widely considered contemptuous. He also passed laws limiting campaign expenditure and lobbying activities. A sort of tyrant himself, La Follett made ruthless use of patronage, and demanded absolute loyalty to the compact from his subordinates, "only because he was devoted to honest government."[19]

La Follett influenced other Progressive governors like Charles Evans

---

[19] Garranty John A./McCaughey *A Short History of The American Nation Fifth Edition*

Hughes of New York, Hiram Johnson of California, and Woodrow Wilson of New Jersey. The great success of his ideas also led the way for massive and sweeping administrative reform in the States of Arkansas in 1901, Oregon in 1902, followed by Minnesota, Kansas, Mississippi, Georgia, Nebraska, and Colorado. The *Progressive* reformers were both Democrats and Republicans.

The thrust they were making for representative government and social reform, with Roosevelt as President, waned in his remaining two years in office. Since most reform measures were aimed at unscrupulous business practices that had proven harmful to the general public, Roosevelt successor to the presidency, William Howard Taft conducted a more vigorous attack on what Roosevelt had called "predatory wealth." These were the railroads that Taft had to tighten Federal control over. He instituted the highly efficient Parcel Post system, and a Federal income tax that was legitimized by the Sixteenth Amendment in 1913. Taft's administration instituted twice as many proceedings against business combinations as Roosevelt had launched.

Prior to this era of progressivism, where laissez faire dominated the order of business, the U. S. Supreme Court's attitude and practice was that of *judicial restraint*. Wherefore, the new era now demands *judicial activism* as the main vehicle for social reform in all business and industrial practices, in the interest of the greater public and safety of the environment.

In the pursuit of a more vigorous involvement by a national leader, Roosevelt challenged the leadership of Taft, who was nominated for a second term by the Republican Party with a campaign for "New Nationalism." This drove a wedge between members of the Republican Party, allowing the opposing Democrats to win the Presidency.

WILSON

"This is not a day of triumph; it is a day of dedication..." declared Woodrow Wilson, the new Democratic Party President in his inauguration speech. My job as President "is a human being trying to cooperate with other human beings in a common service." The service Wilson pledged was to honor Progressives' demands with a radical reform agenda.

His first order of business was a precedent set by only one former President, and that was to bring both Houses of Congress into one session to lay out his program. Legislative achievements under Taft had been very small. An avalanche of important new measures produced by Wilson now received approval of the lawmakers.

The first significant reduction of duties before and after the Civil War, known as the Underwood Taft Act, was passed in October of 1913. In order to compensate for an expected loss of revenue, the Act provided for a graduated tax on personal incomes, which resulted in enactment of the Sixteenth Amendment, ratified earlier in February of the same year.

Responding to Howard Taft's plea in his campaign for a second term, when he stated that the "most crying need of the country" was a proper banking and currency system, congress passed the Federal Reserve Act in November, giving the nation a Central Banking System for the first time since the days of Andrew Jackson- freeing its credit supply from the control of a few private financers.

This measure divided the country into 12 banking districts, each under supervision of the Federal Reserve Bank- a banker's bank, as it were. All the banks in each district, along with state banks that wished to participate had to invest at least 6% of their capital and surplus in the Federal Reserve Bank, which was empowered to rediscount or exchange Federal Reserve notes, or paper money, for the commercial and agricultural paper that member Banks take in as security notes. Thus the volume of currency was no longer at the mercy of the supply of gold, or any other commodity in particular.[20]

When *inflation* threatens, the Federal Reserve could raise the exchange rate, thereby discouraging borrowing, which automatically reduces the amount of money in circulation. Conversely, in bad times it could lower the rate, making it easier to borrow; injecting new money into the economy. This act enabled the nation with a safe and flexible currency. Local and private autonomy was also reconciled with the need for government supervision, preventing the general public from recurring economic depressions.

The following year of 1914, Wilson continued to push for tariff reforms, while lobbyists tried to frustrate his plans. He then set out to

---

[20] Ibid

make a dramatic appeal to the people to show how "insidious" the lobbies of big business were against their intended regulation by government. "The public ought to know the extraordinary exertions being made by the lobby in Washington... money without limit is being used to sustain this lobby. Only public opinion can check and destroy it," Wilson declared, and went on to state that "...control of the system of banking, and of issue must be vested in the government itself so the banks may be instruments, not masters, of business, and of individual enterprise and initiative."[21]

Voters respond so strongly to Wilson's appeal that the Senate passed his far-reaching reduction in tariff Bill as substantially as he had desired it to be. Thus, the most far-reaching series of laws connected with social justice were set in motion with the establishment of the FTC (Federal Trade Commission) to regulate business. The Clayton Antitrust Act that prevented business monopolies made certain business practices illegal, such as price discrimination that foster monopolies "tying up" agreements which forbids a retailer from handling the product of a firm's competitors.

He created an interlocking device and a board of directors as a means of controlling other companies. These acts also exempted agricultural organizations and Labor Unions from the antitrust laws, curtailing the use of Court injunctions in labor disputes; while officers of corporations could be held individually responsible when their companies violate the antitrust laws.

His phenomenal success so far in having his way and getting these progressive measures through Congress caused Wilson to reflect when questioned about it, stating that "running the government was like child's play for anyone who had managed the faculty of a university."

But a more formidable and demanding task was in the making, when he declared in November of 1914 that he considered the era of reform to had come to an end. Progressive reformers demanded more, such as: Federal Farm credits, wages and hours benefits for labor, women *suffrage* (the right of women to vote), and the outlawing of child labor.

---

[21] Ibid

10

WORLD WAR I EVENTS

The President's abrupt declaration to the ending of further domestic reform was on account of a looming immanence of the nation's involvement in a European war that had been ignited and aflame months earlier. In July of 1914, Austria had declared war on Serbia. On August 1, Germany was at war with Russia. Four days later, Germany attacked France.

On August 4, Wilson delivered to the nation the first of a series of neutrality proclamations. Most important about these proclamations was the nation's defense of its own boarders, owing to precipitating conflicts with Mexico. Ever since Mexico's revolutionary change of government in 1910, the country had remained the United States main foreign worry. U. S. troops were sent into Mexico In April of 1914, when Wilson learned that German merchantmen laden with munitions were expected to land at Vera Cruz.

Early in February of 1915 the following year, the Germans declared waters surrounding the British Isles a war zone, stating that they would sink without warning all enemy merchant ships encountered in the area. Since Allied Forces ships often flew neutral flags to disguise their identity, Neutral ships entering the zone would do so at their own risk.

Sailing this route three months later, on May 7th 1915 an English passenger liner, the *Lusitania*, was torpedoed by German U-boat submarines causing the death of more than a thousand persons, including 124 Americans. The mood among prominent Progressives was for an immediate declaration of war, but Wilson declined to commit the country to war, and even refused to ask Congress for increased military appropriations, saying that he did not want to "turn America into a military camp."

This position accurately reflected the attitude of most Americans toward war. Although Wilson made efforts to have Germany stop its U-boat attacks and pay indemnity to its victims, the Germans belligerently rejected his plea and continued their attacks, unabated.

In spite of a brief setback through the death of his wife, Wilson was up for re-election in 1916, and his real problems of handling things scholastically and judiciously had just begun. The nation's dispute and worries with Mexico were not yet over. General Francisco, "Pancho Villa" early in 1916 rose against American recognized President, Venustiano Carranza of Mexico, and began a series of attacks on U.S. citizens. 16 American passengers were killed on a train in Northern Mexico. Villa then crossed the U.S. boarder to the state of New Mexico, burning down the town of Columbus and killing 19 people.

He was then pursued for a brief period by U S Army General Pershing and his troops, encountering several clashes with regular Mexican troops in Mexico. Pancho Villa proved elusive, and impossible to catch, as he drew General Pershing deeper and deeper into Mexico.[22]

In the meantime, Roosevelt had become so incensed by Wilson's refusal to commit the nation to the Allied causes of the war waging in Europe, that he was ready to support any Republican candidate to guarantee the President's defeat. At the same time, many prominent Progressives were complaining of Wilson's unwillingness to work for further domestic reforms.

Their gripes were answered with the passage of legislation that called for: A Farm Loan Act to provide low-cost loans to farmers based on agricultural credit; the Keating-Owen Child Act, a Workmen's Compensation Act for Federal employees, and the Adamson Act, establishing an 8-hour day for railroad workers.

The stance of neutrality, of avoiding the nation's involvement in war seems quite realistic to the majority of working-class voters; simply because the war *out there* created a great boom in American trade and industries. In the meantime, supplies and food were badly needed in Europe. The Democrats, in light of current legislative enactments, have not deviated

---

[22] Ibid

from their platform of shifting from an all-time *States' Rights Party,* to now become the Party of progressive nationalism.

By contrast, the Republicans' agenda to elect a new President did not differ in their progressive plans, save for American policy toward the warring powers that made the key issue in the Campaign. Wilson's opposition and formidable challenge for the Presidency was Republican candidate Charles Evans Hughes, a former Associate Justice of the U.S. Supreme Court, and Governor of New York.

Almost all the Eastern States favored and voted for Hughes In the November election. Wilson went to bed that night feeling he had lost the election, since most of his opposition had come from his unwillingness to commit the country to war. However, returns from California the following day showed he had won the popular votes in this state by a narrow margin of 4,000 votes. This automatically gave him all critical 13 delegates, enough to win the Presidency.

Largely because of his anti-war sentiment, Wilson was victorious at the polls. "He kept us out of war," was the popular mandate that voters expected to continue. But this was only a social delusion. In his attempt to carry-on with this mandate, it became apparent that control of the situation rested more with the warring powers than with the American government.

Less than a month after his election, the President issued an appeal to both *Allied* and *Central* Powers- (as the warring parties were referred to), asking for terms under which hostilities might be ended. Austria-Hungary, and Germany, called *Central Powers,* stood in opposition to Britain, France, Italy, and Russia, who were the *Allied Powers.*

Allied Powers demanded the return of all territories conquered by the Central Powers, as well as repatriations. The Central Powers reply was prompt, stringent, and evasive; indicating that they would make their terms known at the Councils' Chamber. In short, neither side would accept anything less than a victor's terms.[23]

It was within the face of this impasse that Wilson delivered a speech to the U.S. Senate in January; outlining terms which he hoped and believed would become the basis for negotiating a settlement that would bring about "peace without a victory." But Wilson's hope vanished within a week.

---

[23] Ibid

Germany was convinced that an economic blockade would starve the British into submission, thereby reducing Allied armies into impotence, by cutting off American supplies. The Germans then went into unrestricted submarine warfare against merchant-shipping in the war zones, not caring whether they were Allied or Neutral vessels.

The U.S. immediately broke off diplomatic relations with Germany, and events began to move swiftly and relentlessly. On February 24th 1917, Hines Paige, a U.S. Ambassador to Britain informed the State Department of a *"Zimmerman Telegram"* that was intercepted; revealing that Germany had proposed a secret alliance with Mexico in order to receive, "in the event of war with the U.S., the lost territories of Arizona, New Mexico, and Texas."

This telegram was released to the press on March 4th. On March 25th Wilson calls upon the National Guard; and on the 27th, news came that three American ships had been sunk. A special session of Congress was called, asking for a declaration of war against Germany; and a resolution was passed on April 6th by overwhelming majorities.

When the United States entered the war siding with *Allied Powers*, Germany's blockade with its U-boat submarines on shipping food and supplies from all Neutral and Allied sources had proven to be so successful, that *Allied Powers'* resistance was at its lowest morale and dimmest hopes. The British resistance estimated they had only a week's supply of food and material on hand. More than a million lives had already been lost in Russia, while France seemed to be on the verge of collapsing before the *Central Powers'* onslaught.

A decision was now made and got underway to send and transport both merchant and U.S. troops, screened by warships to Europe. Anti-submarine minefields were planted in the North Sea, and U.S. destroyers and airplanes joined British forces in seeking out and combating German U-boats in the Atlantic. Six months after American intervention, Allied shipping losses due to submarine attacks had been dramatically reduced, and not a single American troop ship was sunk during the war. "Results were impressive!"

Dwindling Allied supplies made it imperative for the nation to gear its economy to the war effort with utmost speed. The Emergency Fleet Corporation entrusted to Herbert Hoover, built, purchased, or "confiscated" enough ships to transport American farm and factory products to Europe. By dramatic tax increases, and the sale of *liberty bonds,* the nation funded its war expenses, giving the Allies a considerable boost in assistance. This accounted for a steeply graduated income tax that took away more than 75% of the incomes of the wealthiest citizens, along with a 65% excess profit tax, and a 25% inheritance tax.

The conversion of American industries to war production had to be organized and carried out at the spur of the moment, or without any kind of pre-arrangement. This mobilization required close cooperation between private enterprise and the military. Antitrust laws were suspended, while producers were encouraged- even compelled to cooperate with one another.

U.S. exports in food increased by about 6 million tons. Between 1915, and 1918, real income of farmers increased 30%; unemployment disappeared, and wages rose along with the cost of living. Cooperation between private industry and the military produced unprecedented opportunities that were to become the basis of our modern-day American economy and civilization.

The war itself was now implicating a sense of common purpose among the general citizenry, owing to the nation's commitment and considerable steaks it had in the *Allied Powers'* war efforts. Since 1915, U.S. bankers had been making enormous loans to England and France, totaling more than $2 billion by April of 1917. German loans, by contrast, totaled only $27 million. A break-up of diplomatic relations with the Allies would mean a substantial loss of these funds. On account of this, Wilson felt an inherent need to mediate the war's eventual or ultimate outcome.

The first unit of U.S. troops arrived in Paris on July 4th, 1917; while positions on the actual battle front were taken in October. Although airplane, tank, and artillery construction developed too slowly to affect the war, the country's national prosperity was still interwoven with Allied Powers' needs and demands. Allied Powers were now seen in a new perspective of defending core values to which Americans subscribe.

With the Germans planning a final crushing offensive on the Western front in the spring of 1918, the U.S. provided up to 50,000 troops in order to bring the war to a forceful end; participating in some of the fiercest battles waged with the enemies. It was not until late in September when the greatest impact of American engagement in the war began. And for about two months of relentless horror and sustained terror that took about 120 casualties, they inched their way, closing in with British and French armies staging similar drives from a different direction on the enemy.

The Germans, who were already sensing defeat, seized upon Wilson's Fourteen-point plans as an opportunity and basis for making peace sometime in October. In the meantime, Allied Armies who were advancing against the Germans on all fronts, now finally broke their center offensive when they surrendered. An armistice was signed on November 11th, ending the war with more than 230,000 returning wounded U.S. troops, and the loss of more than 45,000 lives. Russia took the heaviest toll with more than 20million lives lost.

From January through May of 1918, Wilson had belabored himself in producing a Fourteen Point peace plan; principles on which he believed a just and lasting peace could be established between the warring nations. In general, eight of these principles called for the adjustments of European boundaries according "to the ideal of self-determination." Five were enumerated guidelines for the conduct of nations in their relations with each other, which included:

The avoidance of secret treaties, freedom of the seas, and the removal of free-trade barriers; a reduction of arms; and the impartial adjustments of their colonial claims. In his final principle, he noted that it was "for the purpose of affording mutual guarantees of political independence and territorial integrity to all involved." Wilson further proposed a general association of nations, which in effect was a *League of Nations*.

Wilson's plans and the nation's timely entry into the war, tentatively earned him the reputation of a potential savior abroad. However, at home he fell into increasing disfavor with fellow politicians and the public alike. Voters ignored the President's appeal for an endorsement of his policies by returning Republican majorities to both Houses of Congress in the mid-term elections of 1918. A reaction against Wilson's crusading zeal of the war was underway.

Being dealt such strong opposition, Wilson decided to personally lead an American peace delegation to Paris. While there, immediate public response to his Fourteen-Point peace plan presentation was met with open enthusiasm, while the reality of commitment was placed squarely on the U.S.

Personally presenting the peace plans to Allied Prime Ministers, the vagueness and inconsistencies of the document did not match the social reality of demographics, language, nor customs of the locales' disparate traditions. Furthermore, the *Allies* had already made certain territorial commitments to one another in secret treaties, running contrary to the principle of "Self-determination." Neither were the Allies ready to give up all claims to Germany's sprawling colonial empire. Every Allied country rejected Wilson's ideas of "peace without indemnities."[24]

Seventy-eight years old French Prime Minister Clemenceau viewed the document most cynically when he said that, since both man and womankind had "been unable to keep God's Ten Commandments, it is not likely to do any better with the plan." While the British sympathized with what Wilson was trying to accomplish, they also found his plans incomprehensible with his facts of "*right* being more important than *might*, and *justice* being more eternal than *force.*" Individual complaints and criticisms of Allied Nations were reasonable; however their conclusions were not entirely fair in some of their demands. Wilson wound up agreeing to one compromise after another, leaving them with a sole victorious agreement of forming a League of Nations.

On his return to the U.S., Wilson began to mount an uphill battle for ratification of the treaty from the Senate. "Reservations" and "minor alterations" were demanded before the Senates' approval. Wilson refused to budge, consider any modifications, or make any concessions. He became "a moral absolutist," as others have it. His unbending attitude precipitated into an increased stubbornness and loss of good judgment. Some members of the Senate were not in sympathy with his ideals or methods of achieving them. He therefore created the impression of forcing his personal conceptions of world organization on the country.[25]

Trying to rally public opinion on his side, Wilson set out on an 8,000-mile speaking tour throughout the Mid-Western states and Pacific Coast. He collapsed in exhaustion on September 25th after delivering a speech at Pueblo, Colorado, canceling the rest of his engagements. On his return to Washington on October 2, Wilson suffered a stroke that left him partially paralyzed and an invalid. From here on until the end of his term, the

---

[24] Ibid
[25] Ibid

nation carried on without a Chief Executive, in the sense that the President was confined to his bed most of the times- "partially paralyzed, mentally exhausted, and intellectually embittered."[26]

POST WORLD-WAR 1 EVENTS

A Presidential election was nearing during Wilson's illness, which carried the sentiments of Western farmers who believed they had been discriminated against during the war, owing to government price controls placed on their wheat; while allowing the price of cotton to rise up to 500% in two years. The labor market was restive in the presence of peacetime conditions, with swelling unemployment; while businessmen were angry with Wilson's administrations' drastic tax program that funded the war. They also demanded freedom from government regulations. Most important of these issues was Wilson's intentions to break with the nation's isolationist tradition, making the U.S. inclusive in a League of Nations.

The Republican Party election platform embraced by Warren G. Harding and his running mate Calvin Coolidge stood diametrically opposed to the Democrats who wished to continue Wilson's plans. The Republicans keynote to voters was "we must be now and ever for Americanism and nationalism, and against internationalism."

In direct reference to Wilson's appeals for a League of Nations, the platform noted that "the Republican Party stands for agreement among nations to preserve the peace," with a stipulation that this must be done "without compromising national independence." Representative Senator Henry Cabot Lodge farther argued, and insisted "that the nation's right to determine its own interests in every situation is preserved."

The Democrats sentiments carried by Presidential and vice-Presidential hopefuls, James Cox and Franklin D. Roosevelt, which urged for immediate ratification of the League of Nation's treaty, overshadowed their pledged adherence to fundamental progressive principles of social, economic, and industrial justice, between and among the nation's states' citizens'- most

---

[26] Ibid

notably, the disenfranchised returning wounded war veterans, who had sacrificed their lives for a mere pittance of a dollar a day.

Furthermore, hasty demobilization accounted for millions pouring into the job market without a plan. Over 45,000 Americans had lost their lives and none of their surviving relatives adequately compensated. Over 20% of the labor force was on strike at some time during and after 1919. Work stoppage exaggerated shortages, triggering further inflation and more strikes. Between July of 1920 and March of 1922, agricultural prices plummeted, while unemployment soared.

Revival of European agriculture production after the war had cut the demand for American farm products, just when the increased use of fertilizers and the invention of new machinery was boosting output. Labor unrest, terrorists' threats to murder prominent officials, revival of the Klux Klux Klan's program of ethnic and religious groups' purge, and bigotry with its eager followers, had been gaining hundreds of thousands of new recruits in the western and southern states, where the Democrats hold were strongest.

Added to this combination of national outrage and discontent were *Communists* who had appointed themselves as champions of workers, and the rampant labor unrest that had magnetically attracted them, when waves of strike broke out throughout the nation.

From all over the country came demands that these radical elements of society be ruthlessly suppressed. And because of the cruelties, bloodshed, and supposed menace of Communism that took place in the Russian Revolution, the voting public tolerated wholesale violation of Civil Rights of suspects or anyone sympathetic to such ideological cause.

11

FROM BOOM TO BUST

Republicans were victorious in the general election of 1920; while the Democrats who tried to make American participation in the League of Nations their decisive campaign platform did not matter much to voters, owing to the hardships the War had imposed on citizens. A return to normalcy and a peacetime footing was the main objective of the incoming administration of Warren Harding and vice President Calvin Coolidge. A month after inauguration, a special session of Congress convened, laying out a broad program of a long-needed Federal Budget System, higher tariff barriers, cutting down on War taxes, an extreme economy, and restrictions on immigration.

Big business' interests pervaded the administration's atmosphere more heavily than anything else. War-time powers that had included governmental ownership of railroads were slowly liquidated, and a step by step Federal regulation of the nation's business life was eliminated wherever possible. Negotiations were reopened with Germany concerning its indebtedness, and a Peace Treaty was signed on August25, 1921.

Harding and Coolidge used the power of appointment to convert regulatory government bodies, like the Interstate Commerce Commission, and Federal Reserve Board, into pro-business agencies that almost entirely ceased to restrict the activities of industries that they were originally designed to regulate.

In effecting their broad-based program, the Presidential Cabinet is said to have been composed of an alarming number of distinguished people. However, what was later revealed was that much of Harding's administrations' work and real political business took place at evening poker and drinking parties that were regularly attended by various cronies, friends, hangers-on, and acquaintances of dubious repute.

Because the Senate disapproved of the Versailles Treaty ending the War in 1921, separate treaties with Germany and its allies were arranged, that excluded the United States participation in the League of Nations. With Harding's approval, Congress increased protective tariffs to a new high, established a system for preparing a national budget, and vetoed a bonus bill for the veterans of World War I, which Congress had approved.

Perhaps because of his indifference to war veterans, Mid-term elections of 1922 showed that the Republican Party's majorities were reduced in both Houses of Congress. Harding was worried that the election results showed a loss of confidence in his administration. He then resolved to go on a nation-wide speaking tour.

The President was a well-annoyed and badly haggard man, and the general public knew very little when he set out by train from Washington for a "Voyage of Understanding" on June 20, 1923, just when personalities of his distinguished colleagues began to unravel. Though it had been going on from the beginning of his administration in 1920, it wasn't until late in 1922 that Harding began to learn of the epic proportions of dishonesty and the betrayal of public trust within it.

Officers ranging from coroner, policemen, to Cabinet members instituted their stamp of government agents' graft, greed, and corruption. Made law of the land by the Eighteenth Amendment, Prohibition proved to be an enormous boom for bootleggers and the corrupt officials who stashed away millions of dollars- some of which was allegedly appropriated to the Attorney General's aide and confidante.

The first major avalanche of shock waves came in January of 1923, when the head of the Veterans' Bureau was relieved of his duties, (later indicted, tried, and locked-up for siphoning over 200 million dollars of government money for his own purposes). The second tremor occurred two months later in March, with the suicide act of the attorney for the Veteran's Bureau. Aware of further disastrous events in the offing prompted Harding to advise one of his cronies to leave Washington.

On the night of May 29, this crony returned to Washington and shot himself in the apartment he once shared with the Attorney General. Although he is said to have been visibly shaken, Harding continued his voyage of understanding to Alaska. On his return on June 27th to Seattle, he was said to be stricken by food poisoning, which his physician, who was then Surgeon General, first diagnosed. After canceling some of his speaking engagements, Harding seemed to have been recovering when he arrived in San Francisco on July 29[th.] But then he contacted pneumonia. And in the presence of his wife and distinguished physicians attending to him at Stanford University, Harding died.

Vice-president Coolidge, who then succeeded Harding, restored some of the dignity and public trust which the Administration had lost. There were no more drinking and wild poker card parties, and a few heads were changed in the Cabinet. "The business of America is Business," was Coolidge's operational. In spite of the fact that Americans' pursuit of wealth during this period was marked by the administrations' monumental hypocrisy, and immense immorality, any interference with this state of affairs and its material objectives were harshly condemned by all the nations' mainstream Medias.

Most commentators of the times insisted that the goal of Capitalism and precepts of Christianity were identical. Their true religion was business; their God- the United States dollar; and their salvation was to be achieved through productive labor and economic success. "The man who builds a factory builds a temple," declared Coolidge. "The man who works there worships there."[27]

Business boomed, real wages rose, and unemployment declined. Prosperity still rested on the basis of the hands-off attitude of government that bolstered confidence of the business community; while the Federal Reserve Board kept interest rates low. The Auto industry, inventions, new household appliances, the use of electricity, and the remarkable improvement in efficiency of American manufacturing, plus the growing ability of manufacturers to create new consumer demands, and the invention of radio fueled the nation's economy to unprecedented highs. Business advertising and salesmanship were elevated almost to the status of fine arts.

Underneath, a marked shift in political consciousness solidified toward the election of 1924, where Democrats were "violently" split over the fundamental issue of the Ku Klux Klan and their program of ethnic and

---

[27] Ibid

religious purge, and bigotry in the South and Western states. Assembled amidst an atmosphere of wide open dissentions, no amount of reference to the epic proportion of the rampant corruption that took place during Harding Administration's shortcomings could have concealed the fact that the Democratic Party were violently split on the fundamental issue of the Klan's voice.

With Democrats blocking and tackling other Democrats, Coolidge was free to be elected with ease to the Presidency. He tersely repeated his pledge to enforce the economy, reduce taxes, and avoid governmental interference with business. He made no attempt to work closely with Congress, take issues to the people, or to use his executive powers forcefully. This was a period of economic prosperity, and Coolidge's job, as he saw it, was to encourage private enterprise to the utmost, with minimal government interference.

In stark contrast to the nation's business boom was a negative era from the standpoint of government participation in the nation's economic life of many of its smaller productive economic units. While industries and big businesses reaped high profits, the purchasing power of farm communities had been dwindling. Being forced to sell their products abroad, farmers found that world prices depressed domestic products, despite the high tariff walls that the administration had erected. Both Harding and Coolidge had opposed direct aid to agriculture as a matter of principle.

However, Congress did make it easier for Farmers to borrow money, but did nothing to increase agricultural income. Congress also strengthened laws regulating railroad rates, and grain exchanges. Depressed agricultural prices that kept farmers far behind in income gains led to a bitterly contested Bill in Congress, between 1924 and 1929. Put forward by a coalition of Mid-western Republicans and Southern Democrats, who had come together to form what was then called the "Farm Bloc." The Bill sought to separate farm produce for export from those for domestic consumption, in order to keep domestic price levels from being depressed by world prices. This Bill was vetoed twice by Coolidge.

A year before, and during the entire years of Coolidge's administration, indexes of speculative gains rose from 100 to 410; while wages for workers only rose from 100 to 112. As big businesses continue to reap high profits, the purchasing power returns of high agricultural production in farm communities were kept low by comparison. Successful speculators who were amassing fortunes, lulled a sizeable portion of the lower class population into the delusion that their prosperity was going to go on forever.

Service vendors such as cab drivers, barroom owners, barbers, and so on invested and provided plausible lip-service, and helped to spread the notion around. After all, millionaires were being made every week or everyday as the mania spread. So it was shock and disappointment to the Republican Party when in the midst of this prosperity Coolidge must have heard a siren, and decided to get out of the way. [28]

In spite of a population surge of over a million and a half unemployed workers, Farmers, seamen, textile workers, and coal miners had a hard going during this period of economic boom and prosperity. However, in spite of this pervasive fact, Democratic sentiments and representatives' electioneering were unable to solidify this discontentment and incorporate them into their platform, in order to suggest a course of change in government, when the Republicans nominated Herbert Hoover to be President in 1928.

In fact, Hoover's optimism of the nation's economic life was well supported by then Chairman of the Democratic National Committee, stating that "if a man saves $15 a week and invests in good common stocks, and allows the dividends and rights to accumulate, at the end of twenty years, he will have at least $80,000, and an income from investment of around $400 a month. He will be rich. And because income can do that, I am firm in my belief that anyone not only can be rich, but aught to be rich." [29]The prospect of prosperity that pervaded the conscience of less successful Americans was bolstered by the voter's decision for continued Republican rule, with an even more experienced and efficient business executive in Herbert Hoover.

Hoover declared that given the chance to go forward with the policies of the last eight years of his predecessors, "we shall soon, with the help of God, be within sight of the day when poverty will be banished from the nation." The country was at the pinnacle of prosperity when Hoover took office. Prices on the New York Stock Exchange already at a high during the Presidential campaign began to surge, and climbed even higher in the

---

[28] Ibid

[29] Ibid

first half of 1929 when a mania of speculation swept the country, causing thousands of investors to pour their savings into common stocks. In fact, in the single month of January 1929, more than a billion dollars' worth of new securities were absorbed by the eager public.

Amidst volatile fluctuations of the market in the month of September, stock averages started easing downwards. Most analysts then contended that the exchange was "digesting" previous gains; putting out the prevailing view that "stock prices would soon resume their usual advance." But three days later a wave of selling sent prices spinning on October 24th, when nearly 13 million shares were dumped on the panicky market and changed hands.

Within a few weeks, securities lost more than 40 billion worth of their value and neither government nor the speculators realized the magnitude and acuteness of the situation. When bankers and politicians rallied to check the decline it was too late. Their response was a diatribe plea of confidence, asserting that prosperous times will soon return. But days later, the boom was over, bottom of the stock market fell out, and prices took a nose dive.

The crash came with great force. Hoover had only been in office for seven months. He made encouraging statements, but precipitating events proved him and his experts wrong. As purchasing power diminished and merchandize inventories stockpiled on shelves, factories were forced to reduce their production. Legions of the unemployed grew, while those who kept their jobs had to be contented with reduced wages. Department stores' clerks' salary sank to $5.00 or $10.00 a week; domestic servants $10.00 a month. Southern plantation cotton planters were paying as little as 20 cents to get a hundred pounds of cotton picked, at a rate that amounted to a wage of 60 cents for a 14-hour day, for the most able-bodied skilled picker.[30]

As the crisis escalated and more unsold merchandize stockpiled, factories further restricted production and more workers fell out to the streets. The acuteness of the depression spread wider and wider throughout the nation. The President's program for ending the depression evolved gradually between 1929 and 1932. Millions were spent on semi-public corporations that produced cotton and wheat. It also called for cooperative

---

[30] Ibid

action by businessmen, free from antitrust prosecutions, in order to maintain prices and wages for tax cuts to increase consumer spending. He made it easier for farmers to borrow money and set up cooperative marketing schemes designed to solve their problems.

Amidst the crisis, Hoover was obsessed with the idea of balancing the budget, refusing on constitutional grounds to provide relief for destitute individuals or their families. "Prosperity cannot be restored by raids on the public treasury," stated Hoover. He believed that government loans given to businessmen were constitutional, because the money could be put to productive use and eventually repaid. And it was this trust- without legal government compulsion- that led to the escalating decline in public confidence.

From March of 1930 through June of 1931 was a long period of despair for many in the nation. Homeless men wandered the city streets, or drifted aimlessly from town to town, hoping to get a start, when factories closed down, and millions more became hopeless in search of a livelihood. The public grew more resentful of Hoover's dogmatic economic stand and his refusal for Federal intervention, stating that this was the province of charities, state, and municipal agencies. He clung to his laissez faire traditional American philosophy of government, while millions more Americans "kept themselves fed on stale bread, thin soup, and garbage."[31]

Collapse of the stock market did not immediately caused the depression, but activity began to decline significantly early in 1930, despite protests registered by 34 nations, and one thousand American economists, when Hoover signed the Hawley-Smoot Bill, raising the nation's tariffs' barrier to prohibitive levels. The measure made it impossible for European nations to pay their World War I debts to the United States, thereby hastening the depression, and paving the way for the eventual collapse of European economies in 1931.

---

[31] Ibid

12

ROOSEVELT'S CONCEPTS AND
IDEAS FOR A NEW DEAL

Severity of the depression led most well-thinking, and well-meaning educated Americans to favor radical economic and political changes. Disparities between the rich, well-to-do, and poor, which became starker engendered considerable bitterness in the souls of many. This challenge to democracy and freedom within the ideology of capitalism was to be taken up by Franklin D. Roosevelt, the Democratic Party nominee for President. "My policy is as radical as the United States Constitution," was his declaration in his basic opposition to Herbert Hoover's approach in dealing with the crisis. This position was unmistakable.

"There must be a reappraisal of values," and the American people deserves a "New Deal" from their government. Instead of hanging on to old ideas concerning the scope and limitations of Federal power, the government should do whatever is necessary to protect the unfortunate and advance the public good.[32]

He went on to note in a campaign speech that "Only a foolish optimist can deny the dark realities of the moment… citizens face the grim problems of existence … rulers of the exchange of mankind's goods have failed through their own stubbornness and their incompetence.."

Roosevelt was born to wealth and social status, but his desire and ambition to render public service motivated him to take up the burdens of an altruistic leader. While serving as Governor of New York, his administration enacted an impressive program providing relief for

---

[32] Ibid

139

the needy, by creating a program for old-age pension, unemployment insurance, conservation, and public power projects, among the first of its kind in the nation.

Hoover, by contrast was the son of a poor Mid-Westerner who became a self-made millionaire before he was 40. Critics of the day had described him as a person who was doctrinaire, too rigid, and too aloof to win the attention of ordinary people. He was also too wedded to a particular theory of government to cope effectively with the problems of the times. Hoover never thought much of Roosevelt's plight. In fact, he thought Roosevelt was "ignorant, but well meaning."

From the big crash of the market through 1930, Hoover sought for a solution through the same prism and reluctance for direct government intervention. And from 1930 through June 1931, he campaigned for re-election on the shaky ground that the depression was part of the sudden collapse of the international market, and through the inability of the nations affected by it to pay their debts- notably Germany. But the public refused to buy this commodity, and grew increasingly resentful of his dogmatic economic stand, by rendering the Constitution inflexible.

In spite of the fact of the overwhelming inability of private charities, local, and state agencies to even make a dent on the severity of the depression, the President adamantly refused to allow the Federal Government to take up the responsibility. While only the national government possessed the power and credit to deal adequately with the national crisis. Theoretically and traditionally, Hoover was right in maintaining that altruism was the province of private charities, such as church organizations, states, their local and municipal agencies.

And truly, up to this period in our American history, the Federal government had had nothing to do with individual welfare, other than infractions, encroachments, crimes against other individuals and their properties; or violations of state, constitutional laws. Curiously apathetic in the face of so much suffering, as we can witness in today's rampant homelessness, (year of this book's publication) Hoover, Congress, and the nation "drifted aimlessly like a sailboat on a flat calm,"[33] ignoring the unwanted, depressed, and deprived of basic subsistence needs.

It was too little, too late, when serious measures were taken to

---

33

remedy the depression. Shanty-towns called "Hoovers Ville "continued mushrooming, and inundated large cities. Throughout his campaign, vast majority of the people were confident that Roosevelt shared their plight. Like Donald Trump's 84 years later. He had no difficulty adjusting his views to the prevailing attitudes, since he was never afraid to acknowledge conditions of the "forgotten man," and all those who had lost their footing. The election of 1932 gave him a majority of 7million popular votes over Hoover, and his margin of electoral votes were even more impressive, 472 to Hoover's 59.

The depression reached its nadir or lowest point between the Presidential election and Inauguration Day. Hundreds of banks continued to collapse as the nation's banking system disintegrated, and 80% of all state banking systems were suspended. Proving itself incapable of effective action, the last Congress of its kind convened through enactment of the Twentieth Amendment, which provided for the new and subsequent Congress to meet in January, and advanced Presidential Inauguration Day from March 4 to January 20.

Starvation and malnutrition was common. Riots erupted in hundreds of communities for food, jobs, and living wages. Some cities' unemployment rate ran as high as 50%. "The nation asks for action, and now.... in the event that congress should fail.... I shall not evade the clear course of duty that will then confront me. I shall ask Congress for the one remaining instrument," Roosevelt enunciated. "Broad executive power to wage a war against the emergency, as great as the power that would be given to me if we were in fact invaded by a foreign foe..." [34]On all fronts, and with every tool at his disposal, Roosevelt did go to war making a direct assault on the depression.

Donald Trump did go to war making a direct assault on those responsible.

Unlike our situation today, Corrective actions and proposals for legislation in Roosevelt's time came from the White House staff and both Houses of Congress as early as two days later, when a banking holiday was declared. It was an emergency Act to check banking monopolies in order to restore the confidence of bankers and businesses. Putting the Federal government through the greatest upheaval it had ever known in peacetime,

---

[34] i *bid*

within the next ninety-eight days, amateurs, professionals, experts, and cynical politicians cast into a mold, an avalanche of impressive corrective measures and laws that became known as the "New Deal."[35]

Donald Trump's performance accomplishments in his first year in office has been unquestionably impressive in restoring national public confidence. A virtual halt to the process of homelessness is underway that begins with a crackdown on mass illegal immigration and their automatic accommodation.

New Deal measures that were outstandingly significant were: the establishment of a Federal Relief Administration, making direct grants to state relief organizations; and the Civilian Conservation Corps that allowed work for 250,000 in forestry. A Home Owners Loan Corporation was formed to rescue households from foreclosures, and a similar law helped farmers pay their debts. The Tennessee Valley Authority was established to construct hydroelectric power and flood controls, providing more work. A banking law was passed- the Glass-Stegal Law- in order to separate investments from commercial banking operations.

Also passed was an Agriculture Adjustment Act passed to give rise to the purchasing power of farmers by paying them to limit specific crops; and also the National Industrial Recovery Act, designed to unravel riddled knots between manufacturers, such as cutthroat competitions by national planning, and encouraging cooperation between capital investors and labor. These were the first action of the New Deal as partisanship was subordinated to broad national needs.

The NRA was one of the most ambitious of Roosevelt's plans, a non-coercive measure designed specifically for industrial leaders to produce a balance between industrial production and consumer demands. This soluble business design was to be self-regulated by its own code of "fair competition" without the use or force of government oversight. But the NRA never balanced its production and demand. They turned out to be were suckers.

By 1935, the NRA's effects on labor, trade unions, and struggling small businesses was taking its toll with bitter industrial strikes throughout the nation- through its encouragement of monopolies and postponements of Antitrust prosecutions. The act which affected and depressed every

---

[35] Ibid

aspect of the economy, noted by the sentiments of Progressives, came to be disparagingly assessed as the "National Run-around Act" (NRA), before the Courts had declared the Act "unconstitutional."

The NRA blunder which has now produced a listless and sluggish economy gave rise to prominent all-around opposition from Progressives, prompting Roosevelt to go on a renewed offense on the depression with a "Second New Deal." This Second New Deal had a shift in emphasis.

The president was advised to re-assert his fruitless appeasement of big businesses, whose affairs he had considered to be too mercenary, before taking office. He was now characteristically telling business *what to do*. Reforms of the Second New Deal included the dismantling of public utilities holding companies, the re-installation of antitrust suits, and a law that increased tax obligations on the rich.

Milestone legislation exacted from Congress in 1935 was the Social Security Act, providing old-age insurance, through a system of compulsory contribution by both employer and employee; a Federal-State cooperative program for unemployment compensation; and a grant of Federal matching funds to States in the Union to provide for the care of the unfortunate, destitute, blind, crippled, or indigent; mothers and children, and a variety of other social services.

The Wagner Act was another milestone Act passed by Congress, but to Roosevelt's chagrin. This Act became the 20th Century Magna Carta of industrial unionization. The law recognizes the rights of employees to unionize without interference or intimidations; specified rules of bargaining collectively between unions and management; and clearly defines a number of unfair practices. A National Labor Relations Board was thus established to supervise adherence to these regulations.

As part of the Second New Deal Act, the Emergency Relief Appropriations Act, empowered the President to spend almost $5billion on relief measures, putting more than three million people back to work in the construction and development of schools, hospitals, airports, playgrounds, and many other variety of public conveniences that we now take for granted as part of our Americanization. [36]

---

[36] Ibid

SOME PREEXISTING CONDITIONS
BEFORE NEW DEAL

The question and answer to what constitutes *progress* and *change* in Americanization in this treatise is bounded by a specific range of historical activities affecting the nation's entire civilization, from the standpoint of government control under its constitutional limitations, are the unique cultural patterns that have been instituted, developed, and stimulated by the leaders of industry; their ruthless operational framework, their visible historical development, and the dynamic forces which individuals and socio-economic events play in shaping the quality of human lives.

According to the nation's pioneering individualist's theories, the only proper purpose of government was to clear the land, keep order at home, and defend the new settlers from attack abroad, as conquerors of the new territory. Their compact was based on the belief that people, other than those taken to crime, will work out their own salvation in the best possible way, if they were left alone to follow their own self-interest. Settlers will cooperate or compete with each other, and resist their opponents as their own good judgment may direct. As such, the pioneering conquerors were led to believe that small local governments were enough to deal with most practical problems, if and when government attention was needed.

After the Civil War, the American people were still in a stage and spirit of active pioneering, in which each family in the new Western states were largely independent in its daily life activities. The need for attention to a centralized government evolved naturally when their production got larger, evoking the need for regulation to buy supplies, build roads, transport, and sell their wheat, grains, and other products to larger markets. And as they prospered in this chain of dependent circumstance, they found themselves in the grip of monopoly buyers, railway companies, and suppliers.

Cultural homogeneity of these Western communities had already began breaking down since the 1850's, with the construction and initial operation of the National railroad Network. This was accelerated by the development of an increasing urban market in the 1870's, and the application of two new sources of power: the internal combustion engine, and the use of electricity in transportation.

The systematic application of technology through new discoveries of science, applied research, and development, engineering, and management organization led to rising standards of living, new status achievements, and dispensations of wealth. It is from this period in the 1890's that monopolies by big private business really got out of hand, affecting the nation's smaller productive units. The Populist Party was formed among farmers of the South and West, to resist encroachments on their business growth.

Their indignations about monopolies roused the two major political parties to do something on the national scale against monopolies. However, throughout the entire second half of the 19th Century, both political parties clung to the ideology that *freedom* means no interference by government; meaning, in a context, that government had no right to protect the equality of its weakest citizens by restraining other citizens. This idea of government began to change with the Presidency of Theodore Roosevelt. Big business and property owners of the day harbored a belief similar to the original framers of the compact.

Fearing that a strong executive might become an oppressive tyrant, they had designed the Constitution to rest mainly on Congress as the ultimate defender of *freedom* and decider of national policy. As such, Roosevelt was forced to check the workability of this Congress in the interest of the greater masses of Americans, as well as the businesses that served them. Cultural attitudes concerning the role of government that had evolved or developed to this point helped Roosevelt's forcefulness on Congress to set the ethical and legal rules under which big business of the day had to play.

Humans, land, raw materials, natural resources, and cultural patterns are taken as a given. Roosevelt's *Square Dealing* acknowledged that large corporations often act without regard to the common good. The *Hepburn Act* brought the regulation of business in the public interest. It caused a breaking up and major dissolution of monopolies by huge holding companies.

The Interstate Commerce Act of 1877 was the first challenge to the prevailing notion of "no meddling in business" by government, or the laissez faire ideology. The Act did so by describing clearly the right of Congress to regulate private corporations. While the Sherman Antitrust Act, passed in 1890 when applied, curbed the manipulative and oligopolistic attitude of businesses.

The most contentious issue within this post-Civil War industrial boom was *labor*. Both the Courts and organized government will now play an active role in the violent confrontations and disputes that surfaced between management and labor. Master craftsmen, manufacturers, merchants, and small businesses dominated the United States labor policy from 1789 through 1910. Guilds or craft organizations of people in the same trade or craft were the forerunners to labor unions.

These guilds operated to protect trade secrets, promote the trade or profession, maintain professional standards, and train new members. The guilds also set their fees and regulate those within the trade. Under the classical labor policy, the United States government operated to outlaw collective bargaining, which was the primary purpose for the emergence of labor unions in the first place. Government assumed collective bargaining to be illegal and immoral, and was expected to interfere with, and arrest Union leaders attempting to engage in collective bargaining.

Tennant farmers, newly freed black citizens, sharecroppers, and other forms of laborers were now implicated in a new kind of economy, with new developments in oil, electricity, and mechanical engines, which again developed into a monopoly, requiring ever-increasing meddling by government. This then contributed to the emergence of industrial labor organizations and an increased effort towards collective bargaining between management and labor over wages, working conditions, workplace health, and safety. The Progressives labor policy pushed for the outlawing of child labor, minimum working hours, and workmen's compensation, but both state and federal polices continued to push them aside and undermine them.

In fact, the Supreme Court struck down most progressive proposals-Child labor, minimum wage, and maximum working hours. The Court argued that laws against these practices by businesses violated the contract rights of individual workers and the "due process clause of the Constitution." In the year1869, at least 700,000 union members were accountable for in the United States, and their ever-increasing numbers and push for fair treatment as organized employees contributed to violent confrontations with employers and their management.

The Haymarket Riot in Chicago in 1886, where several people were killed and hundreds wounded, is a case in point. Union organizers and speakers were arrested, tried, and most who were convicted were hanged. In the Deep South, their local militia killed about 20, and the rest of union officials mobbed and lynched. By1888 Union membership had thinned down to about 200,000; and by 1895, there were only about 20,000 union members in the United States. [37]

Every strike that the unions undertook after 1886, notably the Knights of Labor, by far one of the largest unions at the time, was lost. Employers organized strong associations to fight the unions by blacklisting participants, using spies, lock-outs, armed guards, and detectives.

The American Federation of Labor founded in1886 had favored industrial unions representing skilled workers and using passive tactics such as: boycotting, or the refusal to buy products of companies hostile to the unions. However, the American Federation of Labor was a direct target of anti-union business organizations campaign, such as the National Association of Manufacturers.

While common laws outlawed collective bargaining, laws favoring employers and business over employees and unions were enacted. The Supreme Court used the Sherman Anti-trust Act of 1890 to destroy unions. It uphold the right of a company to sue the AFL Union over its boycott tactics; a law suit costing the Union somewhere around $420,000. This was enough to cripple its function.[38]

Employers are said to have used *yellow dog contracts*- a condition where a prospective employee is offered a contract, where he or she agrees to refrain from joining or engaging in union activities, such as instigating, or organizing strikes. During President Wilson's *New Freedom* progressive regime, the Clayton Act passed in 1914 was designed to exempt unions from antitrust prosecutions.

LUDLO MASSACRE

This Act was passed shortly after the *Ludlo Massacre* that occurred in September of 1913 in Colorado, between the United Mine Workers, who had organized the coal miners of that area against their employers, calling

---

[37] Ibid
[38] *Ibid*

for Federal intervention to restore the peace. These coal miners had lived in isolated mining camps where the company owned everything- from the land, hospitals, houses, stores, schools, churches, banks, the political set-up, judges, to the cemeteries for their burial.[39]

Miners were paid only for the coal they extracted. The demand to get paid according to the hours they worked extracting the coal, whether any coal was extracted in their mining for it or not. Workers also demanded civil rights to work without guards watching them, shop at stores of their choice, and the right to choose their own physicians. Miners' civil rights had been routinely ignored. About 8,000 miners went on strike in the month of September, and once it began, all restraints by industrial management were unleashed against the miners, who were now openly looked upon as *enemies.*

The company began to bolster its defense against the miners by importing additional deputies and guards; desperados, and thugs from Texas, while the miners moved out of the company camps, armed themselves, and set up tents. Sporadic and precipitating violence ensued, and the state governor was forced to send the militia to keep the peace.

Seven months later in April, a machine gun attack began on the tents of the miners. The miners had already dug-in pits to accommodate their children and women to escape potential gunfire. Others fled the scene, while company-men and National Guards set fire to the tents. When the confrontation was over, 19 people had been killed by gunfire. Going through the ruins of the Ludlow aftermath, and uncovering an iron cot covered pit where a tent was pitched, the twisted charred bodies of eleven children and two women were found.[40]

By the end of World War I, most union leaders belonging to the Industrial Union of the World were dead, in jail, exiled, or annihilated. The Federal government used the Espionage Act of 1917 to go after the union leaders. The union leaders were branded *anarchists, socialists,* or

---

[39] Ibid
[40] Ibid

communists by the Supreme Court, declaring that their ideas were "a clear and present danger."[41]

The popular view of the United States Supreme Court concerning human labor and its collective bargaining, with unions and organized business or industries before, and after the Civil War, until 1936 was that: "Unions interfered with the basic rights of workers; their contract rights, and their freedom of association." When the Court struck down minimum wage and maximum working hours legislation, it did so on the grounds that such laws violated the contract rights of employees protected by the *due process clause* of the Fifth Amendment.

Whether Democrat or Republican, the Sherman Anti-trust Act is cited as one of the foundations of American freedom. Those who violated the Act have usually done so by their interpretations of it- not in defiance of its "sacred" principle. To its adherents, it is wholesome deference to a basic theory and practice of *free enterprise.*

[41] Ibid

13

DISTRIBUTIVE JUSTICE

CIVIL RIGHTS & STATUS CONFLICT

All humans alive are familiar with the needs for air, water, food, rest, recuperation, repose, and so on. However, one of our most commonly ignored need by others, and seldom inclusive in our commonsense response is our fundamental need for *justice*. Our main concern with justice here is equality of treatment under state or Constitutional laws- further broken down to community and customary rules. These laws and local rules circumvent the moral obligations and indebtedness of each individual to the other, in his or her pursuits of social or economic enterprise within territories of the United States. This condition has been aptly referred to as *Distributive justice*.[42]

Distributive Justice is the comparative treatment of individuals. Here, Justice pertains to the similar treatment of similars. Individual citizens as a category or class of people, who share a common status, bond, and allegiances to the system. Conversely, *injustice* is the dissimilar treatment of all categories and classes of people, when parallel issues, variable events, and conventions of rules are broken.

In the struggle for a civil society, a rule of law which is just, known, predictable, and applied equally, even though not perfect, provides the governing framework for, and restraints on the entire population of its constituents. It nurtures this civility in serving as a check against the unjustifiable use of force and the abuse of power. The real purpose for the existence of such status quo of society is for its preservation, growth, and

---

[42] Ibid

improvement. No individual can live in a society relatively successfully, with all needs adequately met, without a basic understanding and allegiance to this governance. It carries the same necessity of responsibility, as well as a principle in individual self-discipline.

Economic, political, associational, and religious paradigms through which people of different ethnic group backgrounds order their lives, and competed for economic power and prestige in the free market system, promoted a natural outgrowth of the objective conditions of status and *status rivalry* in Americanization. Status rivalry begins with competing economic units- basically, families or parents to whom one was born; citizenship, property ownership, and migration; while an adult status here is confined to age, citizenship, and the kind of labor, works, or activity a person engages in to maintain or make a living.

An individual's fundamental struggles with *status* in society stem from the inequality of treatment that he or she is subjected to, may reasonably expect, or would prefer to expect under prevailing conditions of communal rules and laws.

The heterogeneous constitutional heritage of the United States defined *equality* as the natural right of every individual to live freely under self-government, to acquire and retain property the individual creates through his or her own labor, and to be treated impartially before a just rule of law.

The struggle for recognized status and social welfare in our Americanization, on a formal and standardized national level, began with the definition of *who was considered an American citizen?* -A basic sense of identity.

It took a Civil War to reach this consensus, allowing free blacks, and the vast majority who were slaves to become citizens, through enactment of the Fourteenth Amendment. Indigenous tribes whom the new nation of conquerors were still at war with, and bent on vanquishing, were also allowed to become citizens, providing they gave up their tribal cultural identities. Citizen rights were not granted to all, as a result of those who had chosen to retain their native identities, until Congress passed the Indian Citizen Act of 1924.[43]

Prior to the Civil War, the States had been considered the bulwark of individual freedom to practice the kind of self-government they choose,

---

[43] Ibid

against possible usurpation by the central government. With passage of the Fourteenth Amendment, states are now enjoined against tampering with the rights of individuals. The Amendment imposed a complete restriction on *state power*, for it forbids the states to "deprive any person of life, liberty, or property without due process of law."

A Fifteenth Amendment was added to the effect of stating that no person could be denied the right to vote because of ethnicity, color, or previous condition of servitude. With these two Amendments to the Constitution, black citizens of the United States were put on equal political status with white citizens, or any other ethnic group member in the nation. Through insistence of the Radical Republicans, the federal government was now placed in the role as protector of Civil Rights.

Not for long though. Both constitutional Amendments left large enough loopholes by which Southern governments would later infringe. In 1896 in the state of Louisiana, a guy named Homer Plessey who had claimed to be 7/8 or 87.5% white by ethnicity, was arrested for sitting in a railroad passenger car designated for *whites only* (Plessey v. Ferguson).

Providing the legal basis for the emergence of ethnic group segregation, apartheid, and racism, the Courts argued that Homer Plessey wasn't *white*, and that the Civil Rights Act of 1875 violated the reserved powers clause of the Tenth Amendment, which specified that all powers not granted to the Federal government were reserved to the states.

People who were not considered *white* were refused equal accommodation or privileges in privately owned facilities, providing public service, had no recourse in the law of the land. The Courts argued that the Fourteenth Amendment guarantees any potential discriminators' Civil Rights against invasion by the states and not by individuals.

Homer Plessey's case was a case of *injustice* based on a human biological status interpreted by the courts' justices. That is, the biological inherited gene status of an individual, regardless of Homer's skin pigmentation, is, and may be a case of sub-human status to those who define themselves as *white*. This distribution of *injustice* then became the prevailing morality of social enterprise, and a hallmark for economic exploitation in sanctions, persecution, and functions, nationwide.

The court's ruling led to the total imposition of segregation, apartheid, or racism throughout the South- separate hospitals, schools, recreational facilities, and so on. Mississippi led Southern states by denying those people considered *black* the Right to vote. 130,000 registered black voters voted in the election of 1896 in the state of Louisiana. But heavily laden with impediments such as poll taxes, literacy tests, and other obstacles to deny their voting Rights, only 5,000 black voters were counted in the election of 1900.

Nearly All communication mediums and governing intelligence networks of the day commented favorably to the court's validation of biological racism, (if genealogical identity is confirmed or known), apartheid, or *segregation-* the common reference term of the day. Certified crackpot scientists, biologists, physicians, and other supposed experts on the human species (*Race*) agreed to black persons as beings of a *sub-specie* category of quite another race, by comparison to persons *considered white*, or those who consider themselves to be so.

There is no big wonder why President Woodrow Wilson's claim in his first term in office, that "running the government was like a child's play for anyone who had managed the faculty of a racist university at the time." Wilson was a Southerner completely suffused with its ideology of segregation, and was also President of Princeton; the only major Northern University that had refused to admit black students at that time.

Research sources claimed him to be an "outspoken supremacist, and his wife was even worse." Wilson's *New Freedom* movement or regime, as an extension of Progressivism, meant a new form of tyranny for black people that were not to be removed by the Supreme Court until 1957.

Here were the days' commentary on Wilson: "Some historians make out Wilson to be a conservative of sorts, in part because of his Presbyterian faith, but also because he was a vicious racist and segregationist. . . . Wilson screened the infamous movie *Birth of a Nation,* glorifying the Ku Klux Klan, in the White House, and recommended that it be widely viewed."[44]

"Wilson was a vicious racist and segregationist..." His administration submitted a legislative program intended to curtail the Civil Rights of black people, which Congress refused to pass. Unfazed, the punk used his power as Chief Executive to segregate the Federal Government. Offices

---

[44] Hayward Steven F. *The Politically Incorrect Guide to The Presidents From Wilson to Obama,* Topic: *Woodrow Wilson, "Wilson the Conservative" page 39-40*

that the Radical Republicans and Progressives had instituted and reserved for blacks were now offered to Southern whites.

In 1914 he ordered that white and black workers in Federal Government jobs be segregated. This was the first time since the period of Reconstruction that such apartheid, racism, or segregation existed with Presidential authority. All black persons who protested the move were fired!

Aided by the propaganda movie *Birth of a Nation* that opened in the year 1915, American white supremacists, notably the Ku Klux Klan group, rose to their zenith. Extreme civil unrest and social strife were common during the Harding, Coolidge, Hoover, and early Roosevelt's years. It was open season for killing black people nationwide, as their opponents saw fit- with little or no consequence for their actions.

On the poor *whites* side of similar status, whose Civil Rights were also denied, they had took to many forms of law-breaking and made organized crime rose to its zenith; producing violent notorious avengers such as Baby-faced Nelson, Machine-gun Kelly, Al Capone, and many others.

The 1919 riots of Chicago are well publicized, but others such as the one which occurred in 1921 in Tulsa, Oklahoma in a black neighborhood where *whites* dropped dynamite from airplanes on them, killing more than 75, and destroying more than 1000 homes, is just another anomaly infrequently found in American history texts taught to students, about the beauty of our nation. [45]

The real ugliness was that during this period in our Americanization, in most states, black people felt deep down inside themselves that they had no Civil Rights that white people must, or ought to respect as they would for their own ethnic group kind, or whom they believe to be so.

With slavery being the birth of American racism by a dominant warring and enterprising group with superior resources, followed by the outgrowth of apartheid or sanctioned segregation, this American past can always feel ever present today in the body-mind of any of its citizens when certain conditions are kept up with provocations. However, with world-wide human progress in education today, these conditions must be deliberately concocted, provoked, and can be easily avoided or negated.

Just as any individual could draw similar conclusions considered to be the ultimate truth from the holy Bible, written and published

[45] Parenti

before the United States was ever conceived or invented; any person can respond positively to any myth, or body of myths with equal sincerity and deep convictions, just as he or she can to any body of truth, as long as justifications can be sought or found. Thus, the continuing provocations of the very successful and resourceful are set against the ethnic group status of an individual, superimposed, as it were, as a criteria and condition for *just* treatment.

Unfortunately, this is a universal human condition that will never, ever, fade away. Again, it is up to each individual to work out his or her own salvation form this unavoidable human dilemma, even if our parents refuse to do the job for us. Being treated from above or below as a group or ethnic group member It is the bane or curse of individuation and individuality.

That is, even though we are not parties to anything, or anybody, in everything, the pre-judgments are stuck on us. A pre-judgment on innocent individuals, based on a categorized group member's performance, becomes more formidable and believable when most members of the ethnic group subscribe to the form of behavior under scrutiny, under just about any common circumstance of interaction.

Between 1900 and 1956, Congress passed no Civil Rights laws. Key committees were dominated by Southerners and Democrats committed to preserving apartheid, racism, or segregation, and were successful for keeping the struggle for equal Civil Rights off the Congressional agenda. The regime remained in place until the Civil Rights Act of 1964. Franklin D. Roosevelt was the first United states President to exhibit concern about Civil Rights issues of the *forgotten man.*

Prior to the Stock Market crash of 1929, the times of economic prosperity that Harding, Coolidge, and early Hoover administrations were reveling in, were really grinding years of poverty for many who lived in company-owned towns, such as those coal miners in Pennsylvania, and Virginia, and other underpaid workers elsewhere in the nation.

Before and during the Depression around 1930, more than 42% of all farms were worked by tenant farmers who belonged to a sharecropping system, which poor *whites* and *black* families participated in. *Debt peonage* was common. This was a condition where families are perpetually indebted to a land-owner, and state laws prohibit them from leaving the land until their debt is paid. These underpaid workers and tenant farmers were the real workhorse of America's sturdy yeomanry, who prospered during the years of WW1, but their prosperity declined severely with the onset of peacetime.

The United States, including other nations, had become too industrialized, urbanized, and farming commercialized. Technological growth elsewhere, such as Canada, Australia, and Argentina, in the agricultural world of farming, contracted sales and demand for American products in the European markets. These contributed to a radical change in status acquisition.

Meritocracy now confers on a high school diploma as a social selection process. This was all that was required as a vehicle to a middle-class, entry-level job or position, in the new world and hierarchies of sales, manufacturing, production, and the distribution of goods and services in the economic market.

COURTS

Since the authoritative allocation of valued resources is a minimum requisite for the survival and existence of any human society, one of the implicit, understood, and expressed purpose of government (or some form of it), is to have the ultimate say and authority by using its physical backup force- army, navy, air force, local militia, sheriff, and police departments- if necessary, in deciding how differences over issues, or valued resources are resolved.

This ultimate power so vested, is limited by the fundamental written laws of the land, which is the United States Constitution. Elasticity or constrictions of its interpretations are vested in the judicial branch of government which makes laws and public policies. It is the most conservative body of government and its rulings. This conservatism is rooted in the insulation of tradition and judicial tenure, and free from the turbulence of everyday politics.

In all cases, the judicial system lies at the heart of an ongoing struggle for all American freedoms. While the Bill of Rights is the fundamental charter of all American citizens' Civil Liberties. However, it is still the judicial system personnel that legally defines, with the force of the state, how those Rights are to be applied. Speaking as a justice of the Supreme Court, Charles Evan Hughes noted that "We are under a constitution, but the Constitution is *what the judge says it is.*"

The Supreme Court made no effort to systematically apply the Bill of Rights to citizens in all states until 1925. And form around 1890 through 1937, it interpreted the Constitution in such a way that the largest industrial enterprise takes on the character of an individual, thereby allowing government from forcefully regulating them.

Oliver Wendell Holmes, Dembitz Brandies, Felix Frankfurter, and Charles Evan Hughes were all justices of the Supreme Court, whose iron-clad policies were looked at as *Judicial Restraint.* This policy fundamentally required the courts to avoid constitutional questions where possible, and to uphold acts of Congress, unless they clearly violate a specific section of the Constitution.[46]

It was the insistence of the average enterprising productive citizen-settler that actually forced the Bill of Rights into the Constitution. The United States' government as a political governing body and its rendering of justice thus contain a derivative of two major inputs: one, are the demands made by individuals and groups of the general citizenry- basically what the citizens want and realistically can expect. And two, is support of the particular system by allegiance, actions, and attitudes that people take on, sustain, uphold, buttress, or to defend the system- at all levels, allowing it to continue to work.

Thus, people organize a government to express the attitudes they have in common, and to influence their government to respond to those attitudes. These attitudes encompass the moral boundaries of *right* or *wrong* action on behalf of each individual, social, religious, or political group, and industrial organization.

Human existence requires that each person recognizes the Rights of others, and that at times; an individual forgoes, or must forgo his or her own interests in recognition of another person's interest. Without such behavior, there wouldn't be a mother, father, some kind of medical care, pro-social behavior, or concern for any human being alive, for that matter.

---
[46] Ibid

Our interdependence on Group life cannot be argued away. Yet each person must meet the demands of survival, as well as the satisfaction and fulfillment of his or her own needs alone.

These two basic elements provide the grounds of recurring conflicts at all levels of any human social and economic system, thereby evoking necessity for the presence of a stable, conservatively-changing, judicial system; in order to provide a standard of means for the resolution of conflicts between individuals', groups', and enterprising organizations' interests – covering the entire scope of public welfare, self, and others.

Constitutional interpretations by justices represent the output of our ethical, moral, and political system that becomes the binding rules from laws, regulations, or actual judicial decisions handed down. Our primary concern with court decisions up to this time period in Americanization is its service as political action, taken under the ideology of *judicial restraint,* and routinely applied by justices up until 1937.

JUDICIAL ACTIVISM

A new era in Americanization began with the philosophy and ideology of "Judicial Activism." In its total output it has also been referred to as "cooperative federalism." *Judicial activism* peaked with majority of the members of the Warren Courts, which boldly applied the Constitution to social and political questions, beginning in the 1950's and throughout the turbulent and tumultuous 60's.[47]

President Franklin D. Roosevelt's feelings for the *forgotten man* engendered in his New Deal programs from 1932 through 1937, (although they didn't all worked out perfectly, and some were miserable economic waste), wholeheartedly embraced, changed, and introduced this entire new principle of American governance. The overriding Congress and dire straits electorate consensus was that:

The nation's acute state of Depression, and problem with balances

---

[47] Ibid

between wealth, autonomy, and abject impoverishment of the greater population *could, and should be* solved by the Federal government as a form of distributive justice. Not only must the government take a stand and intervene as a referee, it must also institute programs that would benefit its lesser productive units or citizenry.

Origins of the nation's problems arose from the unavoidable conflicts of the kind and quality of status rivalry it had engendered. It became extremely pronounced during the Great Depression: "...They were poor, not because they did the lowest paid and hardest work, but because they were of no use. What happens to a people when they are not needed, and when they are superfluous? One in every four or five persons of working age was unable to find work for long periods, and had to learn how it feels to be unwanted."[48]

Since technological inventions has forced masses of the population to become more dependent on industries, rather than the self-reliance of old, the vast majority of Americans must now rely on the decisions of these enterprising leaders of industry in the organization of their lives.

Throughout the conversion from small independent farmer, slave, indentured servant, and cottage industry productions- to the evolving world of the industrial revolution, the new forms of businesses that were replaced could have cared less about a *Free Market* system, since their tendencies had always been to stifle competition, if it serves their purpose or interests in making a profit, while all this carrying-on was backed by the might of both the Supreme Court, and political leaders of the day, for businesses to achieve their ends.

Emphatically put forth by Coolidge, stating that the order of government is business, and "the business of America is business." The facts which support this condition of Americanization were no longer objects of mere speculation when the nation's new ideology was drafted under New Deal legislations. They had already forced themselves on the experience and sensibilities of the population at large.

These values have become the most important ingredients in cultural heritage. They are created, inherited, and passed on from one generation to the next, in every-which-way. These values that we relate to have five

---

[48] Bird Caroline, *The Invisible Scar*

major components that operate as a single person in all our social relations and interactions.

They are the *biological status* that we inherit through birth, citizenship, the status we achieve or attain through learning, education, or apprenticeship; the *roles* we take up to maintain and aggrandize our status, which generally involve labor or work; and the symbolic representations, that inspires, incites, worry, annoy, or naseauate us.

Humans are the last link, as well as the originators of all values; and the individual is the original and final source.

BIBLIOGRAPHY

INFORMATION SOURCE AND
AUTHOR'S WORKS CONSULTED

Stefan Lorant: *Presidency*. Footnote, 13, 14, 15, Expansion of Populist movement. William Jennings Bryan's presidential campaign. Garret Hobart, succeeded by Theodore Roosevelt. Montage on Roosevelt's character.

Morton Borden: *The American Profile*. United Mine Worker's strike, 1902. Panama Canal

John A. Garranty/Robert A. Mc Caughey: *A Short History of the American Nation 5ᵗʰ Edition*. "Square Deal," United Mine Worker's strike. Panama Canal. Muckrakers. La Follett's Progressivism" footnotes 16, 17, 18.

Morton Borden: Woodrow Wilson's "New Nationalism." World War I. Pancho Villa. Footnotes

Garranty/Mc Caughey: "Zimmerman Telegram" intercepted. World War I. Wilson's "Fourteen-Point" plan. "Moral absolutist." "Peace without indemnities." Wilson's health conditions.
Footnotes 19, 20, 21, 22, 23, 24 25.

Morton Borden: Post-World War I events. The Ku Klux Klan. From Boom to Bust.

Stefan Lorant: Warren G. Harding's administration. Footnote 27

Garranty/Mc Caughey, Borden Morton: Coolidge/Hoover. Stock market crash. Footnotes, 27, 28, 29, 30, 31. New Deal. 32, 33, 34, 35, 36. Roosevelt's election. Depression and New Deal measures.

Stefan Lorant: Haymarket Riot in Chicago. Supreme Court defending industry. Labor Unions versus the Supreme court. Footnote 37

James W. Lowen: *Lies My Teacher Told Me, Everything Your American Textbook Got wrong.* 1913 Ludlow Massacre in Colorado. Woodrow Wilson's racist schemes. Footnotes 38, 39, 40, 41

Garranty/Mc Caughey: Civil Rights/ Distributive Justice. Judicial Restraint versus Judicial Activism. "Plessy vs Ferguson." Separate but Equal doctrine.

Steven Hayward: *The Politically Incorrect Guide To the Presidents From Wilson To Obama. Topic*: "Wilson The Conservative." "Vicious Racist" profile. Footnotes 42, 43, 44, 45.

James W. Lowen: *Lies My Teacher Told Me.* 1921 Riots in Tulsa Oklahoma. Whites dropping dynamite on Blacks

Paul Soifer/Abraham Hoffman*: American Government Cliffs Quick Review.* **Kurland, Garranty/Mc Caughey**: Concepts of Judicial Restraint and Judicial activism.

Caroline Bird: *The Invisible Scar*: The unemployed during the Great Depression. Footnote 48.

PART III

1937 THROUGH 1955

WORLD WAR II ERA, KOREA, & VIETNAM

14

THE DAWN OF WORLD WAR II

REELECTED FOR A SECOND TERM, and defeating his opponent with a higher percentage of popular and electoral votes, Roosevelt candidly admitted in his January inaugural address in 1937 that the nation had not yet reached the "happy valley" he envisioned at the beginning of his first term. He pledged to continue the work of relieving at least 33% of the nation's population, who were still living in acute, and dire straits poverty. Having abandoned efforts to appease big business, which he denounced as "economic royalists," Roosevelt appealed to the votes of workers and the underprivileged.

While newly empowered labor unions had generously poured money into his campaign, and his evident concerns for the welfare of farmers and homeowners in guaranteeing their mortgages, the American voters gave Roosevelt an impressive vote of confidence. Vermont and Maine were the only two states that did not vote overwhelmingly for him.

The landslide victory carried an interpretation of further reform demanded by the majority, and no issue or institution of worry appeared to be in the President's way but the courts. Since a good portion of New Deal legislations that were drafted for a direct assault on the nation's economic problems had no proper regard for the Constitution in vein of tradition.

Owing to the fuss and protests of conservatives about excess waste, and irresponsible spending on many New Deal projects, Roosevelt decided to cut spending. This eventually led to disastrous results. The cuts also led to a dramatic drop in stock prices, a peak rise in unemployment, industrial production slumped, and *sit-down* strikes became commonplace, especially in the auto and steel industries.

While other vigorous inventive body-minds search for more efficient means of distributing the nation's resources and dissatisfactions more equitably, an idea and generalized principle was put forth in a publication by British economist John Maynard Keynes, as a solution for nations going through periods of depression. A brief summary of Keynes' theories states that: the world depression could be conquered if governments would unbalance their budgets by reducing interest rates and taxes, and increasing expenditures in order to stimulate consumption and investments.

Roosevelt never accepted this theory of government, but imperatives from the scope of the nation's depression forced him to consider the proposition and went ahead spending more than what the government was collecting in taxes. So in April 1938, to compensate for the nation's economic slump, the President committed the nation to heavy deficit spending.

Meanwhile, on the international scene, the economic and social dislocations that followed World War 1 created desperate conditions that led millions in European Nations, including the Asian nation of Japan, to adopt totalitarian ideas as a form of government rule. This idea began to take hold when Italian dictator Benito Mussolini came to power in 1922. Shortly thereafter, the Japanese invaded Manchuria in China, Shanghai in 1932, then extended their conquest to the North.

Mussolini annexed Ethiopia in 1935, while rebels backed by Germany and Italy with planes, troops, and military supplies attempted to overthrow the republic government of Spain; and the remainder of German troops occupied the Rhineland in 1936. In july1937, the Japanese again attacked other parts of China, securing Peking, Canton, and then Hankou in 1938.

Prior to these precipitating events, the US Senate in 1928 had signed and approved an agreement called the Kellogg-Briand Pact. Its essence was basically an alliance of countries who had agreed never to go to war with each other; and also that "every nation is free at all times... to defend its territory from attack, and it alone is competent to decide when circumstances require war in self-defense."

With the most powerful country remaining out of the League of Nations, and without an effective organization to block the *Axis Powers*, as Germany, Italy, and Japan are now called, these aggressive countries were able to overrun their weaker neighbors. Each aggressive act drove the country deeper into a bag of isolationism. Congressional hearings and debates yielded nothing but passing neutrality laws.

In a direct response to the escalating dilemma, Roosevelt declared, "I have said not once, but many times, that I have seen war and that I hate war. I say that again and again. I hope that the United States will keep out of this war." The administration was committed to the idea of reform and responsibility for the national welfare, and act to meet specific problems in every way necessary.

Late in October of 1937, Roosevelt became fervently convinced and concerned about the precipitating rash of aggression by the Axis Powers when he counteracted with a "Quarantine speech," warning the nation that "the epidemic of world lawlessness is spreading," with the United States being vulnerable to attack, and that "there is no escape through neutrality." [49]

Both Congress and most of the public paid little attention. The Neutrality Acts kept the country from trading with, or giving financial credit to any nation involved in war. What these laws actually did was to encourage eventual aggression against Britain, France, China, and Russia. Including the United States, these countries were now united and implicated as the *Allied Powers*.

Germany annexed Austria in March of 1938, and in September, Czechoslovakia. Sudetenland surrendered, and by March of 1939, all of Czechoslovakia. Russia and Germany signed a Non-aggression Pact, and in the following month of September, Germany invaded Poland, provoking Britain and France to declare war. This act by the Axis Powers also effected a basic change of attitude in American thinking; causing Roosevelt to abandon further efforts at domestic reform.

---

[49] Ibid

15

A BRIEF SCENARIO OF WORLD WAR II

WHILE CONGRESS CONTINUED TO DEBATE the issue and fates of free democracies in Europe and Asia for about six weeks with considerable rancor, its embargo on arms was lifted, and new legislation permitted warring nations to purchase munitions and other supplies from the U.S. on a cash-an-carry basis. Short-term loans were also authorized.

Mounting dangers of the war, the wave of orders, and the cries of beleaguered allied democracies, caused the Great American Depression to vanish after 1939, when economic mobilization got underway in an all-out effort to win the War. A War Resources Board that planned for the conversion of industries to war production was appropriated $40 billion for national defense, while the President arranged a trade with Britain for Naval bases, in exchange for naval destroyers to combat German submarines.

Between April 9 and June 22 of 1940, Denmark, Norway, Belgium, and France, all fell to Adolph Hitler's German forces. When Mussolini's Italian forces joined the war against France, Hitler decided to bomb the British and starve them into submission. But the British decisively defeated Germany's blitzkrieg, and ended the air battles that they waged in the summer.

In spite of their Arial victories, the British were now pushed back across the English Channel, short of being annihilated. Japan then signed a multi-Non-aggression Pact with Germany and Italy, solidifying their alliance. This alliance then turned into global warfare for domination. Nearly all of Western Europe was now controlled by the *Axis Powers*.

The 1940 Presidential election took place in the midst of these international events. Roosevelt was nominated by his Party for a third term, and was successful at defeating his Republican opponent. His election for a third term encouraged the President to respond to the world crisis more boldly.

While Britain was rapidly exhausting its financial resources, Roosevelt decided to provide them whatever they needed to defeat the Axis Powers. The view that aiding Britain was a form of American national self-defense was presented to Congress in January of 1941, with an expenditure plan calling for $7 billion for war materials that the President could lend, lease, exchange, or transfer to any country whose defense he deem vital to the United States.

U S Armed Forces occupied Greenland in April 1941, and in the following month of May, a state of unlimited national emergency was declared. Germany invaded Russia in June. U S Armed Forces then occupied Iceland in July, and the Draft-law was extended in August. By December of 1941, America was *in fact* at war in Europe, without a formal declaration from Congress.

Meanwhile American-Japanese relations began to worsen after Japan decided to attack Dutch-French colonies in Southeast Asia. A restriction of trade was imposed. War powers of Japan that assumed control of U S-Japanese relations, negotiated with the United States bid for them to refrain from further aggression and expansion. An agreement was reached under conditions that the United States and Britain would cut off all their aid to China, and then lift the U S economic trade blockade. Upon the rejection of these demands by the United States, The Japanese prepared for an all-out assault on the Dutch East Indies, British Malaya, and the Philippines.

To immobilize the U S Pacific Fleet, Japanese leaders planned a surprise aerial raid on the Naval Base at Pearl Harbor in Hawaii. Believing that war was imminent when U S intelligence cracked the Japanese diplomatic code, commanders had anticipated a devastating blow to fall somewhere in the Philippines; while those stationed at the garrison in Pearl Harbor, took precautions only against possible sabotage.

Naval commanders of both stationary Pacific Fleets believed that an attack on Pearl Harbor would be impossible. That impossibility was over in a hurry when planes from Japanese aircraft carriers finding easy targets, rained bombs on Pearl Harbor in the early dawn of Sunday morning on December 7. Within two hours of vicious attacks, the U S Pacific Fleet there was reduced to a smoking ruin.

Congress declared war on Japan on December 8. China declared war on Germany, Italy, and Japan. While formal war with Italy and Germany was still undeclared, the Axis powers had already honored their treaty of obligation to Japan. On December 11, all three declared war on the United States.

About 15 million men and women were mobilized into the U S Armed Forces, while Congress granted wide emergency powers to the President- especially by refraining from excessive dickering or meddling in administrative problems which concerned military strategies. The nation's fate, perhaps that of the entire free democratic world, now depended on delivering supplies and weapons to the battlefronts.

Recruitment and mobilization, along with expanded industrial production, caused labor shortage, thereby increasing the bargaining power of workers. Prosperity and some stiff government controls added significantly to organized labor; having more to do with institutionalizing industry-wide collective bargaining, as workers recognized the positive benefits of union membership. This was perhaps the only time when wages and prices remained in a fair balanced relation.

A steep graduation of income tax on the wealthy, combined with a general increase in the income of workers and farmers, affected a substantial shift in the nation's distribution of wealth. The poor became richer, while the rich collected a smaller portion of the national income.

On January 1, 1942 twenty-six countries subscribed to principles of the Atlantic Charter, agreeing to fight until victory could be won over the Axis Powers. War would be waged until there was an unconditional surrender by the aggressors. Russia was also one of the twenty-six signers of the Declaration of the United Nations in which Allies promised to avoid territorial aggrandizement after the war, and to respect the rights of all people to determine their own form of government. Allied Forces referred to themselves as the *United Nations,* forming the basis of existence of the current organization after the war ended.

Allied planes began bombing German cities in the summer of 1942; while the Philippines fell to invading Japanese forces; followed by a series of land, sea, battles waged in the islands of the Central Pacific in August of 1942. Strategic decisions on points of attack were localized in Germany. Japanese conquests were considered remote and unimportant regions from Allied Forces point of view. Air Attacks on German cities did not destroy their armies' capacity to fight. But war productions were severely hampered, and communication systems tangled.

Allied forces commanded by Dwight Eisenhower landed in North Africa. The Axis Powers' empire at its height had extended from here to entire Western Russia, Norway, and France. During Allied powers air attacks on German strongholds, the Russians had fought off the Germans fiercely, pushing them back out of Stalingrad and Leningrad. Allied troops landed in Italy in September of 1943.

War and conquest in the Pacific belonged to the Japanese, whose empire at its height had stretched from the Netherlands East Indies to parts of the Aleutians. Their expansion eastward ended with the Battle of Midway, and landing of the United States Marines on the island of Guadalcanal. Throughout the remainder of the year, the U S and its allies won several victorious battles that reduced fortified Japanese strongholds and resistance.

On June 6, 1944, a collection of Allied troops and assault forces that had assembled in England under the command of Eisenhower to invade France, stormed ashore the coast of Normandy; supported by thousands of planes, paratroopers, and a great armada. Against fierce and coordinated German resistance, and within a few weeks, a million or more Allied troops were fighting on French soil. Another Allied Army Force invaded France from the Mediterranean south, and then rapidly advanced to the North. Paris was liberated on August 25th; and by mid-September, Allied Forces were fighting at the edge of Germany itself.

In the Pacific, Japanese soldiers fought like Spartans, and almost never surrendered for every foot of ground they had to yield. But the Forces led by U.S. Navy Admiral Nimitz were in every case victorious. American airpower proved to be decisive. In October of 1944, two great Naval Battles were waged along the coast of New Guinea and the Philippines. They were the Battle of Leyte Gulf, and the Battle for the Philippine Sea. Victory in these battles by U S Forces completed the destruction of Japanese seapower, and reduced its air-force to a band of suicidal pilots, who would deliberately crash bomb-laden planes on American warships and air-strips.

It was election year again on the home front, and Roosevelt had been nominated by the Democratic Party for a fourth term- with the condition that current Vice-President Henry Wallace be replaced as his running mate. The President conceded, and Harry Truman, a Senator from Missouri was chosen to replace Wallace. On the Republican ticket was Thomas Dewey, who ran on a platform of censured Democrats' waste in government and their inefficiency in running it. Dewey also pledged to maintain New Deal Reforms, and at the same time save the free-enterprise system. There was little or no disagreement on how the war was being handled.

With virtually full employment nationwide, and the feeling of approaching victory in both Europe and Pacific wars- for the incumbent and fairly competent Commander in Chief of the United States Armed forces, these conditions prevailed in the voters' psyche, and thus weighed heavily against the President's opponent. Roosevelt and Truman won the 1944 election handily against their Republican opponent by more than 3.6 million popular votes, and with an Electoral majority of 333.

His election campaign had weakened him even more, and Roosevelt was in bad health when he began his fourth term in office. Two days after his inauguration, he met with British leader Winston Churchill, and the Russians' Josef Stalin in Yalta, Russia to map the final assault on Germany, and post-war occupation of it. Russia also promised to enter the war against Japan after the surrender of Germany.

On his return to the United States on May 1, 1945, the President spoke to Congress concerning substances of the Yalta Conference. While working routinely at his desk on May 12th, Roosevelt complained of a severe headache, and within a few hours that day, he died of a cerebral hemorrhage.

Truman succeeded to the Presidency. As the war waged on in Europe, Allied Forces were viciously closing in on Germans in all directions, halting their offense in December. While the Russians had knocked out four of the Axis Powers satellite states of Bulgaria, Romania, Finland, and Hungary out of the war, they were stopped by the Germans in their attempt to secure Poland.

A final assault on Germany was planned for April. Meanwhile, Italian leader Benito Mussolini, who was overthrown and imprisoned in July of 1943, was rescued by German paratroopers. He was later captured by

Italian partisans in April 1945 in an attempted escape to Switzerland. He was later tried and executed.

Italy surrendered to Allied Forces on May 2.Throughout the month of April and early May, the Russians shelled and bombed the city of Berlin, reducing it to rubbles. Hitler committed suicide in his bunker on April 30 during the air-raid. And the Germans surrendered on May 8.

THE PACIFIC FRONT

Once the Marianas were cleared on the Pacific front, and the islands of Iwo Jima and Okinawa taken by U S Naval Fleet and Marines, which were only a few hundred miles away from mainland Japan, U.S. B-29s, began a relentless assault with high explosive fire-bombs on the mainland in March through June of 1945. At this point, ending of the war began to seem more inevitable. However, most military experts were predicting another year of fighting, and a million or more American casualties before the Japanese would surrender.

Throughout the conflicts on both European and Pacific fronts, Roosevelt had responded to a warning from Albert Einstein that the Germans were trying to develop atomic weapons. Federal funds were thus committed to a top-secret Atomic Energy Program. To this point, research had proceeded rapidly so that on July 16, 1945 a transportable bomb with the destructive force of more than 20,000 tons of TNT was successfully tested at Los Alamos, New Mexico. All speculations and efforts of bringing the war to an abrupt end were now realistically, fully possible.

On August 6, 1945 the U S detonated one atomic bomb over Hiroshima, Japan, killing about 78,000 people, injuring another 100,000 or more out of a population of roughly 344,000. Still bewildered and shocked, a second atomic bomb was dropped over Nagasaki with the same destructive force. Japan surrendered to the United States on August 15th. On both fronts, the U. S had over 1.5 million wounded, and at least half a million casualties.

16

POST-WORLD WAR II CONSENSUS

ON THE DOMESTIC FRONT, HARRY Truman wanted to extend Roosevelt's New Deal policies, and so prepared a program he called the "Fair Deal," because he thought it would be fair to both rich and poor. Truman asked for an enlarged Social Security program, permanent fair employment compensation to protect Rights of the disadvantaged, aid for scientific research, and money for power utility projects.

Republicans who gained control of Congress in mid-term elections of 1946 blocked most of these domestic measures. The only significant policy they agreed on was to unify the armed forces under one single Secretary of Defense in 1947. International problems were more pressing.

Shortly after the surrender of Germany, almost nothing could be agreed on between the United States and Russia, from the endless talks held on repatriations, territorial concessions, dispositions of colonies, and other details of the truce. Every proposition was interpreted as stemming from the worst motives; since Truman had signed off the Lend-Lease Aid it was giving Russia to help defeat the Germans.

Pressured by communist witch hunters, the aid was cut off when the Russians' need for it was greatest. They then naturally thought this to be a calculated move by the United States in order to weaken and intimidate them. An American offer to share atomic secrets, presented in 1946 fell afoul of suspicion on both sides.

Results of this rift between Russia, the United States and all its former Allies developed into what was called the *Cold War*. Russia began to gain control over one nation after another in Eastern Europe, setting up pro-communist governments. At least eight other nations teamed up for the spread of communism. In response, Truman declared that the United States would give help to any free nation resisting communist aggression.

Congress agreed, and this new notion became known as the "Truman Doctrine." It then developed into a containment policy against the expansion of communism. A $400 million dollar deal for Greece and Turkey was extended to defend themselves against such insurgents.

With spontaneous global assertion of nations between the competing ideologies of *capitalism* and *communism*, Secretary of State George C. Marshall called for an extension of the Truman doctrine. He believed that the war-torn nations of Europe should join in a mutual program of aid for their economic recovery.

As a result, in June of 1948 Western Allies announced plans to unify their German Occupation zones and established a strong West German government, intended to stop the Russian or communist threat. The Russians countered with blocking, and finally shutting down all railroad, highway, and water traffic to Berlin, hoping that the blockade would force the remaining Allied Powers out of West Berlin.

Now all Western Europe seem in danger of falling into the hands of communists. For a while, it seemed as if though Allied Powers must either fight their way into the city of Berlin or abandon it to the communists. Unwilling to adopt either alternative, early in August the United States and its allies ordered airlifts of supplies- about 8,000 tons a day, for nine months, to allied forces in Berlin. The Russian Blockade was eventually neutralized and lifted in May the following year.

Meanwhile, the looming Presidential election seemed like a forgone conclusion in favor of Republicans. They were facing a sharply divided Democratic Party. Party members had splintered into Progressives, nominating former Vice President Henry Wallace, who had strong pro-Russian alliance views. And Dixiecrats, a faction of Southern Democrats who bitterly opposed Civil Rights programs, nominating Strom Thurmond, governor of South Carolina, as their candidate.

Tom Dewey was again the Republican nominee for President. Every public opinion- including experts, pooled Dewey to be the overwhelming choice, with a landslide victory. But with an extraordinary commitment and citizen purpose, Truman made those political experts look ridiculous at the election outcome. Compared to 16 states won by Dewey, with 189

Electoral votes; 4 for Strom Thurmond with 39 Electoral votes, and zero states and zero Electoral votes for Henry Wallace, Harry Truman won out majorities in 28 states and 303 Electoral votes.

This was a major lesson and landmark in our American history on the effects of mass propaganda. (Blatant racism- even within Truman's own political party), what we are led to believe, versus what we know and truly believe. Those facts we are led to know, versus those facts we actually experience or know, and are ignored. This situation will re-surface with the election of Donald Trump as President on November 8, 2016. This time it was an outsider's victory over both Party's' challenge and entrenched corruption.

Although Voters also elected a Democratic dominated Congress, this Congress proved to be just as uncooperative in the resolutions of domestic affairs as the preceding Republican dominated Congress had been. Southern Democrats joined hands with Republican naysayers to defeat most of Truman's domestic agenda. Adding to his woes were charges that the State Department was "harboring communists."

Led by Wisconsin's state Senator Joseph Mc McCarthy, a vicious attack on individual Civil Liberties ensued, leading to the arrest and conviction of several American citizens as Russian spies. Confrontations between the nation's core ideologies of *capitalism* versus *communism* now became the most imminent and vicious battle front for national security and stability.

The President's attention and most government officials, were dominated by news headlines- and so goes leading institutional norms and conscience. Additionally, there was no way to ignore the rampant internal social unrest that it engendered nationwide, for the oppressed blacks and dispossessed whites.

The United States, Canada, Britain, and France, along with 8 other Western European nations met in Washington in April of 1949 to set up a mutual defense. Under this agreement, the North Atlantic Treaty Organization (NATO) was born. Its emphasis was to strengthen communist-threatened countries military defenses. A corollary to this reasoning was that if these nations were strong, the United States would also be strengthened.

Russia ended its Berlin blockade in May. Meanwhile efforts to contain communism elsewhere in Asia exploded into full blown war. Mao Tse-tung's communist armies had defeated the Chinese National Army *Nationalists*. What remained of the Nationalists took refuge on the island of Formosa. The United States had declined in giving them aid in defense of China.

Japan gained control of Korea in 1895 and made it part of Japan in 1910. After the Allies defeated Japan in WW II, American and Russian forces moved into Korea. At the end of September 1948, there were two independent governments. The Democratic People's Republic in the Northern section, backed by Russia; and the Republic of Korea in the South was backed by the United States. The two powers could not agree on a united Korea, and so they referred the problem to the United Nations.

A UN Commission supervised elections in the South; but the communists refused to allow the Commission to do its work in the North, and so a Russian style dictatorship was set up there. Both Russia and United Nation troops eventually withdrew from the peninsula; while American strategists had decided that South Korea was not worth defending.

The Nuclear arms race began on August 29, 1949 when Russia detonated a hydrogen bomb with about 200 times more destructive force than the bombs dropped over Hiroshima and Nagasaki. The disclosure of Atomic secrets by British Scientist Klaus Fuchs in 1950 to Russia, heightened fears in the United States that led to the arrest, conviction, and execution of two American citizens considered to be "spies." Along with this hysteria came a speeding up in the development of nuclear weapons.

Every major move the United States made in the containment of communism evoked a Russian response. Enactment of the Marshal Plan led to Russia's seizure of Czechoslovakia. The build-up of Germany led to the Berlin Blockade. And the creation of NATO led to Russia's creation of the Warsaw Pact, which was an alliance of pro-communist nations.

THE KOREAN WAR BRIEF

Communist armies invaded South Korea on June 25, 1950, which was in direct violation of International Peace Agreement made with the United Nations. Members of the UN demanded a withdrawal, but the communists kept on fighting. At this point the UN asked its members to intervene. Ninety percent of troops, military supplies, and equipment were provided by the United States, while 16 other countries provided troops, and forty-one others from around the world sent food supplies and equipment.

China, which has now become under total communist rule, fought along with Russia on the North Korean side; providing them military supplies and equipment. When their drive into Seoul in South Korea had reached its periphery, both Truman and the UN took action to halt their advance. Air and Naval forces were ordered into action with General Dwight D. Eisenhower as Commander of both forces. As two agonizing years of bloody battles continued, peace talks had begun in July of 1951.

Meanwhile at home, with the sensational accusations and enormity of his charges directed at innocents, Joseph McCarthy had the public well distracted on the fears of communism and worse things to come. The President was no exception to the prevailing heed, and McCarthy's attack-claiming that his administration was riddled with communists, and that he was too soft in dealing with them.

Truman's popularity with the media hype on communism was at an all-time low, as McCarthy relentlessly attacked him for his handling of the Korean War, and his "mistreatment" of General Douglas Mc Arthur. Truman had relieved Mc Arthur of his military duties as Commander in chief of the war- more specifically for Mc Arthur's derision of Truman's policies.

Mc Arthur blamed Truman for the Chinese take-over of mainland China, since the U.S. had refused to intervene when Mao was on a roll against the *Nationalists*. Truman's refusal to use nuclear weapons or bombs in North Korea, as Mc Arthur was demanding, landed heavy accusations of the U.S. Army "coddling communists."[50]

In the upcoming Presidential election that was to follow in November of 1952, Eisenhower was nominated to lead the Republican Party. He had also pledged to end the Korean War; while Truman had proclaimed his fill with the fulfillment of his duties, and did not desire to run for a second term. There were also widespread beliefs that the Democrats had been in power too long.

---

[50] Ibid

Illinois Governor Aldi E. Stevenson, grandson of a Vice President under Grover Cleveland was the Democrats nominee for President. The publics' confidence and convictions that Eisenhower was indeed capable of his pledge to end the anguish of war, along with the nation's inner socio-economic turmoil was made clear on Election Day, with Eisenhower receiving 34 million popular votes and 442 Electoral; to Stevenson's 29 million popular votes, and 89 Electoral.

Truce talks about ending the war began on July 10, but for months, both sides were stalled and firmly deadlocked on the issues of *voluntary repatriation of prisoners*. The United Nation's command then adjourned on October 8, 1952. Shortly after Eisenhower's inauguration in January, Russian leader Josef Stalin died in March. Its successive leader Nikita Khrushchev now sought a softer peace with the United States for obtaining communists objectives.

This was to be accomplished by Russia appealing to the prejudices of underdeveloped nations just emerging from the yoke of colonialism; using the parities that it had reached with the United States in weaponry, science, and technology, and by offering them economic aid.

Meanwhile Truce Talks about the fate of Korea resumed on April 26th when the Communists had agreed upon voluntary repatriations. A truce was signed on July 27, 1953, and the fighting ended. Casualty counts left more than 54,246 dead Americans, 103,000 wounded, and about 6,000 missing. The Koreans and remaining UN troops had over 61,000 troops dead, 187,000 wounded, and more than one million civilians killed.

VIETNAM

While ending of the Korean misery was in the making, trouble erupted elsewhere in Indochina. Nationalist rebels who took over China, led by Ho Chi Ming had been terrorizing the French-colonial stronghold in Vietnam since 1946. When China began supplying arms to the rebels, Truman applied the containment policy by giving economic and military assistance to the French.

With Eisenhower's succession to the Presidency, there was continued and expanded assistance. But early in the spring of 1954, the North Vietnamese Army besieged the French garrison at Dien Bien Phu, inflicting a death toll of 20,000 soldiers leading them to surrender. France, China, Britain, and Russia, then signed an agreement at Geneva, Switzerland, dividing Vietnam.

The North was to be controlled by Communist forces under Ho Chi Minh, and the South was to remain in the hands of Emperor Bao Dai. Meanwhile an election was scheduled for the settlement of the future of all Vietnam. The elections were never held. Sensing that the Communists were more than likely to win the election, Bao Dai was overthrown by Ngo Dinh Diem, who was supposed to be an anti-communist.

The U S continued its aid to Diem's regime, while it, and seven other nations signed the Southeast Asia Defense Treaty, designed to prevent further communist expansion in Southeast Asia. After the Defeat of France, the U S came to believe that if one Southeast Asia nation fell to communism, others would topple. This was referred to as the "domino theory." The U S had therefore found it to be of absolute necessity to increase military and economic aid to South Vietnam.

17

PROVE YOUR DEMOCRACY

TORN BY CIVIL STRIFE AFTER World War II had ended, questions concerning *democratic rule* and *equality of treatment under the law* took on an exigency of national importance, because of its ideological competition with *communism*. Harry Truman's attempts in pressing for Civil Rights, desegregation, Anti-Poll Tax, and Fair Employment Practice Commission were filibustered to death in the U S Senate. Eisenhower, on the other hand, thought that the ethnic group divide between black and white people, and their cries for *equality of treatment* under the law was practically an insoluble problem.[51]

Convinced that the courts must take the offensive position in the cause for American Civil Liberties, he appointed the Governor of California, Earl Warren as Chief Justice of the U S Supreme Court in 1953. The wrath of Earl Warren's Courts in the transformation of American attitudes towards their less fortunate fellows began with a deliberate goal to uproot the inherent tyranny of our so-called democratic virtues. This was the prevailing racist apartheid ideology of *separate but equal,* that the nations' operational had hinged on for more than fifty-eight years of terrible brain-fucking.

This doctrine was challenged at the elementary public school level with an extraordinary involvement of the NAACP Civil Rights movement in the case, *Brown V Board of Education* of Topeka Kansas. Speaking for a unanimous court, Warren reversed the Homer v Plessey Ferguson's decision made in 1875, declaring that "separate but equal has no place in the field of public education." This case marked the beginning of active

---

[51] Ibid

181

judicial participation (*judicial activism*) in the official honoring of human Civil Rights in the United States.[52]

Because of the awareness, turmoil, and transformation in consciousness this court was to bring to the nation, Eisenhower would regrettably look back in hindsight, declaring that his appoint of Chief Justice Earl Warren to be "the biggest damn-fool mistake I ever made."

But he was absolutely wrong! Facing Jesus had just begun. The entrenched values of a semi-apartheid state were beyond the range and realm of resolution in his lifetime, as Eisenhower saw it.

In all areas of social life, and in all parts of the country, *segregation* was still the order of business after the 58-year rule was overturned. Ethnic group relations between Southern whites and their black counterparts remained firm against the court's decision, while Northern whites showed more willingness to accept fellow blacks and their fates as co-equal citizens, residents, or workers.

Differential economic progress, and the limited extent of actual integration into social life of the political state, now produced a greater frustration among progressive thinking black Americans. Most notable of these were those who served in World War II, before, and when *desegregation* began in the armed forces on a trial basis. Desegregation was completed when Truman issued a 1948 executive order, calling for equal treatment for all enlisted persons.

In fact, when Hitler was on a roll in Germany with his *Master Race* psychobabble, the fear of God in rousted intelligent members of the Supreme Court's bench had declared the word "Race," when used in identifying a person, to be a "suspect classification."[53]

How do you like this shit today? What Race is it you belong to, other than human?

Eisenhower's administration's purge was yet compounded- perhaps even more seriously from the standpoint of national security. The question of social inequality based on ethnicity, coalescing with the ideological competition of communism, took on the urgency and importance of national security. Awareness of criticisms from Russia and other foreign nations concerning oppression and ethnic group prejudice smeared the nation's self-image wherever competition for trade, influence, and strategic bases existed.

---

[52] Ibid
[53] Ibid

The critical problem on the home front, needing a work-in-progress solution revolved heavily around human relations and internal security. The nation's attachments and concern for external events became inseparable from concerns for its own internal events.

Joseph McCarthy's crusading zeal to get rid of undesirables of all sorts suspected of being affiliated with *communism,* sanctioned the discharge of almost 500 State Department employees- not a single one of whom was proved to have engaged in communist subversive activities. He went as far as accusing the U S Army of "coddling communists." This led to the demise of his nation-wide public influence, and was censured by the Senate for contemptuous conduct. The misery died in 1954.

In the midst of the social upheaval, economic conditions became depressing for many in the labor market. Eisenhower's Administration discovered that a balanced economic budget sent the economy into a slump. A federal policy resembling the New Deal was thus assumed and expanded with the usual Keynesian method- "easy money, and a deliberately unbalanced budget." [54]

MIDDLE EAST

Eisenhower, along with Vice President Richard Nixon, faced their same Democratic opponent, Aldi E. Stevenson, for the November election. This time they got re-elected with an even larger majority of popular and electoral votes. Just before the election though, two major concerns in foreign affairs gripped the Administration's attention. Britain, France, and Israel had invaded Egypt on October 23, while Hungary, revolted against communist rule and asked the United States for help.

A revolution in 1952 had overthrown King Farouk of Egypt, and Gamal Abdel Nasser emerged as the nation's new leader. Angered by the creation of the state of Israel in 1948, Nasser had nationalized the Suez Canal and began sinking ships in the channel in July of 1956. This move was what galvanized the British and French to take back the Canal by force. Without consulting the U S, war between the three nations ensued.

Our national interest in the Middle East was fundamentally influenced

---

[54] *Ibid*

by the huge oil reserves in the region. War waged on with Egypt, Britain, and France, While Russia and the U S introduced resolutions at the United Nations for a cease fire, which was vetoed by both Britain and France. At this point, Russian President Nikita Khrushchev threatened with a declaration that he might send volunteers to fight in Egypt, and then launch atomic missiles against France and Britain if they did not withdraw. Eisenhower also demanded the invaders to pull out of Egypt. The British then announced a cease fire, nine days after the attack before the crisis subsided.[55]

INTERNAL PROBLEMS

Early in January of 1957 Congress approved the Eisenhower Doctrine, which stated that the U S was prepared to use armed force anywhere in the Middle East against aggression from any country controlled by international communism. Then when Eisenhower announced his plans to rely more heavily on nuclear weapons as a deterrent, Europeans panicked.

With the presence of Russia as its main competitor in the arms race, if there really was a nuclear showdown, those nations in Europe would surely be destroyed. Given this reasoning, the French became a receptive ear, while both the United States and Russia continued talks on peaceful co-existence, and adopted an accommodating attitude about nuclear weapons, as they continued making them.

In June of 1957 the Russians successfully tested an ICBM missile. Later in October, they launched the first man-made satellite named Sputnik I. The U S launched its first earth satellite three months later than the Russians. Russian rocket science power was more advanced, but the whole world stage had been clearly established by two powers with a questionable nuclear balance of terror.

The fright and awakening of the matter now made education the nation's top priority. A National Defense Education Act was passed, authorizing federal loans and grants for science, and aid was given to the nation's hard-pressed schools. Meanwhile, the contentious problems of social inequality based on ethnicity, and many forms of segregation, willful

---

[55] Ibid

negligence, injustice, and social integration continued to burden the social order and nation's stability.

In spite of the Court's decision eliminating the *separate but equal* doctrine in public schools, and the quest for broader areas in social life, White Citizen's Councils in 17 states, dedicated to an all-out opposition to the court's ruling, sprang up throughout the South. The governor of Virginia called for a "Massive Resistance," denying aid to any local school system that wished to desegregate."

"The fellow who tries to tell me you can do these things by force is just plain nuts," [56]was Eisenhower's response to those who did not wish to carry-out the Court's decree of *desegregation*. Nonetheless, precipitating events in 1957 compelled the President to act with the use of force when 1,000 Paratroopers and 10,000 National Guardsmen were deployed to Little Rock High School in Arkansas, in order to allow black children to attend classes there.

Congress passed the first federal legislation since Reconstruction, to help black people in gaining the exercise of full citizenship. These were the Civil Rights Acts of 1957 and 1960, authorizing the Attorney General to stop Registration and election officials from interfering with black people seeking to register to vote.

The other side of this problematic social coin was the rampant fear of communist subversives, which led to the repression and infringement on the Civil Rights of many progressive thinking whites sympathetic to their less fortunate fellows. National attitudes of moral indignation coalesced with international attitudes of other democracies' colonial political rule. Simplified Marxism exploded to its zenith.

SPANISH SPEAKING AMERICA & THE COLD WAR

In 1959 Fidel Castro overthrew the Cuban ruler Flugencio Batista. He began his rule by driving many of his opposition into exile, seizing American private industrial properties, suppressed some Civil Liberties,

---

[56] Whitney David C./Whitney Robin Vaughn, *The American Presidents:* Eisenhower.

and then entered into a relationship with Russia. A *movement* called *Fidelismo* then began to make inroads throughout Central and South America.

The United States reacted to Castro's regime by putting an embargo on sugar imported from Cuba. Russian President Nikita Khrushchev then declared that "the Monroe Doctrine had outlived its time." Khrushchev even dared that if the United States intervened in Cuban affairs, Russia will defend the country with atomic weapons.[57]

"Kept in power by bayonets, because the alternative seemed to be communist revolution," the United States continued the support of colonial empires or "democracies" considered "conservative" regimes throughout Latin America. Events that were now precipitating in Cuba provided no easy solution.

A temporary thaw in Cold War relations began in the spring of 1959 when the Foreign Ministers of Russia, France, and Britain met in the month of May; and Vice President Richard Nixon visited Russia and met with Khrushchev. Khrushchev visited the U S in September, conferring with the President in Maryland and Camp David, where a top-level Summit Conference was agreed upon to be held at a future date, and Eisenhower cordially accepted the Russian President's invitation.

The Summit Agreement never matured. Why? A U-2 American spy plane was shot down with its pilot while snooping over Russia a few weeks later. The Russians captured the pilot, (Gary Powers) who confessed to be a US spy. While the United States publicly admitted that it had been flying U-2 missions over Russia for over five years. This incident abruptly ended the thaw in the ongoing Cold War relations.

Beginning with Germany, other countries in Europe, Africa, the Middle-East, Indochina, and Latin America, communist ambitions were ebbing high against oppressive democracies. A meeting was held by the United Nations' General Assembly in New York, in September of 1960, and was attended by Russian President Khrushchev, who openly expressed his anger over the U-2's spying. At this meeting he made an attempt to destroy the power of the U N to send troops into the world's troubled spots,

---

[57] Ibid

where overt rebellion against oppressive rule were becoming commonplace and ubiquitous.

As Eisenhower's Presidential term was coming to a close, he "reluctantly" endorsed Vice President Richard Nixon to be his successor. Nixon had come to national prominence the same way McCarthy did, by exploiting public fears of communist subversives, charging that "traitors in high councils of our government have made sure that the deck is stacked on the Soviet side of the diplomatic tables."

Although Nixon won much praise for his defense of American values in his confrontations with Khrushchev in Moscow, and no prominent Republican candidate rose to oppose his Party's nomination, the rising population of progressive independent voters, and the intimidation of media personnel, taking on the constant scourge of being potential communist subversives themselves, denied his election to the Presidency. In fact, reporters generally had a low opinion of Nixon.[58]

JOHN KENNEDY

The Democrats had nominated John F. Kennedy, a Senator from Massachusetts to be President, along with Senate Majority leader, Lyndon B. Johnson from Texas as Vice President. Both were elected. Kennedy accused the Republican administration of losing the Cold War, and neglecting the importance of national defense. A former World War II P. T. Boat Commander, who sustained some serious injuries during the war, John Kennedy nevertheless maintained a youthful vigorous world vision for America in his political career as a Senator. This outlook allowed him to secure a paper-thin victory over rival Republican candidate Richard Nixon in the 1960 November Presidential election. Although speculation has it that some 9,000 votes from the state of Illinois that accounted for his victory in that crucial state were supplied by "unlawful means," by Then Chicago mayor Richard J. Daily.

Whatever its merits, John Kennedy is said to have had a genuinely inquiring body-mind, and stood out to teach Americans the true value of the individual- regardless of status; and seemed intent on teaching the country

---

[58] Ibid

to respect its pool of superior creative and productive talents. Contrary to his train of thinking were the old formidable wall of segregationists- ever rebuilt, now made of a coalition of Republican *nay-Sayers*, and *won't-do* Southern Democrats.

Both parties blatantly resisted his plans to provide federal aid to education, urban renewal, medical care for the elderly, and a higher minimum wage. Commentators often spoke of a "deadlock of democracy" in which Party discipline crumbles, and positive legislative action become next to impossible. His proposition to lower personal and corporate taxes in order for the public to have more money to spend on consumer goods, allowing corporations to invest in new facilities for producing these goods, was to go nowhere.

Economic growth remained sluggish. The lagging rate, persistence of unemployment, worries about continuing inflation, and grass-roots Civil Rights' movements that were now becoming commonplace, getting stronger and more radicalized in their demands, alarmed Kennedy.

John Kennedy also hoped to reverse the Truman- Eisenhower doctrine that was catered to the backing of reactionary regimes of other nations, simply because they were anti-communists. Meanwhile, angry protests demanding Civil Rights attention and action got deeper and more forceful. The real inspired grass roots of protests were initiated back in December of 1955.

In Montgomery Alabama a weary black female public transportation commuter had refused to comply with a bus operator's demand to give up the front seat she had occupied on a public transportation bus to a white patron. This action was against the internalized, institutionalized, established standards and espoused values of Southern states apartheid system against black people.

Be they male or female, they must be treated as a sub-standard and separate species. The female's arrest for Civil Disobedience because of her refusal to comply with the bus driver's orders to give up her seat and move to the rear of the bus, was what lead to the first major act of Civil disobedience by black citizens.

Inspired by the Act, the Reverend Martin Luther King became an icon in ongoing boycotts, protests, and other non-violent forms of Civil Disobedience as a strategy for change and swift legislative action. It took a whole year for Montgomery to desegregate its transportation system, after the Supreme Court ruled in favor of Rosa Parks, the black female public transportation commuter dissenter.

In extreme, and demanding a totally different kind of social system were black segregationists. Elijah Mohammed and Malcolm X, both Moslems, were such paragons and advocates. "This white government has ruled us and given us plenty of hell, but the time has arrived that you taste a little of your own hell" (Malcolm X),[59] summarized their mood and the thrust of their movement. The Kennedy administration was relentlessly pushed for a radical policy change. And as the President saw it, America must address itself to the roots of poverty, war, disease, and ignorance.

CUBA & COLD WAR TENSIONS

Shortly after his inauguration, a plan that had been in the coop hatching was executed on April 17, with a band of trained commandos landing at the Bay of Pigs in Cuba, to overthrow the government of Fidel Castro. The invading troops had been promised direct US military support, which included air cover to insure success of the invasion which Kennedy had approved. During their execution of the invasion, Kennedy reneged on his promise, refusing to provide the promised military air support, and Cuban forces crushed the invading insurgents. Most of the captured who were Cuban themselves, were exiles living in the US were later released back to the U S in exchange for non-military supplies.

The chemistry of Cold War tensions frothed in Europe when Khrushchev threatened to give communist East Germany control over the West's air and land supply routes to Berlin. This was part of the Russian effort to end Allied troops presence and control of Berlin that began at the ending of World War II.

Besides Russia's presence there, the remaining Allied nations: France, Britain, and the United States opposed any threat to the freedom of West Berlin. Kennedy met with Khrushchev in Vienna, in June to discuss this matter. Nothing was settled; and the crisis deepened.

Russia began erecting the Berlin Wall in August, and with aggressive

---

[59] Ibid

initiative resumed testing nuclear weapons by exploding a big-ass hydrogen bomb. This time with a power 3,000 times that of the bomb detonated over Hiroshima!

Goddamn! Son-of-a-bitch! Is this enough overkill?

We think not. The US followed suit in the testing of nuclear weapons, greatly expanded its space program, and Russian superiority in space was gradually reduced. In an effort to counterbalance the failed invasion of the Bay of Pigs and bolster the image of the country, Kennedy established an agency for International Development to administer economic aid to nations throughout the world. The Peace Corp became the vehicle and organization that mobilized his plans of technical skills and American idealism.

In the competition for image, and influence, the Russians could have cared less about this world-wide campaign led by the United States, as they continued their plight, and then brought on the most reckless daring and challenge yet to the United States post- World War II consensus.

In the experience of many, it brought the world to a heightened awareness of the real possibilities of a nuclear disaster in the month of October, when U S intelligence reports were fully acknowledged that Russia had established missile launch pads in Cuba, capable of striking U S cities. On this premise, the President ordered a naval blockade; the activation of 14,000 Air Force Reserve troops; and US Navy ships ordered to stop, search, and turn back all ships delivering Russian missiles headed for Cuba.

Kennedy went on live television on October 22, informing the nation that "A deliberately provocative and unjustified change in the status quo" had occurred; and should there be any Cuban-based nuclear attack on the country, it would result in "a full retaliatory response upon the Soviet Union."

Kennedy then called on Russian leader Khrushchev to dismantle the missile bases, and to remove all weapons capable of striking the U S form the island. The world remained panic-stricken for several days as the Russians continued their work on the missile bases.

For those of us alive during this period in history, this was the most tense and dangerous moments in the nation's and world history that hung heavy in the air until October 27, when the Russians agreed to remove the missiles. Both sides were appalled at the narrowness of the escape and avoidance of war. The crisis brought a deep change in U S-Russian relationship- an immediate thaw that produced a relaxation of tension, and a call to "live together in mutual tolerance."

Meanwhile, Russia's widening split with China, and being deeply affected by the narrow escape of involvement in a nuclear confrontation, was now genuinely interested in easing the tension. Realizing what an all-out nuclear war would mean, Russian President Khrushchev agreed to the installation of a "Hot Line" between the White House and the Russian Kremlin, so that in any future crisis, or the risk of a nuclear war that could be started by accident, leaders of both nations could be in instant communication.

NEW FRONTIER

Kennedy's vision for a "New Frontier" for the nation was largely an attempt to set a mood, to draw the citizenry into the spirit of a national discipline and self-sacrifice, so that the nation might attack its internal and external problems with renewed vigor, energy, and imagination. It was a search for a spirit of dedication- especially amongst the young- backed by a set of proposals for national action. Instead, the nation swelled and seethed with more than 800 demonstrations and protests nationwide for immediate Civil Rights action, in practically all major cities.

Twice, the National Guard was called into service in Alabama, to protect blacks in the integration of their schools. Then later in August, more than 200,000 black and white demonstrators came down on the capital (March on Washington), demanding action on Civil Rights legislation, which were already sent to Congress. Flooded by these demonstrations and protests, the President was now fully engaged.

In a televised broadcast addressing the nation, Kennedy noted that "... one hundred years of delay have passed since President Lincoln freed the slaves, yet their heirs, their grandsons, are not fully free. They are not yet freed from the bond of injustice. They are not yet freed from social and economic oppression, and this nation, for all its hopes and all its boasts, will not be fully free until its citizens are free..."[60]

A Virginia and Mississippi Senator stalled the Bill Kennedy planned to pass in a committee. On November22, 1963, while riding through the streets of Dallas, Texas in a motorcade, Kennedy was shot by an assassin, and died shortly. Vice President Johnson, who was also in the motorcade riding behind the President, was unharmed, and later sworn into office.

Theories concerning this Presidential assassination continue to be the American political cult of inquiry, conspiracy, sliding into a never-ending body of verified and unverified truths, of how things really went down at this particular time in our history, defying adequate closure for many.

Johnson pushed for legislation that had been proposed by Kennedy. He also proposed a national "War on Poverty." The national mood after Kennedy's death seemed to create and produce a will for favorable and decisive political action to remedy and resolve the nation's domestic problems. Without further fudging, Congress passed the Civil Rights Act in July of 1964, made financial appropriations for a variety of retraining, and there was an Urban Improvement program, to help Johnson with his "War on Poverty" declaration.

[60] Ibiod

18

VIETNAM WAR & THE NATIONAL DIVIDE

A BRIEF OVERVIEW OF VIETNAM'S PAST began with the French founding Catholic missions there in the 1600's. Led by Napoleon III in the early1860's, the French sent forces there to gain control of the area and make it a part of its colonial empire. Saigon and South Vietnam were seized in 1860's and colonized in 1864. They then gained control of North Vietnam. These three divisions of Vietnam, along with Cambodia and Laos were combined to form what became French Indochina.[61]

France ruled the area until 1940 when Japanese invaders seized it during World War II. At the end of the war, all Vietnam declared its independence by communist leader Ho Chi Minh. Shortly thereafter, the French returned to resume control. Their intentions were for the Vietnamese to retain "independence sovereignty within the French union." This meant France would retain all the important aspects of its government, including military and foreign affairs. Attempts for negotiating this deal failed, and war broke out between the two in 1946.[62]

With the spontaneous eruptions of communist challenge on multiple fronts that began with the Berlin Blockade, Mao's revolution in China, and the invasion of South Korea in 1950, the driving theme of United States foreign policy was anti-communism. The NSC considered South-East Asia as the "greatest target of coordinated offensive directed by the Kremlin," Russia.[63] In its activity to contain communism, by 1952 the US

---

[61] Ibid
[62] Ibid
[63] Ibid

193

had provided substantial assistance of military and aircraft equipment to the French for use in Vietnam.

As the French situation deteriorated, demand increased for the US to enter the war. Eisenhower's decision in 1954, not to intervene when the French were about to be defeated was intelligent. The imminent collapse coming only after a year he had brought the Korean War to an inconclusive end, would put enormous pressure on a war-weary nation. He thus refused to intervene directly when asked for an aerial bombing campaign to support a last-gasp French effort.

The last French-held position, Dien Bien Phu was overran by North Vietnamese communist forces on May7, 1954. Three months later an agreement was reached on July 21 in Geneva. This agreement separated Vietnam at the 17 parallel, giving the North to the communists, while the South remained briefly in the French union until it was declared independent by Ngo Dinh Diem.[64]

"....based on wishful thinking and academic abstraction," John Kennedy, our next President in line committed the US to the Vietnam War. "Flawed from the start... it began with Kennedy's impulsive and disastrous decision to approve a coup against South Vietnam's leader, Ngo Dinh Diem." The Joint Chief of Staff called Diem's killing the 'Asian Bay of Pigs.'" Then Vice President Johnson commented on "playing cowboys and Indians in Saigon." The whole American-Vietnam Conflict story began to snowball from here on.

With the ever-increasing presence of American troops now supporting South Vietnam, fighting began on a small scale in 1957, then escalated into a savage full-scale war that threatened world peace. There were 3,200 American military personnel there in 1961, but South Vietnamese forces could not hold off the rebels. By the time Kennedy was assassinated in November of 1963, the presence of military troops had increased to 16,000 and more than 120 Americans had already been killed.[65]

Anti-US riots broke out in the Panama Canal Zone early in 1964. But Vietnam got to be more demanding on the Johnson administration in August. Threatening to turn the Cold War into a Hot War, the U S continued to step-up its support for South Vietnam against communist

[64] Ibid
[65] Ibid

forces. Following six months of covert naval operations in the Gulf of Tonkin, 30 miles off the coast of North Vietnam, three North Vietnamese PT boats allegedly fired torpedoes at a U S destroyer on August 2. A full retaliatory attack took place on August 5 after a second such alleged attack. At a later date, many reliable sources claimed the attacks to be false.

On August 7, Congress gave Johnson a blank check, authorizing the President to "take all necessary measures to repel any armed attack against forces of the United States and to prevent further aggression." This was the "Tonkin Resolution" approved by 416 to 0 in the lower House, and 88 to 2 in the U S Senate [66]

"I've got Ho's pecker in my pocket," a confident Johnson believed. "I am not going to lose Vietnam. I am not going to be the President who saw Southeast Asia go the way China went."[67] Well, maybe not.

THE HOME FRONT & VIETNAM

A strong back and a willingness to work no longer guaranteed that the possessor could earn a decent living in America; while educated workers with special skills could easily find well-paying jobs. On the other hand, there were entire regions in the country- notably the Appalachian area, that had been bypassed by economic development, technological advancement, rising living standards, and where job requirements had totally changed.

To attack the problem head-on, Johnson's *War on Poverty* passed the Economic Opportunity Act that combined the progressive concepts of a welfare state, with the idea of individual responsibility. The administration pledged to support the weak and disadvantaged, and giving each citizen a fair chance.

"The welfare was not designed for breeders...", Johnson said in his war on poverty speech. Naturally, with such enforced rule and regulation that should accompany the act of aid, poverty and its sanctioned institution in

---

[66] Ibid
[67] Ibid

the United States would have been held to its most insignificant level in the country. But look at the *breeders* in California.

Legislative action along these lines helped boost Johnson's Presidential candidacy by unanimous support from the poor in the up-coming election. He also garnered business interests, and the allegiance of organized labor. He won 61% of the popular votes in the November election, carrying all but six states over his Republican opponent Barry Goldwater, who was advocating a return to *lassies-faire* type government rule.

Johnson pressed ahead with his program by proposing a compulsory hospital system for persons 65years or older. Also passed, and amended by Congress were, Medical and Medicare, a combined hospital insurance for retired people, funded by Social Security taxes. This law provided grants to states to pay the medical expenses for people below the retirement age of 65. This part of the system is called "Medicaid." An Elementary and Secondary Education Act supplied funds to improve the education of poor children in areas where they were educationally deprived and needed extra help. Project "Head Start" was one such related program.

Johnson's success in getting Kennedy's proposals through also engendered the government's atomic energy and space program, a boom in the aircraft and electronic industries, and efficient machinery in the merging of scientific technology with commercial utilities. The victories of World War II had left the nation great and prosperous. "...but we have no promise from God that our greatness will endure. This fragile existence... tower beyond the control and even the judgment of men..."[68] noted Johnson.

Change was happening so fast that parents who transmitted the accumulated wisdom of their years to their children, found their advice rejected; often with good reason, because that wisdom had little application to the social problems their growing children had to face. The modern educational-military-industrial complex society was beginning to recognize our true interdependence, and thereby began to place an enormous premium on social cooperation as *the tool* for national security.

But no real consensus of method emerged or unraveled in the building of Johnson's "Great Society." As some authors of the period aptly noted:

---

[68] Ibid

"American society remained fragmented, its members divided against themselves and often within themselves."

The vexing character of modern conditions was visible in practically every American social life. Black anger erupted in a series of destructive rage and urban riots. Resentments were directed at the social system and its "domineering attitude of mind." The "white racism that deprived them of access to good jobs, crowded them in slums, and the erosion of hope of escape from such misery." Progressive white middle classes, with education as its main catalyst, join the foray in the spring of 1965. [69]

NAM- 0UR TURMOIL

Rather than see all Vietnam unified under the Communist government, in "an air of crisis," Johnson made a commitment and ordered the first U S combat troops into South Vietnam under the pretext of protecting American bases, and to stop Communist forces from overthrowing the government of the country. From its inception, the war in Vietnam divided the American people sharply. Those who understood the dynamics of the war expressed and stressed the undemocratic character of both sides of the South Vietnamese regime, and opposed American intervention.

George Romney, father of Mitt Romney, who was the Republican Party front runner in the 1968 election, explaining why he dissented against the war he once supported, noted that it had been a result of "brainwashing" he received from generals he met with in Saigon in 1965. This took him out of the presidential race, making way for Nixon to become the GOP nominee, and President.

The massive aerial bombings, use of napalm, and other chemical weapons sprayed in forests, and on crops that wreaked havoc among civilians, was considered and looked upon as unnecessary, and immoral. The "war hawks," as the pro-war faction of government were called, continued to argue that communist subversion must not be allowed to topple the South Vietnamese government, lest all Southeast Asia fall.

Rather than yield to social reform domestically, the nation endured

---

[69] Ibid

a string of sweltering protests, violent confrontations, and deadly riots; beginning with the Watts Riot in Los Angeles, in August of 1965; Detroit, and Newark in 1967; Cleveland and Chicago in 1968, which claimed hundreds of lives. The most frightening aspects of the riots were the mixture of anti-war sentiments, and their tendency to polarize society along ethnic group lines of *black* and *white* power. *Black power* meant a radical transformation of identity than what American society had nurtured up to this time in our history. Conversely, *white power* meant the perpetuation of the undesirable conditions of identity degradation.

As Johnson escalated the war, casualties and criticisms mounted-reaching unknown levels of anger, and an avalanche of ambivalence that the nation had never before experienced through any other military engagement. Fever-pitched protests resonated from the Senate, universities, the press, and churches' pulpits. Civil disorders and riots broke out every summer subsequent to 1965; and in 1967, 41 serious civil disorders took place in 39 cities.[70]

As bombing, ground attacks, American casualties, and the cost of war mounted in Vietnam, so did the destructive riots and demonstrations on the home front that haggard and challenged the post-World War II consensus of America's unquestionable dominant world power, in relation to its citizens' welfare. Notable critics of the administration urged young adults of draft-age to resist or refuse to fight in Vietnam, while tens of thousands evaded the draft by fleeing the country.[71]

At the end of 1965 there were about 184,000 American troops fighting in the fields. After a year of continuous heavy fighting, the number of troops had increased to 385,000, and 485,000 the following year of 1967. By 1968 that number had peaked to 538,000. Conversely, in a corresponding increase of U. S. troops' presence, there was also an increase in Viet Cong guerrillas fighting the war. The nation was now engaged in another a full-blown war that was never declared by Congress.[72].

As the war dragged on, it became increasingly clear that a quick military victory was impossible. Air power proved ineffective in halting Viet Cong guerrilla attacks. Yet, U S leaders and experts repeatedly advised

---

[70] Ibid
[71] Ibid
[72] Ibid

the President that one more bombing escalation would break the enemy's will to resist. But they were miserably wrong.

"Ho's pecker" in Johnson's pocket wreaked havoc and hell in both American and Vietnamese lives simultaneously.[73]

Our overkill and build-up for a quick victory turned into a nightmare on the Viet Cong Lunar Year of January 30, 1968. North Vietnamese forces launched a general offensive blitz, striking 39 of the 44 provincial capitals, with many other towns and cities- and every American base throughout South Vietnam. The greatest toll of American lives in a single day of confrontations was recorded on this day.

Although U. S. retaliation cost the North Vietnamese heavily, because large sections of cities were leveled with bombs, and elsewhere- destruction was total! In the words of one experiencer, it became necessary to destroy a whole town in order to "save it." (One such incident of reference that came to public notice and scrutiny could have been the *My Lai Massacre* that was officially documented on March16). In any case, the psychological impact of the coordinated Tet offensive made it a clear victory for the communists- both in their country and the ebbing Anti-Vietnam sentiment in the United States.

In a democratic effort to show seriousness in seeking peace negotiations with the North Vietnamese, Johnson, in a televised address to the American people on March 31, 1968, announced that he was calling a partial halt to the bombing of North Vietnam. When Army General Westmoreland declared Tet as a communist defeat, and when it was understood that the administration was considering sending an additional 200,000 troops or more to Vietnam, thousands of students took to the streets and became activists in political affairs of the nation, supporting any Presidential candidate opposing, or ordering an end to the war.

Democratic Senators Eugene McCarthy, former Attorney General, Robert F. Kennedy, and Hubert Humphrey of the Democratic Party were such paragons. As a result, Johnson withdrew from the race as a candidate for the Presidency.

Making things worse in decision-making for a divided party was the candidacy of Governor George C. Wallace of Alabama, advocating the Old South's racist ideology, and an end to all Civil Rights reform, as the

---

[73] Ibid

American Independent Party's candidate. Richard Nixon and Spiro T. Agnew were the Republican Party's choice for the Presidency; proposing the sentiment of a gradual or "phased" withdrawal of all American troops from South Vietnam, and ending the war "on honorable terms." [74]This plea was more reasonable to voters.

On April 4 of 1968, Civil Rights leader Martin Luther King Jr. was killed in Memphis, Tennessee. In response, riots, looting, and burning exploded in more than 100 cities across America. The President was forced to call Federal troops to put down the riots. Two months later, Democratic Presidential hopeful Robert F. Kennedy who had become leading contender for the nomination, after winning the California Primary, was also killed by an assassin on June 5, 1968.

Pressure mounted on delegates at the Democratic National Convention held in Chicago, when thousands of radical students and other young activists protesting the Vietnam War descended on them to repudiate the administration's Policies. Another common sentiment that prevailed among the youth culture of the day was that they truly believed that funds they should be receiving from their government for subsidies were being diverted to the war effort made in Vietnam.

Robert Kennedy's death, and Johnson's choice not to run for re-election, changed the political picture for the Democratic Presidential nomination. Vice President Hubert Humphrey accepted the nomination, while violence erupted between protesters, National Guardsmen, and club-wielding policemen, injuring hundreds outside the Convention, as TV cameras broadcast the violence live into millions of homes.

Peace talks on ending the War had dragged on through the summer and fall, with no positive results. North Vietnam continued its insistence that all US bombing must be halted before any agreements could be reached. An all-out effort to end the bombing of North Vietnam was then announced by the President on October 31, 1968. Perhaps this was done in a gesture for the Democrats to continue their administrative rule. But they were disappointed when Republican Candidates Richard Nixon and Spiro T. Agnew won the election by a narrow margin of electoral votes, while Democratic candidate Hubert Humphrey had won majority of the popular votes.

---

[74] Ibid

NIXON

Public hopes and expectations remained high, that a breakthrough for peace would come through the new presidency, with the long Peace Talks that began in January- but to no avail. In June of 1969, Nixon announced that although there had been no progress in the Paris Peace Talks, he planned to begin the gradual withdrawal of US forces from the war zone, with the first 25,000 due home by September. Meanwhile, fearing for their lives through compulsory conscription, thousands of draft-evaders continued their exodus to Canada or Europe; while other draft-age college students continued their protests on most campuses throughout the nation.

As promised, the first 25,000 US combat troops did came home from Vietnam in September. However, in less than two months, protests ebbed again, reaching a new climax when more than 300,000 demonstrators this time gathered in Washington DC on November 16. The anti-war sentiment was heightened and frenzied when it became publicly known that US troops had massacred hundreds of Vietnamese civilians in the village of My Lai, on March 16, 1968.

In the midst of it all, while at the White House during the uproar, Nixon maintained an attitude of wait-and-see outcome of the immense commotion. To insulate himself from being influenced by the protesters, he comforted himself in the Oval Office by watching a televised football game.[75]

Soon after military leaders overthrew the pro-communist chief of Cambodia, the new government that replaced it appealed to the US for assistance and military supplies, as North Vietnamese troops began to close in on its capital. While concealing the bombing from Congress and the American public, the US Air Force had been bombing communist forces in Cambodia since 1969. On April 30, 1970, Nixon announced that the US and South Vietnamese troops were marching into Cambodia, in an effort to capture Viet Cong troops and supplies.

Under protests from Senators and Congressmen from both political parties, stating that only Congress has the power to declare war on another country, troops were removed from Cambodia on June 30. Congress

---

[75] Ibid

then voted to cut off all funds for further American military operation in Cambodia.[76]

On domestic issues concerning the ethnic group divide, the Nixon administration pursued a course and policy of "benign neglect." The drive to integrate blacks and whites into previously segregated public schools slowed down, and unrest developed within the administration with protests that resulted in many resignations within the Department of Health Education and Welfare. Runaway inflation was blamed for the major economic problems of the nation, due primarily to heavy military expenditures, and the *easy money* policies of the Johnson administration.

During this same year of 1970, Congress passed a law giving the President power to regulate wage and prices. As a result, there was a ninety-day price and wage freeze, and a 10% surcharge on imports. These controls did not check inflation; rather, they angered union leaders who believed labor was being shortchanged, since controls slowed down their upward spiral. The Dollar was devalued in December, making American products more competitive in foreign markets.

Nixon advocated shifting the burden of welfare payments to the Federal government, and equalizing such payments in all states, as well as a "minimum income" for poor families; but these measures got nowhere in Congress. Meanwhile, the administration considered a solution to the Vietnam problem as the President's chief task.

And as the level of American troops' presence was reduced, the communists merely waited for further reductions. Then late in April Nixon escalated the war and resumed bombing targets in North Vietnam and neutral Cambodia. "Let's go blow the hell out of them" was Nixon's go ahead command to the Joint Chiefs of Staff.[77]

Students took the lead in opposing the invasion of Cambodia with many campus demonstrations. One college where feelings ran high was Kent State University in Ohio. For several days students clashed with local police and caused heavy property damages. Four students were killed. While the nation was still reeling from this shock, two more black students at Jackson State University in Mississippi were killed by State policemen.

---

[76] Ibid

[77] Ibid

This was followed by the closing down of hundreds of colleges- even those that had no previous unrest on campus.

Demonstrations and huge protests continued in Washington, DC from May 3, through May 5. At the instigation of Attorney General John N. Mitchell, the largest mass arrest in the nation's history was made, when more than 13,000 youth demonstrators and protestors were clobbered and jailed.

In June of 1971, the Senate passed a Bill extending the military draft; at the same time it also passed a measure calling for all American troops to be withdrawn from Vietnam within nine months. Shortly thereafter, the North Vietnamese at the Paris Peace Talks proposed that if the US would withdraw all its forces from Vietnam by the end of 1971, the communists would release all their Prisoners of War simultaneously. Further, a cease fire would be agreed on, as soon as a withdrawal date was set.

Accusations came on, charging that the President was prolonging the war so that he could bring it to an end during the election year of 1972, to help him with his campaign for reelection. In June, the Federal government obtained injunctions to prevent the *New York Times* and other newspapers from publishing documents concerning the Vietnam War. The claim was that if published, it would jeopardize national security. By a 6 to 3 vote, the US Supreme Court ruled to uphold the newspaper's right to publish the so-called *Pentagon Papers,* which were a part of the history of the Vietnam War, compiled by the Department of Defense, and classified as "Top Secret."[78]

Nixon's ideological views of dedicating his energies and wisdom to bring about a "generation of peace among nations" began in February of 1972, when he decided to go on an 8-day diplomatic visit to China. For more than 20 years now the US had refused to officially recognize Communist China. The "Bamboo Curtain," (since Russia is deemed the "Iron Curtain"), that had separated the country from the Western world throughout the period of the Cold War, parted widely. An estimated 60 million people watched the pomp and ceremonies of the President's historic visit to China.

Back from his trip across the bamboo curtain, Nixon stressed that his meeting with the *Dragon* was a success. Noting that cultural, educational,

[78] Ibid

and journalistic contact between both countries were established to broaden trade and communication between both governments. "...most important, we have agreed on rules of international conduct which will reduce the risk of confrontation and war in Asia and the Pacific. We agreed that we are opposed to the domination of the Pacific area by any one power. We agreed that international disputes be settled without the use of threat or force; and we agreed that we are prepared to apply the principles of national relations. We agreed that we will not negotiate the fate of other nations behind their back and we did not do so in Peking. There were no secret deals of any kind."[79]

Incidentally, unknown to the public or Congress, Nixon secretly promised North Vietnamese leaders $4.75 billion in American aid in order to rebuild their country should they choose to end the war. The promise went unfulfilled, and was not disclosed to the public until after the North Vietnam had conquered all of South Vietnam, four years later.[80]

Nixon's next shattering historical pledge was to visit the Soviet Union's capital of Moscow on May 22, 1972, also for an 8-day Summit. During this visit, there was a sharp escalation of fighting in Vietnam when Viet Cong forces from Hanoi committed most of its main forces to a full-scale invasion of South Vietnam. In spite of the fact that Russia was the main supplier of war materials to the Viet Cong, Nixon made it clear that he was looking forward to better relations with the Soviet Union's leaders.

A new spirit of goodwill came about through five days of ceaseless rounds of talks and ceremonies. The President was invited to address the people directly on a Russian TV station on May 28. His address was keynoted with these words: "As great powers, we shall sometimes be competitors, but we need never be enemies..." Nine agreements and treaties were signed, the most import having to do with restrictions in the production of Atomic weapons.

Other notable agreements were for shared discoveries and improvements in medicine, environmental protection, space, science, technology, the prevention of incidence at sea between military ships and planes; creation

---

[79]

[80] Ibid

of a joint trade commission, and a twelve-point declaration of guidelines to provide peaceful coexistence.[81]

Diplomatic meetings with China and Russia produced a feeling of milestone achievements among Americans who considered themselves *conservatives*, owing to the polarity in relations that once existed between these nations. Meanwhile, Democratic Senator George McGovern, a Presidential hopeful was chosen at their convention in July, to challenge the Nixon administration's handling of the war.

To ensure his reelection, Nixon set up a campaign organization called "CREEP," a short form for Committee to Reelect the President. Over $60million in campaign funds, most of what had been illegally donated was to be used for criminal purposes. This had included an illegal break-in at the Democratic National Convention Headquarters in Washington called the *Watergate*, and another Illegal break-in at the office of Daniel Ellsberg's psychiatrist, in Beverly Hills, California.

Daniel Ellsberg was a distinguished serviceman in Vietnam who disagreed with our involvement there. As a civilian employee within high levels of the administration, he was able to have access to details of the history of our involvement in Vietnam. These were the set of documents called the *Pentagon Papers,* and labeled "Top Secret." He wanted the American public to know how immoral the War and our National position there was.[82]

Although newspapers carried these stories during the 1972 Presidential campaign, Nixon and his colleagues were so vehement and convincing in their denials, including having any connection with the burglary incidents of Ellsberg's psychiatrist, and break-in at the National Democratic Convention Headquarters. The administration's attacks on the press as being "irresponsible" lulled the public's sense of inquiry, as voters' attention remained focused on symbolic gestures at his efforts to end the War.

Hopes and spirits were high when Presidential adviser Henry Kissinger announced at a White House press conference, twelve days before the

---

[81] Ibid
[82] Ibid

election on October 26 that "peace was at hand" in the Vietnam War. Even though a Cease Fire had not been signed, he declared that he had reached substantial agreements in secret negotiations with the North Vietnamese diplomats in Paris. Voters went to the polls in record numbers, reelecting Richard Nixon and Vice President Spiro Agnew- this time with a landslide victory with over 60% of the popular votes, and 521 Electoral to 17 over their Democratic opponents George McGovern and Sergeant Shriver.

Negotiations with North Vietnam continued after the election, but talks went poorly. Talks were suspended because Le Duc Tho, the chief negotiator of North Vietnam, according to our negotiator, "tried to change previously agreed-upon matters." On December 18, about two days after the postponement of Talks, Nixon ordered the heaviest bombing attacks of the war against North Vietnam. In spite of protests from most of our allies, including Canada, the US continued intense and relentless bombing for two weeks.

On December 30, the White House announced that Negotiations would resume in Paris, and that the bombing of North Vietnam's capital and main seaport would be halted. As Talks progressed, the President halted all bombing on January 15, 1973. Then three days after Inauguration Day, he declared that an agreement had been reached "to end the War and bring peace with honor in Vietnam and Southeast Asia." Formal signing of Peace Agreements took place in Paris on January 27, and a *cease fire* began in Vietnam.[83]

As provided in the agreement, the remaining 25,000 American troops were withdrawn from South Vietnam by March 27. On other side, during the same period, North Vietnam released 590 American POW's. At this point, more than 46,000 American troops had died and over 300,000 physically wounded. More than 200,000 youths had deserted the draft, and over half a million deserted after having being drafted.

---

[83] Ibid

19

WATERGATE

AFTER ALL THE MASS CIVIL Disobedience, protests, and demonstrations, net effects on the publics' psyche concerning the War was that traditional patriotism and respect for government had been seriously damaged. But this was only half of our national sentiments and moral indignations that were to surface and disentangle. After a brief respite, fighting resumed between the Viet Cong and South Vietnamese. North Vietnam regained and retained control of large sections of South Vietnam.

Bringing a greater divisiveness and more seriousness to the American people were challenges to the United States Constitution, as interpreted by the President, under the clause of *National Security,* when the "Watergate Scandals" began to unfold. The scandals began to transcend all other domestic concerns; beginning on March 19, 1973, when James McCord, a former FBI agent employed as a Security Officer for CREEP, accused of burglary in the illegal Watergate break-in, wrote a letter to the judge presiding over his trial.

As investigations about the scandals developed and expanded during 1973 and 1974, some shoddy, low-life, wheeling and dealing by the President and all his men, extending back into his first term in office surfaced, and were made for public scrutiny. Most people had accepted Nixon's words when he declared "I can say categorically that no one in this White House staff, no one in this administration presently employed, was involved in this very bizarre incident."[84]

The break-in at the Democratic Convention Headquarters was an attempt by CREEP officials' to disrupt the campaign of leading candidates,

---

[84] Ibid

207

in subversive ways. The intruders had been caught rifling through files, and installing electronic eavesdropping devices. When brought to trial, most of the defendants pleaded guilty. The head of CREEP and the President's lawyer also admitted their involvement.

Among their disclosure was that: the Acting Director of the FBI had destroyed documents related to the case; and large sums of money had been paid the burglars, at the instigation of the White House, to insure their silence. The CIA supplied equipment used in the burglary; CREEP officials attempted to disrupt the campaign of leading Democratic candidates; that illegal wiretaps had been placed on newsmen phones, and also on the administration's own officials. Nixon steadfastly denied these testimonies, insisting that he would investigate the Watergate affair thoroughly, and see that the guilty were punished.[85]

The Senate Watergate Investigating Committee was set up as a result and televised public hearing began on May 17, 1973. James McCord Jr, a former CIA agent and Security Chief of the Committee to Reelect the President, told the Senators that he had been offered Executive Clemency in the name of President Nixon, if he would refuse to talk. On the following day, the wife of the now former Attorney General John Mitchell told newsmen that her husband had been too occupied protecting the President, and that Nixon should resign, rather than wait to be impeached.[86]

White House Counsel John Dean shocked listeners when the Senate hearings resumed on June 25, testifying that the President had misled the nation by denying involvement in the Watergate cover-up. He also accused him of raising $1million to pay "hush money" to the Watergate defendants; revealed a list of "political enemies," and told of efforts to get the IRS and other government departments to harass these people.

John Mitchell testified before the Committee in July and denied authorizing the Burglary, but admitted being present at meetings when the affair was discussed. He claimed that his main role in the conspiracy was one of trying to protect the President from finding out details of the botched operations and those involved, and that knowing this would have ruined his chances for reelection.

The Senate Investigators heard more testimony on July 16, and

---

[85] Ibid
[86] Ibid

the White House confirmed that all phone calls and conversations in the President's office had been automatically recorded since 1971. The revelation of the existence of these tapes had come through the routine questioning of an uninvolved White House aide.

More problems plaguing the Presidency was further compounded a month later in August, when newspapers revealed that US Attorneys in Baltimore were investigating charges that Vice-President Spiro Agnew had accepted bribes of more than $100,000 while he was Governor of Maryland, and as Vice President. Surprisingly, it was Nixon who ordered the investigation. In response, an irate Agnew held a televised press conference denying the charges as "damn Lies."

Less than a month later on October 10, 1973, what was expected to be a routine court appearance, turned into abrupt dramatic resignation by the Vice President instead. Two days after his resignation, Republican Congressman Gerald R. Ford, who had been a Minority Whip of the House since 1965, was nominated as Vice President. He was confirmed and sworn in on December 6, 1973.

The U S continued to bomb Cambodia after the Vietnam Cease-fire in January 1973, "in order to make them join the Cease-fire." Then Congress voted to cut off all funds for the bombing. Nixon vetoed the measure, and Congress upheld his veto. But on June 29, the veto was overridden by Republicans, and the President was forced to accept new legislation to end all military action in Indochina on August 15, 1973. Further, fears of future involvement in another prolonged war prompted Congress to approve legislation to limit the President's war-making powers.[87]

Again, for the fourth time, fighting broke out in the Middle East between Israel and Arab states in October, and the U S rushed military supplies to Israel. While the war was brief, bloody, and inconclusive, a truce was soon signed between Russia and the U S. In retaliation, Arab nations cut off all oil shipments to the United States, Western Europe, Japan, and all other nations friendly to Israel. The embargo brought the nation a

---

[87] Ibid

shortage of gasoline and other fuel oil, long disgusting lines at the pump, fueling inflation and a world-wide "energy crisis."

Confrontations with Congress began when the Courts asked that the White House recorded tapes be turned over as evidence to clear the President's involvement in the Watergate affair. Nixon refused. Yielding to relentless public pressure, he agreed to appoint a Special Prosecutor to investigate the affair. Archibald Cox, a distinguished Harvard law professor whom the President had appointed, quickly raised his ire when Cox sought access to White House records and tapes. Nixon refused to cooperate; so both the Committee and Justice Department's Watergate Prosecutors subpoenaed the tapes.

Nixon declared on July 26 that he would not honor the subpoenas. The administration appealed and lost in court. While the case was heading for the Supreme Court, Nixon ordered the new Attorney General, Elliott Richardson to dismiss Prosecutor Archibald Cox, (since John Mitchell, the former Attorney General was now on trial for his involvement had resigned). Both Richardson and his assistant resigned rather than carry out Nixon's order. It was the Solicitor General, the third ranking officer of the Justice Department who did the execution. [88]

Other improprieties plagued the President concerning money owed to the government- some$400,000 or more in back taxes. The Watergate affair reached a new level when Special Prosecutor Leon Jaworski replaced Archibald Cox, and continued the pursuit to secure the White House tapes and documents. This prompted Nixon to release some drastically altered tapes.

After listening to a portion of the tapes recorded in June 1972- a conversation held between Nixon, John Dean, and Bob Haldeman- three days after the Watergate break-in, it was discovered and made public. Leon Jaworski had found it to be "most repulsive" for the President of the United States- himself a lawyer, coaching Haldeman on "how to testify untruthfully and yet not commit perjury. For the number one law enforcement officer of the country it was… as demeaning an act as could be imagined."[89]

In their concerted scheme to avoid testifying before the Senate

---

[88] Ibid
[89] Ibid

Watergate Committee, the suckers came up with an idea of having the officials testify before a Special Grand Jury that could be rigged, and controlled through other suckers (friends) in the Justice Department. During this particular meeting, Nixon's stern advice to Haldeman was: "...Just be damn sure you say I don't remember. I can't recall. I can't give any honest...answer that I can recall. But that's it."[90]

The heart of the White House claim, and Nixon's contentious denials of surrendering the tapes were that disclosures of the Watergate break-in and cover-up were in the best interest of "national security." This claim was contested by the Prosecutor's brief, which held that "not even the highest office in the land had the authority to break the law in the name of national security."

"While the claim of national security give these claims of legalized burglary and perjury a deceptively compelling right, ultimately they rest on a wholesale rejection of the rule of law and espouse a doctrine that government officials may ignore the requirements of positive criminal statues when they feel the circumstances dictate..."[91]

By a unanimous vote of 8 to 0, the Supreme Court ruled that the President must turn over all subpoenaed tapes to the Special prosecutor. The president had repeatedly claimed "Executive Privilege" in his refusal to do so. Judge Sirica's objection to such claims noted that executive privilege "had its place ... but no person ... not even the President could withhold evidence that is detrimentally relevant in a criminal trial."

Former Attorney General John Mitchell was Indicted on March 1, 1974 by a Grand Jury and found guilty on charges of: conspiracy to obstruct justice, making false statements to a Grand Jury, perjury, and sentenced to 2 ½ to 8 years in prison. H. R. Haldeman, and John Ehrlichman, both Assistant to the President, and former Chief of Staff were also found guilty on all counts, and sentenced to the same term of imprisonment.

Nixon's fate was sealed, after careful transcription and analysis of the tapes that were turned over. The recorded conversations between Haldeman and the President on June 23, 1972 proved conclusively that Nixon tried to get the CIA to persuade the FBI not to follow up lead in the case, on the spurious ground that *National Security* was involved.

---

[90] Ibid
[91] Ibid

On June 6 the Watergate Grand jury declared the President an "un-indicted co-conspirator" in the cover-up, and forwarded its evidence to the House Judiciary Committee to consider impeachment. Republican Congressional leaders advised the President that not only will he be impeached, but only a handful of Senators would vote to acquit him. Those who had voted against impeachment were now willing to reverse their pledge to the President, saying they would indeed impeach him.

On July 24, six Republicans joined Democrats on the Committee to vote for impeachment on July 27. Three Articles were adopted. The President was charged with: obstructing justice, misusing the powers of his office, and failing to obey the Committee's subpoenas. The Grand Jury now forwarded its evidence to the House Judiciary Committee considering impeachment. The next day, former Attorney General Richard Kleindienst, having misled a Senate Committee, received a suspended sentence.

Meanwhile, Nixon's chief advisers pressed him to release the remaining Watergate material. Seeing that his impeachment by the House was virtually a forgone conclusion, he did so on August 5. Richard M. Nixon announced his resignation from the U S Presidency on August 8, 1974, and Vice President Gerald Ford was sworn in at noon the following day on August 9.[92]

POST-NATIONAL POLITICAL TRAUMA

Four-time Governor of New York (1958-1973), and one of the world's wealthiest persons, Nelson Rockefeller was nominated for Vice President on August 20. Exactly one month after Nixon's resignation on September 8, 1974. Without prior consultation with Congressional leaders or the Special Watergate Prosecutors, Ford was shot through the head with compassion-for. It was during and after church services he had attended on a quiet Sunday morning in Washington- Ford granted Nixon a "full, free, absolute pardon for all offenses" committed during his administration.

Outraged, and angered that Nixon was allowed to escape indictment

---

[92] Ibid

and trial, Congressional leaders of both parties called the pardon a "misuse of power." Raising questions as to the constitutionality of granting pardon prior to conviction in the court of law. But Ford was still considering pardons for everyone connected with the Watergate affair. The Senate quickly voted 55 to 24 for a resolution that the President should not pardon anyone prior to conviction.[93]

To appease the nation's voters' collective sense of unfairness, eight days after he had pardoned Nixon unconditionally, a Conditional Amnesty was extended towards tens of thousands who had opposed the Viet Nam War by evading the draft, or deserting the armed forces. The Amnesty called for a two-year service in a low-paying job in Public Services.

Very few resistors accepted the terms or turned themselves in. They were afraid to get fooled again. The vast majority believed the amnesty should have been unconditional. While there were also many who believed that the draft-evaders should still be punished. Ford repeated to his critics that his pardon and conditional amnesty was a "conscientious effort to heal the wounds."

Rockefeller was confirmed and sworn in as Vice President on December 19, 1974. During this month, more than a million additional workers had joined ranks of the unemployed. Hard-hit automobile manufacturing companies were laying-off workers, and closing down plants. Stock market values plummeted close to 50% from the previous years' high. The nation was in a full-scale recession at the turn of 1975. Blaming it all on the economic disruptions of the world, and the U S raising the price of world petroleum four times the prevailing price of 1974, the Ford administration proposed a program to make the country independent of foreign energy imports.

With the death of more than 56,000 American troops- and still counting, the war in Vietnam still had not ended. North Vietnam broke the Truce of 1973, and Ford called on Congress to provide emergency funds to the South in order to stop the North Vietnamese. But Congress refused. Consequently, South Vietnam, Cambodia, and Laos collapsed; while remaining American military personnel and diplomats fled to awaiting ships in helicopters, in the month of April 1975, when the communists closed in on their strategic locations in Phnom Penh, and

---

[93] Ibid

Saigon. Hundreds of thousands of refugees fled to neighboring countries, while the United States absorbed more than 130,000 of them to find new homes.[94]

After the fall of South Vietnam to the communists, Cambodians captured an American freighter, the *Mayaguez* on May 12, and 39 American crewmen were taken as prisoners. A rescue mission was ordered by the President on May 15. The Marines landed on an island by helicopter where the freighter was held and attacked the abductors. The incident ended on the same day when the Cambodians freed the freighters' crewmen. 41 American servicemen were killed, and 53 wounded during the action.

This operation, which was conducted from U S bases in Thailand, angered the Thai government because it was never consulted by the United States beforehand to use the bases during the operation. It then insisted that the U S withdraw all its planes and military personnel from Thailand. In forced compliance with the Thai government, the last of about 50,000 U S servicemen were removed in 1976, leaving behind some 93 military installations that were built up during the war. This ended the U S military presence on the mainland of Southeast Asia.[95]

---

[94] Ibid

[95]

20

MORAL ANALYSIS OF

S OME BELIEFS ARE GENERATED BY our constant exposure to regularities in both Nature and Nurture. The more repeatedly and regularly we are exposed to such natural sequences and occurrences, the stronger is our belief in their persistence- even in spite of their absence, or the fact our assurance is only a matter of feeling, and not something for which we can readily give sensible or good reasons.

The growth of human awareness, cooperation, and relatedness begins at a place we call *home,* where we experience relative stability and the fulfillment of basic needs. It then proceed ever outward, embracing greater varieties, covering greater distances, and lasting a longer time in some of our chosen activities and relatedness. This is the essence of our liberty or constitutional freedoms.

Andrew Jackson's Vice President, John C. Calhoun, whom he was seriously thinking about hanging, thought "it is a great and dangerous error to suppose that all people are entitled to liberty." [96]Meanwhile, justice Felix Frankfurter noted that "It is the Justices who make the meaning. They read into the neutral language of the Constitution their own economic and social views." [97] While the United States is a society where "the essential conditions of liberty prevail for all."

Vice President John C. Calhoun, Justice Taney, and all succeeding Justices of the United States' courts- along with President Woodrow Wilson, and a vast pool of influential religious moralists and their true

---

[96] Ibid
[97] Ibid

believers never agreed on this universal consensus as incorporated in the constitution, embracing its full breadth.

With the exceptional and outstanding dissent of Justice John Harlan Marshall in (Homer Plessy v. Ferguson); It wasn't until the Warren Courts came along, that greater breadth of the constitution was interpreted to make all citizens more inclusive.

In our moral allegiances to the nation, there is no questioning that Justices of the courts are the foremost authority of the social order. Their decisions install itself in us, in some measure, the living conscience of each individual citizen in the nation or local community. In this community there is always a "we" and a "they." Be "we" individuals, family, or ethnic group members, or "they" the same- we have been, and always will be divided at times on the most basic issues- unable to agree on the nature of what is *good* or *bad*.

To kill, love, or befriend an individual, family, or members of another social group are profoundly expressive of human nature. However, when one person or social group is designated as *Right* and the other as *Left* or *Wrong*, we have separated ourselves from *Nature*- what a Christian would call *God*, and hold ourselves to a standard of our own making. What is this standard? The symbolic displays of Freedom, Justice, and brotherhood, in which we enact the most vicious, hideous, and monstrous crimes ever- against our own fellow men and women!

In the balance of Nature, all humans and every other species of living organism value our lives- the chicken oppose its head being chopped of, its feathers plucked, body boiled, fried, or cued for human chow. The deer and the fish oppose being game-meat too. If we are going to treat another member of our own species as a totally different species, then we have elevated them as a super-specie category, or degraded them to a sub-specie classification.

Because this social authority operates within us, as citizens to the superordinate state, and as the quality output of this authority embodied in justices, leaders in government, educational, religious, economic, industrial, and social institutions diminishes, the balance within the individual citizen's conscience is also upset, or destabilizes.

Those of us who require this internal reinforcement of prohibition, or moral restraint by positive examples, to prevent us form going over the edge or lawful boundaries, now begin to act on impulse- monkey see, monkey do, basically to serve our own interests, and be accountable to no one. It then promotes a variety of reckless daring, and a pervasive sense of "anything goes."

"If he, she, or they can do it; then why can't we, or I?" The United States Presidency and its expansive bureaucracy of power has demonstrated this phenomena in its most practical form with the toppling of Nixon's presidency; and arguably, erosion and end to the Post-World War II consensus- where secrecy and the covert actions of government is forced to the forefront of public scrutiny.

What we learn here in the absorption of American values from both the courts and government leadership at its highest level, is that any individual, family, group, or organization, who wants to circumvent the intent of any code, or principle of consensus, law, or agreement, can freely do so, and find loopholes when self-interest is placed first ahead of public duty, performance, or an organizational interests.

The heart and power of human *Nurture* is in direct relation to the ways a society is organized. Fundamentally, it encompass the physical defense of a geographical territory, against all other territories that are not its claims- against disease, and against wars among its citizens, to ensure growth and social harmony. How this is done are the many ways we have learned to live within the state.

RUSSIA & COMMUNISM

Observance of the rules of law anywhere, and everywhere on the planet, is a cooperative enterprise. In turn, a cooperative enterprise is a willful agreement; and this agreement is a consensus among similar and dissimilar people sharing common interests. Common interests can range from local to national, to international, to cooperative, and antagonistic sides wanting the same concrete things. The common interest amongst some world nations, notably Allied Forces during World War II in Europe and Asia was specifically to end hostile German and Japanese take-over and conquests of other nations.

During the course, before the Russians came to lose some 20 to 25 million lives, every instrument of mass persuasion in the United States was directed at convincing the people that Russia was fighting for the same common values Americans were fighting for. A U S Ambassador to Russia in a 1941 publication titled *Mission to Moscow* noted that "Soviet leaders were a group with honest convictions and integrity of purpose devoted to the cause of peace for both ideological and practical reasons." Our bond with Russia was further solidified when he stated that "communism is based on the same principle of the brotherhood of man which Jesus preached."[98]

Our bold and admirable General Douglas Mac Arthur, Commander of the Pacific fleet, along with the nation's Vice President, Henry Wallace at the time, both took strongly to pro-Russian positions. Further, the nation's general attitude was whipped-up with propaganda action films sympathetic towards Russia. Complimentary to the Alliance for an all-out victory throughout the struggle with Germany, Russian leaders repeatedly pooled their willingness in working with other Allies engaged in the war, also to deal with post-war problems. Their leaders conferred regularly with their British, French, and American alliances, and fulfilled their obligations.[99]

All this changed when Germany surrendered and the war was over. Beginning with the Berlin Blockade in 1946, and the Russian rejection of a U S proposal for an international agency to control atomic energy production and research. Communist challenges rose up on many fronts. Cold War tensions between the two nations began to develop with intensity in 1947 and 1948; with the U S becoming increasingly aware that Russia did not intend to free the countries of Eastern Europe that it had liberated during the war. They were now parts of its Warsaw Pact.

Communist invasions of China, and South Korea in 1950; then Malaya, and Indochina, swept the region. The countries of Greece and Turkey successfully resisted the communists' takeover, largely with the help of $400 million in aid that Congress granted those nations. A new American policy that was now known as the Truman Doctrine, developed

---

[98] Ibid
[99] Ibid

into a containment policy which states that the U S is willing to help any nation resist communist aggression.

Believing that a strong and stable Western Europe would further block the spread of communism, a Marshal Plan began in 1948. In like response, after creating the Warsaw Pact with 8 other Eastern European nations, the communist countries had a plan to spread communism, uniting them economically and politically.

The French who were fighting the Communist in Indochina, were fighting to preserve their colonial empire. U S aid to the French fighting began in 1950, and by 1954, it was funding 75% of the cost, before the French army of almost 20,000 were decimated by the communist Viet Cong army. In their desperation to fortify a sabotaged runway for the landing of supplies where there wasn't much timber in the valley, The French Army tore down the villager's huts and used the wood as their timber supply!

It was the Chinese, led by Mao Tse Tung, who had become fully communist, that made their push into Vietnam. When Russia was putting down revolts among its Eastern European Warsaw Pact allies during this period, the U S was also busy trying to prevent communist expansion in the Middle East.

The United States offered Egypt help in its construction of the Aswan High Dam. Egypt refused and courted communist aid to build the dam, and also bought communist arms. The U S and Britain then cancelled their offer to help with the project. Egypt then seized the Suez Canal from international control.

Israel invaded Egypt in 1956, while Britain and France immediately joined in the attack, with a desire to return the Canal to international control. After a few days of fighting, the U S and Russia supported a United Nations resolution, demanding an immediate truce.

The Arms Race continued as Russia tested its first ICBM in June of 1957, and a few months later, launched the first man-made earth satellite in January of 1958. Having attained parity and superiority in technology and science with the U S, Russian ambition spilled into surrogate wars with other less developed nations throughout the remainder of the world.

From neighboring Cuba in North America, the Dominican Republic, Latin America, countries in Africa, the Middle East, Europe, Asia, and Indochina, with America being its only rival.

Events which precipitated after the botched invasion at the Bay of Pigs, twenty-one months later, the Cuban Missile Crisis and communist uprisings in Eastern Europe, thawed into a delicate equilibrium, whose basis is the probabilities of nuclear confrontations, by agreeing to a treaty to stop the testing of nuclear weapons. As a consequence, direct relations between the United States and Russia began to improve.

China began to break away from Russia's influence when it launched a "cultural revolution." The Chinese then accused the Russians of betraying world communism by being secret allies with the U S.

Because U S air power proved ineffective in halting guerrilla attacks in South Vietnam, Johnson ordered American ground troops into action on June 28, 1965. And as the war was escalating into a hot war when the U S began some heavy bombing of designated targets, Congress granted the President broad powers to protect U S troops from communist aggression. This was the *Tonkin Resolution*. Both Russia and China lent support to the Viet Cong and North Vietnamese.

Charles De Gaulle of France, challenged the leadership of the United States and Britain, by establishing diplomatic relations with China in 1964, sharply criticizing U S policy in Vietnam. He then requested NATO to move its military headquarters from France in 1967. The French refused to join the Nuclear Ban Treaty. They then blocked Britain from entering into the European Common Market. The French then strengthen their relations with Russia and Eastern European nations. In their surrogate war of 1967 in the Middle East, France sided with the Arabs against Israel, then exploded a hydrogen bomb in 1968.

Meanwhile on the home front, the fear of communist subversives in the United States was whipped to a hysterical pitch with Congressional investigations, beginning with, and throughout Truman's administration. Two of the most prominent figures in these investigations were Richard Nixon, when he was a California Congressman, and Joseph Mc McCarthy, a Senator from Wisconsin. According to the Presidencies of Eisenhower, Kennedy, Johnson, and Nixon, the foremost public issue of the Post-War era was not a consensus on the civil strife of ethnic groups for equality of opportunity, nor the cultural fragmentation that resulted; rather, it was the fear and containment of communism.

Executive deception of Congress and the suspension of Civil liberties in the name of anti-Communism were enforced on all citizens- including executive branches of the government, as witnessed in the unfolding and ending of Nixon's administration. Under the Omnibus Crime Control Act of 1968, for the first time in American history, legal sanctions were provided for telephone wiretapping and bugging by federal, state, and local law enforcement agents investigating just about any kind of whimsical infraction against the law or status quo.

I say *whimsical* because although a "court order" is required, and subjects had to be informed of its issuance, these conditions were routinely ignored by the law encroachment officers in the execution of their duties. Even so, victims were to be "informed"- not before- but after the information gathering and surveillance had taken place.

21

SKUNK WORKS

"ND IT IS NOW, WHEN the Cold War is history, that many of our accomplishments can finally be revealed..."
The book *Skunk Works*, was published in 1994, revealing some of our governments' most covert and most pre-eminent research and development operation in the nation's Defense System. The CIA was created by Congress in 1947, and the U S Air Force was also established in 1947. The CIA was created to advise the National Security Council (NSC), in order to acquire and analyze economic, political, and military information about other countries, individuals, and social groups- as well as our own, on which the President could base his foreign policy decisions.[100]

In the collecting and gathering of this intelligence, *Skunk Works*, under the distinguished leaderships of Kelly Johnson, and Ben Rich, in Burbank California, were the main clients of the CIA in researching and developing its primary tool for gathering information. The U S Air Force relied on Skunk Works for high precision combat aircrafts that could evade and vanquish the enemy with its payload delivery.

For America, Skunk Works invented, developed, and produced: the P-80, its first jet fighter; the F-104 Star-fighter; which is its first supersonic Jet-Attack plane; the U-2 Spy Plane; the SR-71, dubbed the incredible Blackbird, which was the world's first three-times-the-speed of sound surveillance airplane; and the F-117A Stealth Tactical Fighter, that many saw on CNN scoring precision bomb strikes over Bagdad during Operation Desert Storm.[101]

---

[100] Ibid
[101] Ibid

Skunk Works projects were initiated at the highest government level, out of an imperative and acute need "to tip the Cold War balance of power in our direction." The years of Eisenhower, Kennedy, Johnson, and Nixon were marred with highly secretive projects that were in the making at Skunk Works. Only a few people at the highest level of our Defense Department knew about their operations. What came off their drawing boards "provided key strategic and technological advantages for the U S government." Proof of this success was that airplanes built by Skunk Works, were manufactured and operated under tight secrecy for eight to ten years, "before the government even acknowledged their existence."[102]

I have always had, and still do have a strong belief that the many UFO sightings that people all over the U S have witnessed at different places and times, between the early 50's and 1970's, can be easily attributed to the experimental "tinker-toy crafts" produced by Skunk Works, or other private aircraft manufacturers such as: Northrop, General Dynamics, Boeing, and Mc Donnell Douglas- that have direct contact and contracts, or vying for contracts with the Defense Department; since there were three or four other competitive bidders to produce the Government's most sophisticated and advanced technological tools.

The UFO sightings could also be induced by hallucinations. We cannot argue away nor dispute intelligently a persons' true experience. However, there are broad verifiable consensus by two or more people of what exist, could possibly exist, or logically happen.

After reading Skunk Works, it's hard for me to believe anything else, other than that the claimed sighting of these UFOS being no other than contractors or potential contractors for the U.S. Department of Defense testing their experimental models. Today, people bear witness to, and the government does not deny the proliferation of *drones* in the sky as the modern workhorse of national security surveillance world-wide. Drones are now freely owned and flown around by the general public.

---

[102] Ibid

WHERE SOME SECRETS SPILLED

Somewhere during the two years of the Ford administration, executives at Lockheed, where *Skunk Works* is headquartered, along with the Senate Sub-committee on Multi-national Corporations, admitted and disclosed that Lockheed paid Japanese Prime Minister Kakuei Tanaka, who had "both political influence and underworld ties," over 2 to 7 million dollars in bribes, to use his influence to persuade all Nippon Airways to use Lockheed's built "Tri Star" jets. The Dutch Government also conceded that Prince Bernhard received "dishonorable requests" from Lockheed Aircraft Corporation, which resulted in his resignation of his position as Inspector General of the Dutch Armed Forces, and some 300 other posts he held in the Dutch military business, and public organizations.[103]

Other consumers that the aircraft company bribed and persuaded were: West German politicians, Italian officials and generals, and to "highly placed figures" in Hong Kong, and Saudi Arabia, in order to get them to buy their planes. This unfolding produced a huge outrage and ruckus among the NSC brass, and some heads began to roll.

Was this a compromise of American intelligence and Aerospace technology? Or, was this a strategy for corporate domination and control, while undermining the economic base of these nations?

Skunk Works thought so; if we consider the devastating loss of 109 latest and most advanced Jet Attack Aircraft in 18 days, used by the Israelis with comparable pilot skills as our own, during their 1973 war- with Syria and Egypt using more advanced Russian technology. It didn't take much skill to operate the highly accurate radar-guided ground-to-air missiles built by the Russians. The key to their superiority was that in our "Lend-Lease Policy" with them during World War II, the Russians vastly improved and excelled on the radar technology we gave them, while we had hardly made any improvement on our own. Besides economic wheeling and dealing, hundreds of American lives lost in spy mission flights over Russia also compromised our technology.

Having discovered this fatal flaw in our defense system, *Skunk Works* went back to research, and drawing board, then came up with a Stealth Technology; proving its devastating effectiveness and accuracy over Russian technology in the Persian Gulf War.

---

[103] Ibid

BIBLIOGRAPHY

INFORMATION SOURCE AND
AUTHOR'S WORKS CONSULTED

Garranty/Mc Caughey: British economist John Maynard Keynes 'deficit spending. World War II events. Quarantine Speech.

Stefan Lorant: Roosevelt's 1944 election. Source for World War II events. The Pacific Front. Post World War II consensus. Dewey's run for the Presidency.

Garranty/ Mcaughey: Joseph McCarthy's communist purge. The Pacific Front. Truman, Mc Arthur, and McCarthy clash. Footnotes 49, 50. Nuclear Arms Race. Russia's explosion of hydrogen bomb.

David C. Whitney/Robin Vaughn Whitney: The American Presidents. Eisenhower's Administration: Russia. ICBM. Sputnik 1. Footnote 55, 56. The Warren courts. Resistance to Supreme Court's decision on Desegregation (Brown vs Board of Education). Fidel Castro. U2 Spy Plane shot down over Russia.

Borden Morton: Middle East conflict. Russia's intervention and allied with Egypt over Suez Canal. Kruschev. "The Eisenhower Doctrine."

John W. Spanier: American Foreign Policy Since World War II. Copy. 1960 From topic: "The Truman Doctrine," p. 29, "The Missile Gap," p. 169 "The Indochinese War And SEATO," p.107

Garranty/Mc Caughey: A Short History of the American Nation 5th Edition. Kennedy's election. Protests: Rosa Parks, Martin Luther King, MalcolmX. Botched Bay of Pigs. Footnote 59.

Borden Morton: The American Profile. Russia's erection of the Berlin Wall. John Kennedy's Peace Corp established, "New Frontier" agenda.

Garranty/Mc Caughey: Kennedy's "New Frontier" agenda. Kruschev's nuclear disaster threat in Cuba.

Whitney/Whitney: John Kennedy's Presidential profile.

James Trager: The people's Chronology. Copy. 1992. Footnotes on history of Vietnam 61, 62, 63, and 64. French Indochina.

Steven Hayward: The Politically Incorrect Guide to the Presidents from Wilson to Obama. Gulf of Tonkin Resolution. "Ho's pecker." Footnotes 65, 66, 67.

Garranty/Mc Caughey: Medical, Medicaid. Kennedy's proposals passed. Black protest and anger. Tet Offensive in Vietnam. Footnotes 68, 69. 70, 71, 72, 73

Borden Morten: 68, 69, 70, 74, 75. My Lai Massacre. Election year, Johnson's Withdrawal from the Presidency. Civil Rights/Vietnam protests. Martin Luther King Jr.'s and Robert Kennedy's assassinations.

Whitney/Whitney: Presidential profiles of Lyndon B. Johnson and John F. Kennedy. Nixon's election. Nixon's second term. The "Bamboo Curtain." Trips to China, summit in Moscow. Re-election bid. CREEP. Watergate. Daniel Ellsberg. Archibald Cox. footnotes 76, 77, 78, 79.

Leon Jaworski: The Right And The Power. Copy. 1976. Watergate's Prosecutor. Issues: "National Security." CIA, FBI, Attorney John Mitchell. Nixon's advice to Haldeman. Footnotes 80, 81, 82, 83, 84, 85, 86, 87, 88, 89, 90, 91, 92, 93.

James Trager: 1973 Collapse of South Vietnam, Laos, and Cambodia. The end of U.S. presence on mainland. Footnote 94, 95

Garranty/Mc Caughey, Whitney/Whitney: Closure of U.S. base in Thailand. Charles De Gaulle. Removal of NATO fro France. Footnote 96, 97, 98, 99.

Ben R. Rich/Leo Janos: Skunk Works. Copy. 1994 The secret For the U.S. Government and the CIA. Spilled secrets. Footnote 100, 101, 102, 103. building of aircraft and other intelligence projects

PART IV

1980 THROUGH 1992

END OF COLD WAR ERA

LATIN AMERICA & THE MIDDLE EAST

22

FOREIGN AFFAIRS & THE MIDDLE EAST

A FTER THE DEMISE OF RICHARD Nixon's administration, my lay or elementary thinking was that the Republican Party was completely demolished, and that the Democratic Party was in for a windfall of allegiance and following; not according to any polls taken, but according to prevailing sentiments of national betrayal and moral indignation. But this was clearly not the case in the Presidential election of 1976. I didn't play too much football without a helmet on, but I guess my pattern of thinking was as soft as President Ford's sympathy for the devil. I'll tell you again, "I'm not a crook!"

Voters showed their resilience in their Party preference when Democratic nominee Jimmy Carter narrowly defeated Republican President Gerald Ford. According to strategic political speculations, a switch from Carter to Ford ticket of 3,700 votes in Hawaii, and 4,700 in Ohio, would have been enough to have given the electoral victory to Ford; even though Carter still would have led Ford in popular votes. Approximately 50 percent of voters gave their votes to Carter, and 48 to Ford.

Carter's desire to be President was to introduce practical social change in attitudes- radically despising those that were entrenched toward his Southern black counterparts; and eager to bring international relations into harmony and common understanding. The "defense of basic human rights in foreign affairs" was to transcend all other concerns. "...My determination is very deep," insisted Carter.

On his first full day in office, a pardon was granted to about 10,000 Vietnam War Era draft-evaders. Later during the year, he made it possible for almost 500,000 veterans who *did serve*, and had less than an *honorable* discharge to have their beef revisited or reviewed. Carter was given somewhat of a free hand to re-organize the government in order to make it more representative to the people. The dykes were then open for repressed women, Civil Rights activists, and consumer advocates to fill government employment positions where there was once none, and even new agencies and positions created.

Meanwhile, with the worsening of the national and international oil manipulation, so-called "energy Crisis," auto workers who were among the highest paid workers in American industries were severely hit with tens of thousands of layoffs. Hard times began to hit harder, with the competition given off by Japanese and European automakers, whose vehicles give better gasoline mileage, and built comparably good and comfortable like American automobiles. Income tax cuts were approved for low income families, and de-regulation in airline, railroad, and trucking, industries were some of Carter's pledge to flex the nation's economy.

"Over-consumption and wasteful use of energy" were the issues to blame for the nation's "likelihood of a national catastrophe," as Congress was now plagued with a wide range of measures for conservation, bringing about the establishment of a Department of Energy. Although the Democratic Party held control of both houses of Congress, Carter, being a nominal leader (meaning-not an entrenched Party politician), found it difficult to have his domestic legislative proposals adopted without "drastic change."

FOREIGN AFFAIRS

Their fingers are really in our pie now, as I understand it-"If you can do that to us, then we can do this to you- and get real results" is the *now* answering machine, with all sincerity, sympathy, compassion, and full aggression.

With this tit for tat motion around the world, there were marked decline in traditional and customary American influence. The Marshall Plan that had enabled Western European nations to rebuild their economies had became less dependent on outside aid; and in the course of pursuing their own interests, adopted policies that were not in the best interest of the United States.

Military regimes in Argentina, Brazil, and Uruguay refused to accept further U S military aid, owing to criticisms regarding the treatment of their citizens. Meanwhile, aid that was accepted by other underdeveloped countries to help improve their economic base allowed them to act more independently, rather than in ways which benefits the United States.

More detrimental to U S influence were ineffective aid given to nations to bolster regimes that were localized, and were very unpopular with their countries 'majorities. The Middle East was a case in point that proved to be very crucial in American relations. Mohammed Reza Pahlavi, called the "Shah" of Iran had been a close ally of the United States ever since the CIA helped him regain rule over Iran in 1953. As a result, billions of dollars' worth of American arms and other supplies were traded for oil imports. Our relationship with Iran was so smooth for many years, that early in 1977 Carter said that the country of Iran seem like "an island of stability in the troubled Middle East."[104]

What was never publicly disclosed to the American people was that our ally in Teheran, the Shah, ruled Iran with an "iron hand," or the hand of an oppressive punk, and was extremely unpopular with the people. His army was American supplied; his death squad, as well as his secret service police who kept him in power were all trained and supplied by the CIA. Those who opposed him hated and despised him as much as they did the U. S.

The Middle East was considered to be the greatest immediate threat to world peace when Carter became President. Arabs and Israelis had fought four successive wars since 1948; the last being in 1973. A tentative agreement was reached in 1974, lifting the Arab nations oil boycott that had went into effect at the outbreak of their 1973 War.

Up until this period, the U S was importing one-third of its oil from that region, making the situation of peace negotiations crucial. Any further provocation of war would result in the cutting off of our oil supplies from Arab nations. In the meantime, both the Arabs and Israelis have been engaging in continued arms build-up for future conflicts, ever since the 1974 truce obtained by Henry Kissinger.

While engaged in their traditional territorial feud, Carter labored

---

[104] Ibid

extensively to broker diplomatic agreements between leaders of both nations in 1978. These negotiations were crucial. He went further by unlocking relations with Cuba, China, Vietnam, and with leaders of other nations around the world. In his own efforts at bringing world peace and reducing the proliferation of atomic weapons, he deferred production of a neutron bomb, which was supposed to be a tactical nuclear weapon designed to kill people with minimal damage to buildings or other structures.[105]

On May 22, 1977, Carter was quoted in a speech at Notre Dame University saying: "Being confident of our own future, we are now free of that inordinate fear of communism which once led us to embrace any dictator who joined us in that fear.... The unifying threat of conflict with the Soviet Union has become less intensive..."

Meanwhile in Iran, Massive demonstrations, strikes, and riots had been directed at the Shah's oppressive regime. The whole nation seemed to have risen up in arms against his rule, and so he was forced to leave the country. The Shiite leader Ayatollah Khomeine, exiled by the Shah in 1963 returned from France to the capital city, Tehran on February 1, 1979 and seized control of the government. By February 11, pro-Khomeine forces had defeated the Shah's army. Hundreds of his officials and military officers were then executed. He began a theocracy, which is a religious rule on February 14. Meanwhile, the Carter administration had been involved in secret talks with members of Khomeini's staff.[106]

Iranian students seized the U S embassy on November 14, taking at least 62 American hostages, while a hundred other Americans were rescued and spared by Khomeine's troops. Hostages were blindfolded and held as prisoners before chanting crowds, who threatened to execute them unless the Shah and his wealth was returned to Iran. U. S. Envoys were then dispatched to Iran to negotiate release of the hostages taken, but Khomeinie would not allow them to enter the country.

Congress then reacted with an uproar and outrage, prompting the President to take action on November 12; banning any further purchase of oil from Iran, rejected Khomeine's demands, and froze over $6 billion worth of Iranian funds in American banks. Diplomatic ties with Iran still continued as efforts were made through the Palestine Liberation

---

[105] Ibid

[106] Ibid

Army (PLO), who made themselves accessible to garner U S support, to negotiate with Khomenie, since their leader had direct contact with him. But Khomeinie refused to budge.

In an effort to win solidarity with radical elements and dissident groups, fed-up with their government in America, eight blacks and five women were released and allowed to fly out of Iran on November 19, and 20. Then Khomeine went viral, stirring up hatred against America throughout the entire Moslem world.

While Carter had taken his diplomatic Salt II talks with Russian leaders as a positive gain for disarmament of certain weapons, and progress towards a greater peace for granted, Russia's invasion of Afghanistan on Christmas day, 1979 now became a major debacle in his campaign for world peace. Russia justified its invasion by claiming that the U. S. had been financing guerrilla forces attempting to overthrow Afghanistan's existing communist rule; and describing the president they ousted as an agent of imperialism. Carter denounced the invasion, responding with an embargo on American grain and advanced technological equipment shipments to Russia, and a boycott of the Summer Olympic Games held in Moscow.

Meanwhile, the nation felt increasingly humiliated by the Iranian hostage stalemate, while public opinion was steadfastly united behind the President. An abortive effort to rescue the hostages was taken up in April. Against the better judgment and advice of his Secretary of State, Carter ordered a secret military mission to free the hostages; but only to announce on an early morning TV broadcast some details of the aborted mission.

Three out of eight helicopters failed in executing the mission, one colliding with a transport plane, killing eight highly skilled servicemen, and injuring others. The stalemate continued. Then the U. S. broke all diplomatic ties with Iran on April 7, and the Shah died in Egypt on July27, 1980.

With the upcoming election right around the corner, Carter had the feeling that voters supported his confrontations with Iran; while many Democratic leaders were convinced that he could not win a second term, even though he controlled the outcome of the nomination by accumulating enough pledged delegates. With reference to the heightened state of the Iranian hostage situation and the administration's management of it,

Carter accused Ronald Reagan, his Republican opponent as being a movie fanatic who is "dangerous and belligerent" and "could put the whole world in peril" with them ideas of his.

Timing the event so that it would have maximum effect on voters and election outcome, with only two days before the national election in November of 1980, Iran made some stiff and harsh terms for release of the hostages. Now with Algerian diplomats acting as intermediaries, serious negotiations to release the hostages did not commence until the assurance of Carter's defeat. Voters gave Ronald Reagan 4.3 million votes with a huge majority of the electoral, totaling 489 to Carter's 3.5 million popular, and only 49 electoral votes. Republicans won control of the Senate and made deep inroads into the democratically controlled Lower House.

Reagan's campaign promised a "New Federalist" approach; which involved the transference of some of the functions of the federal government to the states; on the assumption that local government reflected both the will and wisdom of the citizenry, better than the remote bureaucracy-ridden government in Washington. His intentions were to reduce government spending on the redistribution of wealth allotted by government programs for lower classes, cut taxes for the wealthy, and cook-up a balanced budget.

Overshadowing election outcomes was the hostage crisis; while Iran and Iraq had just started a war that began on September 22, 1980, over a dispute of the Shatt Al-Arab waterway situated between the two countries. It was Iraq that started the invasion and occupation. Meanwhile, negotiations to release the hostages continued. Consisting largely of restoring the release of frozen Iranian assets in U. S. banks, the new administration gave public details of an agreement with Iranian demands in exchange for the American hostages. After 444 days in captivity, the release of 52 remaining hostages on Inauguration Day January 21, 1981, the day Ronald Reagan was sworn into office as President, was finalized.

23

THE STATE OF AFFAIRS- HAVES & HAVE-NOTS

WITH IRAN AND IRAQ AT war- literally killing each other in their territorial feud, the freed hostage situation shown as a sign of *bold and decisive* action on part of the new administration and the position of the United States given to the public via television as being *neutral*. The new focus of immediate concern now shifted to restructuring of the American economy.

Bolstered by Ronald Reagan's rhetoric on the "evils of communism" on the international scene, and Russia being looked upon as the "evil empire", the Department of Defense was allotted its generous share of the administration's budget for its containment; thereby resuscitating the aerospace and other defense-related industries that provided immediate employment for a few.

Cutting taxes for the very rich by 25% over a three-year period, and cutting spending on social services and Social Security programs for the needy and lower classes of Americans was Reagan's top priority. This "supply-side economics" as it is called in political salads, claims that the rich would have more money to invest with the tax cut, and would invest the money in productive ways, rather than on consumer goods; and that their investments would lead to increase production, more prosperity, more jobs, and therefore more income tax for government- in spite of the lower tax rate that they pay. This was the same chimeratic hope and practical reasoning of Herbert Hoover in the onset of, and during the Great Depression.

A murder attempt by John Hinckley was made on Reagan's life in March of 1981, while leaving a Washington hotel. Reagan quickly recovered from the wound his attempted assassin inflicted. Official reports claimed that it was a case of "insanity" that purged John Hinckley, the would-be assassin.

What has been referred to, and taken for granted in American social life is that any person who strives to be progressive, upholding the values of education or learning, and the application of it by participating in some form of productive enterprise, labor, or work, owning property or a home, and is relatively successful in maintaining that status dynamically, by thrift and investments- is considered middle class.

Those with earnings and incomes over the million-dollar mark are the very rich in status whom we may conveniently refer to as the *Haves*. Power, money, security, and luxury are in their keeps, and they possess ample surpluses. They want to keep things the way they are, and are generally opposed to, or could care less about needed social change.

Just below the *Haves* are the *Have-a-Little,* who sustain their middle class standards by filling key positions of management and power in society, have relatively stable incomes, and are owners of a smaller amount of property. Torn between the status quo controlled by the *Haves*, the prospect of acquiring more, and to protect the little that they have, they could be described as social, economic, and political schizoids in the protection of their properties and social status.

The *Have-Nots* make up the vast majority of man and womankind, through mere ignorance, more than anything else. They are the vast majority of ignorant people and perpetrators who wallow in the vicious institution of poverty, which begins with the propensity for sexual reproduction as an ultimate defense of identity.

Those who escape through education or other legitimate means in hoisting themselves into the middle class orbit of *Having-a-Little,* are relatively satisfied and feel a little lucky and successful in handling social life. While those who are born and raised in the middle class atmosphere claw their way to the top in wanting more, and change, not only for themselves, but also for some of their less fortunate *Have-Nots*. Simply because they have a better understanding, and closer to their situations in many ways.

General conditions of the *Have-Nots* are so commonplace for those who show a consistent disregard for reading as a main source of knowledge, formal education, self-discipline, and emotional control, through lack of understanding and preference for the tyrannical hold of elementary learning from surface or popular culture. Their smug and callous behavior bears semblance of the kind of conservatism that the *Haves* show, which makes them very resistant to *change,* or cultivating and maintaining progressive attitudes.

The work and jobs of practically all middle class Americans are skilled jobs that pay well, or modestly well. According to Reagan and old Hoover economics, these people are fucking stupid. They are programmed stupid. Specifically- to consume beyond their *real needs.*

The powerful ruling corporate enterprise of *Haves* function "just like extraterrestrial beings, they are only interested in enslaving us by granting favors to terrestrial creatures who cooperate with them. Their primary medium of operation revolves around a device whose purpose is to create awareness that dulls our senses to our real needs, and of permanent forms which controls our way of life in any particular region or state in the nation."[107]

Having virtually unlimited resources and surplus, the *Haves* take their powers to be eternal and ubiquitous. Feeling par excellence, that it is their duty to decide morally, and ethically, what is economically and politically right; what masses of individuals, who are the *Have-a-Little* and *Have-Nots*, collective needs are and ought to be. This is justified by suggestive intelligence in all major mediums of communication which leads the population to consume needless goods.

These are the many models of social life that steer away our thoughts that might otherwise inspire us to take adequate action to consume wisely and to better our social environment. Their common stock in trade of mass communication are: analogies, allegories, metaphors, knowledgeable leaders, experts in their fields of research, and other influential people in sports, movies television, and other forms of entertainment, who help us understand something as complicated, intricate, and sometimes perplexing as the events which overwhelms us in everyday social life in the most simplified ways.

The most primary medium for the creation, proliferation, and perpetuation of these forms, in ways accessible to our most prurient interests

---

[107] Ibid

and sensibilities are tactile, visual, and auditory- covering the entire range and mediums of human sensibilities and communication. In spite of its all-encompassing effects- it is still all predicated on *individual choice*. In other words, we are forced to choose intelligently at every moment, every turn, and every twist in social life.

Retooled for the idiot box and Washington, Reagan's presidential image is now fused to keep the general American public "informed," that is- misinformed in a deliberately concocted false sense of social reality. The breakdown of Reagan's "voodoo economics" or fiscal policies now began paving the road to mass homelessness across modern-day America. There was a further breakdown in public trust, and an irreversible decadence that became more and more endemic with homelessness.

State governments nationwide have not been willing to make all-out assaults to re-structure their economies to avoid the inevitable causes of economic shifts, simply by refusing to create comprehensive programs for the displaced to remain housed, fed, re-educated, or re-tooled in order to compensate for unemployment caused by transitions and new forms that industries take on with the churning out of new technologies.

The main shifts are the de-skilling processes made by the onset of computers and other forms of new technology. State governments throughout the nation will not reflect on the true purpose and meaning that forged the Social Security Act of 1935, which was care and concern for the dispossessed, disenfranchised, and indigent American citizen. I am deeply interested in the lot and fate of these Americans, because I am one of them- not given to the dominant stereotype image of the disadvantaged.

The deception and misleading device of the voodoo thing called "Reaganomics" unfolded within three years of the Presidency; Reagan's second term, and into George Bush's Presidency. The entire twelve-year period must be treated as the Reagan-Bush Era. Our modern-era's twisted Republicans, who consider themselves "conservatives," now more than often fall back on this situation as a cornerstone and reference to proper and efficient governorship- and particularly through the schizoid persona of Ronald Reagan.

According to alert and watchful eyes on our national affairs, Ronald Reagan did more to uncouple business from its traditional moorings than any political ideology in the country's history- "...an abstracted form of fiscal revolution by which every company, whatever its grounding in former practice or principle was led before the guillotine of credit." Not only that, "he left his country a little stupider in 1988 than it had been in 1980, and a whole lot more tolerant of…" bullshit. His eight years in office produced an orgy of shenanigans and a "banal drama of pumped-up optimism, as the public face of politics dissolved into theatre." Programming and propaganda got even stronger. According to Robert Hughes in his book *Culture of Complaint. Copy. 1993.*[108]

The administration terminated social security benefits for hundreds of thousands of disabled Americans, legal services, subsistence for the low-income household, the aged, and other legal services. Reductions were made in public housing, and veterans' health care services. Aerospace and other defense-related industries got an elevated budget boost, while the deregulation of public air transportation, railroad, and other major industries like banking got an upsurge in their business.

The nation's sense of morality was given a token uplift by businessman Charles Keating, a prototypical figure of the time who sustained a staunch ethical look for a while, and was the person who co-founded the National Coalition Against Porno. He was considered "a major agitator of traditional values in the mid-west." [109]I believe Americans were already convinced, definitely by Playboy and various sexually-oriented videos and magazines, and probably by some quack physician experts, that it is perfectly normal and healthy to insert a penis or other objects in any human anus as a source of pleasure- without any serious consequences, as a female vagina would respond.

This business side of Reagan's middle class values, and Reganomics was concerned with preserving American innocence about screwing. We must believe. Because cheating the innocent out of their *real* must now be considered the supreme virtue.

According to David Brock, the Federalist Society and their lawyers in the Reagan administration- "devoted to restricting privacy rights and reproductive freedoms (abortion), rolling back civil rights gains, and thwarting the authority of government to regulate business in the public interest- worked to strip away civil rights. A resurgent religious revival in

---

[108] Ibid
[109] Ibid

what became known as the age of the 'angry white male,' the holy war broke out. ....the religious right had won control of the conservative movement, and the movement, in turn, now was dictating Republican Party policy. In search for post-Communist bogeymen, Republicans officially embraced right-wing fundamentalism as their own."[110]

A free market system depends on fairness, trust, and integrity among buyers, sellers, employers, and employees. Ethical issues are not absent from the marketplace because *power* is not equally distributed, and neither are *information* and *knowledge*- the two main commodities of control, and inherent forms of power today. This human situation calls to the need for ethical rules and standards. Ethical elements enter every human contract- and no market, business, or socio-economic enterprise could function adequately without these elements in place and not causing severe disruption of the social order.

The extension of *deregulation* that began during the Carter years as a fiscal policy and now enacted in the administration was really an abandonment in the strict enforcement of antitrust laws, and massive cuts in government spending on social programs, opening the dykes for a tidal wave of mergers, consolidations, hostile takeovers, leverage buying, and acquisitions. Antitrust laws safeguard ethical rules, provide guidelines and oversight, and are enforced to ensure the distribution of fairness among participants in the market's socio-economic system. This fine government check, in place on the books, was routinely ignored.

Many, including Charles Keating, Michael Milken, Dennis B. Levine Kohlberg, Kravis, Roberts, and Ivan Boesky- all convicted thieves or criminals who were knowledgeable of inside information, deliberately misleading and robbing people of their hard-earned securities and lifelong trusts were given a free reign by the administration. They then began making aggressive loans and investments in *junk bonds* and stock trading. High-yield junk bonds were used to facilitate both friendly and hostile takeovers, as well as buyouts of companies "going Private" or buying up publicly owned stock.

Under the deregulated thrift market adopted by the administration, Savings and Loan Associations could take any investment risk they wanted to with depositors' money. This is often at great profit to themselves, with

---

[110] Brock David

the understanding that failures and bad debts would be picked up by the U S government. As hundreds of these thrifts failed in the short-run of three or four years, our government compensated their depositors, 90% of whose net worth accounts to $100,000 or more. By the end of 1990 more than $500 billion in welfare money was appropriated by government for the bailout of Savings & Loans Associations!

At a time when Congress was tightening bankruptcy rules for ordinary citizens, the *Haves* evaded all regulation by putting their money in the riskiest investments, which, because they are risky, offer them high returns. When their investments fail, the "hedge fund," as it is called, falls into the federal safety net. Of course, this federal safety net is subsidized by the *Have-a-Little* and *Have-Not* American taxpayers' money.

In the merger and takeover business that was going on, companies can write off debts that they assume, in order to finance the takeover of another company, in order to raid the pension funds set aside for its employees; strip its assets, and liquidate the company. The mergers then act as a fuel for the flame of stock speculation that adds to a company's debt. Share prices of the business overtaken suddenly skyrockets, and the banks wind up financing the upsurge. The end result is that debts of the merged company will soar as wealth disparity worsens, while stockholders get seedier than before!

The 1982 Garth-St Germaine Depository Institutions Act, a Bill that Reagan signed into law that removed the "artificially" regulated restraints on federally insured savings and loans companies began taking its victims in March of 1984 when Home State Savings & Loans in Ohio fell. Panicky depositors then made runs on other federal insured institutions. Over 70 other thrifts were closed by the governor of Ohio, while federal regulators took over a Beverly Hills Savings & Loan.

Reagan-filled Republicans constantly make reference to the Reagan years of a booming economy. The mergers and acquisitions that were fueled by his deregulation, low interest rates, and a booming stock market benefitted big stockholders, and the top tier of corporate and company executives, who walk away with mega-profits from sales, while employees, and other public consumers pay the cost.

Blitzed by waves of international events, and "by the mutual consent of both rival political parties, the government kept us in the dark, as the public face of politics dissolved into a theatre." No one foresaw that the administration's fiscal policies was to buy a short-term expansion of the American economy that led to a national debt of- *who's counting now?*- A recession, painful unemployment, a way for mass homelessness, and an irreversible decay of public trust in business and government leaders was well in the making as new waves of criminal charges, and convictions of national corporate business leaders unraveled. The stark truth that taxpayers must now literally pony up several billion dollars to bail out the S & L system was not announced until just after the 1988 election, when Bush's Presidency was assured.

APARTHEID

The other side of Reagan's paradoxical and schizoid moral boom was a hatred for communism and a benign relation with apartheid states-specifically South Africa, a so-called *white* dominated supremacist state surrounded by others at the time. I am a so-called *black* person. I don't have a problem with it. And will never be offended by being referred to being categorized as a black person or black ethnic group member.

For the sake of classification of people and their ethnicity or social group category in the United States, I wouldn't want to be referred to any other way as my identity by national existence. I am not an African-American. This categorization and classification of all black native born Americans is an absolute insult brought on by our last president during 2002 through 2016. I wasn't born anywhere near or in the continent of Africa. I was born in Belize, Central America, a former British colony, and I'm a naturalized American citizen. Connect the birthplace and citizenship and this is my American Aztec.

If a person of a lighter shade of skin than me want to classify or refer to him or herself as *white,* so be it. I don't have a problem with it. That is their identity problem to reckon themselves with their surrounding human world, society, or people where they must live out their lives. Calling me and referring to me as african-american is demeaning and outright insulting.

According to author Thomas Frank in his book *The Wrecking Crew,*

Copy. 2008, for many years *apartheid* had been America's friend, and its staunchest supporter in the global battle against communism. The regime's onerous racist policies are capitalistic in origin too, with Christianity written into its constitution.

"South Africa was the place where all the strands of the 80's of Ronald Reagan's conservatism came together. You don't have to dig very deep in the conservative literature of the 80's before you hit apartheid South Africa." Only a few Americans would own up to the passions with which they once worked so hard to rationalize the apartheid system, or vilify its enemies.[111]

Human nature is everywhere the same, and morality is a solid enduring and changing part of any national social system of beliefs. Agreeableness and utility are the root of morality- nothing else. To kill or befriend another are equally expressive of human nature. When one person or a nation state's system is designated right, and the other wrong, we have separated ourselves from human Nature to human Nurture, by holding on to a standard of our own making, including our whole ultimate moral authority being God of some fucking kind.

For us the sane, this standard has been called "American freedoms." For Ronald Reagan's ideology, these freedoms, under God, fundamentally exist only for the prosperity of corporate enterprises and the so-called "white supremacist" regimes they engender within the world of the South African government that our nation had been doing business with so robustly.

The United States, among other nation-states of the human world have- and continue to commit the most hideous and heinous of crimes of body-mind injuries against individuals and groups of other human beings, by denying them their inalienable Rights, and an equal standard of justice. The clear and simple truth we must arrive at is that: standards of morality and justice are nothing but artifacts imposed or enforced by an individual, social group, social system, or nation on another. Morality stands as their limit. "It is not meant to make anything happen, but to prevent certain kinds of things from ever happening."[112]

Human tastes are undisputable. What exists in the nature and utility of things is the standard of our judgment; and what each person feels within

---

[111] Frank, Thomas
[112] Allen Wheelis

his or her own body-mind is the standard of sentiments; the seat of our *morality*. For all the talk about Human Rights and democracy, American business and government leaders have propped-up pro-capitalist regimes throughout the human world- regimes that have used assassination squads or agents, torture, terror, brutal murder of dissidents, outlaw fairness, limit acquisitions, and deliberately kept populations living at, or below bare subsistence levels- all this ordained in the name of a caring and loving God.

South Africa's internal strife, along with its neighboring states drew world media attention in December of 1984, shortly after Ronald Reagan's historic landslide victory for a second term. Anglican bishop Desmond Tutu a black South African, and winner of a Nobel Peace Prize visited the United States and met with Ronald Reagan. In their meeting, Tutu publicly denounced the U. S. policy that was in place toward South Africa as being "immoral, evil, and un-Christian." By implication, he called for total disengagement of the United States doing business with South Africa, as a sanction to free its apartheid held population.

Reagan asked Congress to "resist this emotional clamor for punitive sanctions." He did not say much about the desperation and plight of black people to escape the tyranny of apartheid, but spoke eloquently of "the whites in this country they love and have sacrificed so much to build."[113] He cared not an iota for the senseless brutality and waste of the black populace or people considered to be none-white. Reagan saw the influence and economic system of communism to be more heinous and evil than the socio-economic system of gross human subjugation.

But the United States Congress was not in for duping on this serious state of human affairs. Negative media commentaries generated "a bipartisan storm that slammed into the White House, with legislation carrying sanctions against trade, investments, and financial dealings with South Africa that passed by an 84 to 14 vote", according to Secretary of State George P. Schultz. 75% of Republicans who resented Reagan's plea had a better grasp on the human condition and its quest for freedom from the involuntary tyranny and forceful subjugation of others.

Incidentally Reagan had vetoed the Sanction Bill, but in October of 1985, U. S. Senators voted 78 to 21, to override his economic sanctions veto against South Africa.

---

[113] Ibid

24

THE RAZZLE DAZZLE OF NATIONAL SECURITY

"**S**ECRECY IS TO GOVERNMENT WHAT privacy is to persons" – Joel Brenner, (former senior counsel NSA and counter intelligence executive director's office of National Intelligence, and NSA' inspector general). May I add from the common local citizen level: intrusions and invasions are no different.

The National Security Council (NSC) was established in 1947 to coordinate the defense work of the American government, and is one of the Executive Offices in its Executive branch. Its major function is to keep the President informed of threats to national security, and to suggest methods of strengthening the nation's defense establishment. The Vice-President, Secretary of State, Secretary of Defense, Director of the Office of Defense Mobilization, and other key officials are members of the Council. Operating as a branch of the National Security Council is the Central Intelligence Agency (CIA).[114]

The CIA is charged with the duty of gathering information of the military preparedness of foreign nations- information that is not available through the normal channels of public information. Much of the information gathered is intimate, temporarily secret, and is accomplished through covert, clandestine, and subversive activities; and a variety of means in gaining access to key persons of power, leadership, honor, or prestige, worldwide.

There is a stark contrast, and parallel between this form of information gathering, and the form gathered by news media. News media often report and exploit the drama of human tragedy and misfortune after they happen

---

[114] Ibid

today, while they are happening, and whether they occur or not. While all the potential dangers, of some human tragedy and misfortune, on a wider scale, that the nation's leaders should be aware of are taken up by *timely* intelligence, the province of the NSC and CIA, where action can be taken quickly to prevent misfortune, or remedy failing structures, and always involve an international outreach in their operational action.

Actions can range from simple interventions through electronic or digital communication, destabilization of individuals and social groups, to the overthrow or set-up of new national governments that *are*, or *are not* in favor or compliance in doing business with the United States. The CIA conducts violent covert operations against foreign nations, individuals, and political parties. The source of their directives?

Is it the President or the NSC? Covert actions are always undertaken by the Executive branch of our government; "which typically lies to the legislative branch about what it has done, and plans to do, thus preventing Congress from playing its constitutionally intended role." [115]

Communications on all levels either suppress or ignore what the NSC or CIA personnel do. Among the less savory examples are: various attempts to assassinate leaders or people of great influence; train, and equip death squads, bring down governments of other countries, or de-stabilizing their economy; domestic spying, mind-control projects, and the shipment of narcotics to inner city populations in the United States that contributed to the cocaine epidemic that began in the mid-80's.

In short- actions taken by the NSC and CIA under their *intelligence gathering* and *national security* missions can be virtually limitless, since their actions are not impeded by rule of constitutional law, and or the rule of other governments, or any ethical system they wish to overthrow or transform.[116]

This fucking God thing. Pay attention.

During his tenure as Secretary of State, George Schultz noted that "with authority, ambition, and power, the NSC staff could operate without anyone's full knowledge, even the President's, and was not subjected to Congressional oversight. Laws that limited the behavior of regular government agencies could be read as not applying to the NSC."

---

[115] Ibid
[116] Schultz,

The National Security Act recognizes the general need for secrecy and discretion by providing that the President must notify Congress about covert operations in a "timely manner."[117]

Meanwhile, *Executive prerogative* or privilege granted to the President by the Constitution is a concept that cannot be de-limited through legal means. Historical behavior of the federal judiciary have consistently demonstrated its reluctance to intervene in limiting or defining it. Several lawsuits brought on by members of Congress to clarify the concept have been dismissed; and no modern constitutional lawyer can accept the concept of *Executive privilege* or prerogative, declared by the President, with action dispensed of through the all-encompassing clause of *national security* easily.

Each of the three branches of government created by the Constitution-Executive, Legislative, and Judicial, has a duty to interpret the constitution in the performance of its official functions, and every official in those branches take an oath precisely to that effect. [118]

Our main concern as citizens are the President's decisions. And every decision the President makes or authorize has a direct link to the concept of National Security. The CIA gathering of intelligence is the real American Politics that defines our military policy in the affairs of other nation's governments. Former President Nixon's dilemma was clearly an abuse of power, and all for the wrong reasons.

Ever since Russia and the United States attained somewhat of a strength of rough equivalence in the production of nuclear weapons, the ultimate destructive tool of war that essentially stabilized, and stalemated the war the US fought in North Korea during the 50's, a surprise attack by either side would result in the destruction of both countries.

This was a situation that came to be called "mutually assured destruction (MAD);" deterring both sides from launching a nuclear attack. Sobered by the threat of mutual nuclear destruction during the Cuban Missile Crisis of 1962, when the United States demanded that Russia removed its intermediate–range missiles from Cuba, the world balance of terror has been threatened this close only once. Since then, both Russia and the United States eventually agreed to a Strategic Arms Limitations Treaty

---

[117] Ibid
[118] Stedven Hayward

(SALT 1); sought, and continued negotiations for more than 50 years and ongoing to maintain an amicable relationship.

Both the US and Russia are looked upon as the two rival super-powers of the world. Ever since the breakup of their alliance in World War II, both nations have faced each other as leaders of conflicting political, economic, and ideological alliances. Engaged in a nuclear arms race, both nations continue to fight surrogate wars around the globe- this is to say that for every war and conflict waged by nations of lesser military might throughout the world against the United States or its interests, Russian Influence is automatically inferred as being at the bottom of it all, and vice versa. If for nothing else, in the business trade of weaponry, or the influence of its socio-economic system- so-called *Marxism*.

Domestically, the stability of national security is ever-dependent on intelligence gathering for sound execution of the people's will through their elected representatives. And nowhere is the President's claim to executive privilege or prerogative more pronounced than in regards to national security- an area sometimes removed from Congressional oversight and public scrutiny.

GRENADA

In the President's decision on some military matters, the need for speed, unity, secrecy, and the concentration of authority in the Executive branch of government, means that the public is likely to be excluded. Under the threat of National security, "the President is required to "find" compelling national security reasons as a basis for coversive action taken by CIA."[119]

Two of those recent compelling *finds* were directed to invasion of the island of Grenada, and Soviet ambitions in Latin America, through its support of Nicaragua's new government setup. The *finding* reported that in 1979, the ruling government of Grenada, a former British colony, was replaced by a new government that stressed "socialists and nationalist ideals; ridiculing 'English-style democracy as hypocrisy,' and turning to the Cuban model of 'revolutionary democracy'."[120]

---

[119] Schultz

[120] Ibid

Since the new regime was bent on containing human rights, the safety and security of about 1,000 American students attending medical school on the island were feared, or were at risk of being taken hostages. Conditions are said to have deteriorated as the years progressed, and panic had spread throughout the rest of the Caribbean nations.

Efforts were made to evacuate the medical students through a chartered Pan AM Airline, but the plane was refused the right to land. A second attempt was made by chartering a cruise ship; but the ship was denied permission to dock. With the unanimous consent of the Eastern Caribbean States, the US was given authorization to intervene by force, "acting in a manner consistent with its national interests and with international law." [121] Some claim this was not the case.

Not to say that the British government and its Parliament did not respond to the crisis of its sovereign and former colonial possession- it did. According to Secretary of State Schultz, British Prime Minister Margaret Thatcher did not understand the reality, nor the exigencies of the situation as it related to our hemisphere and national interests. For sure, Americans were still reeling from the last hostage situation in Iran that lasted 444 days, rippling into our real-politick at home.

SOME TROUBLING EVENTS

six months earlier in April of 1983, a pick-up truck packed with over a thousand pounds of explosives rammed into a US Embassy in Beirut, Lebanon, killing 8 CIA members and 17 other Americans amounting to a death toll of 63 people, and many others with major injuries.

Flying through a restricted airspace where a U S reconnaissance plane was spotted by Russians only two hours earlier, on September 1, 3:30 AM, Korean Airlines 747 flight with 247 passengers and flight crew, bound from New York to Seoul was shot down in violation of Russian airspace in the North Pacific. Everyone on that airliner died. The Russians made no apology; insisting that the jet liner was on a U S spy mission.

Some merits to their claim: "Since the plane trespasser did not obey

---

[121] Ibid

the order to proceed to a Soviet airfield and attempted to evade, an air defense interceptor carried out the order of the command post to stop the flight. Such actions are in full conformity with the law of the USSR state boarder... The boarders of the Soviet Union are sacred." [122]

According to former Senator William Fulbright, Chairman of the Senate Foreign Relations Committee, "...Suspicion that surfaces when something like the downing of the Korean Airline plane occurs. It is still a great mystery to me why the pilot was not warned because we hoped to gain some intelligence advantage as the plane flew over Soviet military bases."

Were the people on that airline sacrificial lambs in the name of *national security* and Reagan's *anti-communism* zeal?

We don't know. The fact remains that the pilot was asked to land somewhere, according to Russian constitutional law or rule, and at least the passengers and its crew would be safe. But the asshole refused! And Why?

On October 22, a truck that carried more than 15 hundred pounds of explosives attacked a US Marine barracks- in the same city of Beirut at its international airport, killing 241 Marines, and wounding hundreds. These Marines were part of a contingent force of 1,800 deployed to Lebanon as a multinational peace-keeping force.

On October 23, a plan that was more than four months in its making, the US invaded Grenada. With a few American casualties, most of them killed by friendly fire, because of the overkill in the presence of US troops and Commandos, the budding Cuban-Russian military alliance on the island of Grenada surrendered. The students were rescued and landed on American soil on October 27. Although preliminary CIA reports were insufficient in determining the extent of Cuban-Russian engagement on the island- after all said and done, a conformation of extensive evidence of involvement between the two nations and their true intentions were uncovered.

Catching hell from the British House of Commons because of the "unauthorized invasion," Margaret Thatcher was coyly referred to in the British media as "Ronald Reagan's poodle." Both Thatcher and members of her government vehemently opposed the rescue operation; although

---

[122] Ibid

adequate information and logistics were provided by the US government beforehand, through the proper channels of their official British power lines. The French and other nations throughout Europe also opposed the US invasion of Grenada.[123]

---

[123] Schultz

25

LATIN AMERICA

A NOTHER *FINDING* ACCORDING TO CONGRESS, late in Carter's administration and early in the Reagan-Bush era, stated that the ultimate ambitions of Russia is to topple Latin American governments in our hemisphere, through what had occurred in the country of Nicaragua. Secretary of State George P. Schultz noted that in the 1970's there was only one democracy in Central America, which is the country of Costa Rica.

The rest of the states were oligarchies governed by a combination of landowners who were the real power, while the military provided the muscle. Since 1776 and now, a pattern of economic oligarchy, political despotism, and military repression continue to assert itself as a form of rule throughout the nations of Central America.

Led by rebels at all levels of their socio-economic system in 1979, a revolution in Nicaragua had successfully overthrown the ruling dictatorship of Anastasio Somoza in that country. The broad opposition that overthrew the government had promised to have "free elections, political pluralism, and non-alignment," (according to the United States definition of these terms). Former President Carter was in favor of the new government and proceeded to provide it with about $175 million in aid over its first year of existence, as a result of emergency appropriations signed by him.

Before the end of Carter's administration though, it became apparent in its estimation that the new Nicaraguan government called the *Sandinistas* "were intent upon creating a Cuban-Soviet-Style state," and that every one of their original promises were betrayed. As a result, Carter suspended aid to Nicaragua in his last days in office.

U. S. intelligence reports noted that the real intentions of the

Sandinistas was to create a process of revolution in Central America that will have a domino effect throughout countries of the region, beginning with the overthrow of El Salvador. The incoming Reagan Administration reviewed and confirmed Carter's decision. As disenchantment grew with Nicaragua's government, its opposition that was overthrown called the *Contras,* now coalesced as a resistant movement to reclaim their rule.

With all requirements under the authority of a shared and discussed presidential finding by the intelligence committee of Congress, and "compelling national security reasons," the Reagan administration put together a program for covert assistance for the *Contras,* to avoid the Sandinistas from creating another Cuba, the reasoning goes. "Certification" was Congress's way of saying it will curtail funds needed in Central America, "unless we (NSC operatives) could demonstrate that notorious problems in the countries we supported were being solved- particularly the implementations of land reform, the elimination of death squads, and progress in bringing about to justice those who murdered American nuns and representatives of the AFLCIO in EL Salvador."[124]

Determined to destroy communists' ambitions, Congress was persuaded to provide the *Contras* with $100 million in aid to the military adventures of overthrowing the *Sandinista* Regime. Funds were appropriated for release every six months; but before the next six-month increment could be released, the Secretary of State must certify that progress was indeed being made. Confirmed reports claimed that the Salvadorian military did not use the military aid as effectively as possible to contend with the Sandinista guerrillas.

Congress then snarled at the security assistance given to the *Contras,* stating that it was a waste, and decided to ban further military aid in October of 1984. Reagan sought to persuade other countries and private American groups to help the Contras. In 1985 he allowed the indirect shipment of arms to Iran by way of Israel- hoping that this will result in their releasing a new set of American hostages that the Iranians were now holding and manipulating in Lebanon.

When this did not happen, in January of 1986, he authorized the secret sale of US weapons directly to Iranians. A $12 million profit sale and

---

[124] Ibid

private donation was then supposedly directed to the *Contras* to provide weapons.

It was during this time that the shipment of nearly 75 metric tons of cocaine came into the United States- up from 19 tons shipped in 1976; and prices dropped from $125 per gram to $75 ...in 1986. Congress passed new Anti-Drug laws on October 17. The use of crack cocaine will soon became epidemic, and nationwide.[125]

All this came to light in November of 1986, when both a Presidential and Joint Congressional Committee began investigations into what is now known as the *Iran-Contra Affair;* since as a matter of principle, law, and rule, the United States aught not make such concessions for hostages with nations like Iran, under the threats of terror.

---

[125] Ibid

26

IRAN-CONTRA AFFAIR & MIDDLE EAST POLITICS

Since World War I, the United States, Britain, and France have dominated the Arabian Peninsula, the Gulf Region, and its oil resources, called the Middle East. Naturally, this was accomplished by superior tools, military conquest, coercion, economic control, and exploitation through surrogate governments and their military forces.

Yemen, Sudan, Afghanistan, Turkey, Iran, Iraq, Israel, Lebanon, Syria, Jordan, Saudi Arabia, Kuwait, Egypt, and Libya- are all allies, friends, and enemies of the United States, who participate in the same game of power and dominance, by whatever means necessary; and where human life is worth less than seventy-five cents, a few chemicals, a bucket of ashes- eternally grieving loved-ones, family members, friends, and acquaintances called societies.

My Western conquerors are my true friends. But when they let me down and bully me around, I can make good friends with a bully as big as them. These stand-up bullies have been Russia, and the United States. The United States attitude toward sovereign nations was captured when Chileans in our Western hemisphere voted for Salvador Allende as their President. Kissinger, then Secretary of State, openly stated: "...the United States should not and will not respect the electoral process or sovereignty of another country *if the results do not please us.* -Colonel David Hunt, (italics mine, for emphasis.)"[126]

Furthermore, what was designated as American Republican Affairs in the State Department that deals with countries throughout south of the US Border, Asian, European, Near Eastern, and African affairs, Schultz

---

[126] Hunt David, *They Don't Get IT*

noted that the U S policy "does not have a geographic designation... It is intended to suggest a sense of community in our hemisphere and of attraction of the nations in this sector of the world of the idea of a government of, by, and for the people."[127]

Since World War II, Britain, France, Italy, Russia, Germany, and many other countries around the world, the United States has always been at the very bottom of aid and other things from which their existing rule have risen to their current status. Its main organization of infiltration and set-up of these governments, since Post-World War II has been the NSC and the CIA.

On November 13, 1985 in a nationally televised address, Ronald Reagan stated that he had authorized a small shipment of arms to Iran, but not as a part of a hostage deal. He nevertheless contended: "...we did not- repeat- did not trade weapons for hostages, nor will we....." Since Iran's 8-year war was still going on with Iraq, and since Russia, Britain, Germany, France and Italy were big suppliers of arms to Iraq, Iran began to capitalize on its surrogate Shitte terrorist organization operating in Lebanon, and demanded weapons from the United States for the nominally valuable people they continue to take as hostages.

The urge for war means big money for arms merchants all over the world. Meanwhile, among the rest of the U S population, resentments ran deep of doing business with Iran. It was contrary to the Nation's principles, and sentiments were still ebbing strong after the seizure of our embassies, the people there taken as hostages, the casualties of over 240 plus Marines, and thousands of life-threatening-lifelong limb injuries to both military and civilian personnel in Beirut, Lebanon by the terrorist groups Iran was supporting.

Again, Reagan publicly insisted that our U S policy with any nation-state, and specifically Iran, was "no arms for hostages." On January 6, 1986 John Poindexter, the highest ranking individual in the National Security Council presented the President with a Draft "finding" authorizing arms sales to Iran, which Reagan signed, while Iran's surrogate Shiite organization were still taking in American citizens as hostages. This did not come to public awareness until November of 1986, which then sets in motion Congressional hearings that began in 1987. The hearings were to

---

[127] Schultz

reveal "a pattern of deliberate deception, lies, and misinterpret relations," according to then Secretary of State George Schultz.[128]

"Bush, I said, had been perfectly aware that arms sales to Iran along lines I had argued against was an 'arms-for-hostage deal.' ...at least on one occasion to my knowledge in January 7, 1986 meeting not objected to the proposal for arms sales to Iran, with clear objectives of getting hostages released in the process." Besides Schultz, Casper Weinberger were the only voices of dissent in that meeting.

"...Ireland had been dragged into the affair I knew nothing about, by use of Irish passports apparently forged by officials of my own government, without my knowledge." Schultz.

Ollie North with a pseudonym of "Willie B. Goode," Bud McFarlane, member and representative of the NSC Staff, and four other American businessmen had come secretly to Iran carrying military equipment. "The envoys carried Irish passports, a Bible signed by President Reagan, and a cake that was made in the shape of a key- supposedly the key to Iranian-American friendship." Also in this transaction "questionable characters were involved who were clearly playing us for suckers," by noting that the alleged pretext for arms sales were "to help Iran protect its Soviet boarder."[129]

As part of an operation to bypass Congress, laws, and the Constitution, funds from the arms sales were funneled to the Contra mercenaries in Nicaragua, El Salvador, and among other pro-American political and military leaders. CIA planes transported the guns and supplies. Once the payload was delivered, the planes "were then reloaded with cocaine for their return trip to the U S. The CIA itself admits having known and done nothing about narcotic shipments to inner city populations in this country." In addition, the CIA also "admitted to carrying out at least "149 mind control projects at over 80 institutions."[130]

Meanwhile Reagan admitted full knowledge of the arms sale to Iran, a country he repeatedly accused of supporting terrorism, but was now asking the American public to believe that "these operations were coordinated

---

[128] Ibid
[129] Schultz
[130] Parenti

and conducted by "subordinates" who happen to include his own National Security Adviser, "without being cleared by him."

Schultz: "The President's speech convinced me that Ronald Reagan still truly did not believe that what had happened, in fact, happened. I have seen him before like this on other issues. He would go over the 'script' of an event, past or present in his mind, and once that script was mastered, that was the truth— no fact, no argument, no plea for reconsideration could change his mind. So what Reagan said to the American people was true to him, although it was not the reality."[131]

The Tower Reports submitted in January of 1987 by the Senate Investigative committee with charges that members of the administration deceived Congress and each other, and that the President bears ultimate responsibility for the wrongdoing of his aids came to stark public knowledge when Ollie North testified saying that his "secret operations had approval from higher-ups."

National Security Adviser John Poindexter testified that he "authorized the use of profits from the Iran arms sale to support the Contras." His charges documented the distribution of up to $48 million from the arms sale. It was dubious whether some $12 million or more hustled from concerned donors and contributors ever reached the *Contras*. Secretary of Defense Casper Weinberger testified to "official intrigue and deception;" while Secretary of State George P. Schultz gave testimony to being "repeatedly deceived."[132]

"They told the President what they wanted him to know and what they saw he wanted to hear, and they dressed it up in 'geostrategic' costume. And they kept me as well as others who had constitutional responsibilities to advise the President in the dark… that the intelligence about Iran was fragile at best and obtained from parties with strong interests and bias of their own. …What had been going on here was a Staff con job on the President. Playing on his human desire…."

In spite of ample evidence supporting the Congressional Investigative Committee's charges against the administrative Security council, CIA involvement in the arms-for-hostage deals with Iran, and the diversion of funds to the Contras in Nicaragua, which were all clear violations of

[131] Ibid
[132] Ibid

existing laws; the charges were unable to hold ground, because "laws that pertain to these actions were poorly written or ambiguous" [133]

Waves of adulation and popular approval was generated by North's testimony in July of 1987. In 1982 Reagan had made a proposition to the British Parliament about a "Project Democracy." In his second inaugural address in 1985, he announced that Project Democracy was to be carried out under the "Reagan Doctrine," a document published by then CIA Director, William J. Casey. Casey died in May of 1987.

Project Democracy was intended to be a large scale program of covert action "with Congressional support when available, by other means when Congressional approval was not forthcoming or not sought." William Casey is said to have been the real mastermind behind all of Reagan's plans. "The activist lieutenant to a passive President."[134]

The administration's approach to Iran for release of the hostages began with Casey's concern about William Buckley, the Chief CIA Operative stationed in Beirut, Lebanon; who was reportedly kidnapped and tortured to reveal CIA secrets. Casey persuaded Reagan to say "yes" to the arms deal with Iran, when Schultz and Defense Secretary Weinberger counseled "no."

While testifying, Ollie North spoke about his reverence and veneration for William Casey and his intimacy with him: learning about covert operations and clandestine activities; time spent in each other's office, time shared out and about in airplanes, trains, and cars; as well as time shared at the CIA Director's home.

Reagan, on the other hand, had dreams of spreading what he considers to be democracy throughout the Third World; and Casey, his longtime friend and campaign chairman, was the one who turn them into plans. Reagan was also mesmerized by Casey's dare-devil heroic character performance during World War II as an OSS Officer. [135]

From the arrangement for the arming of guerrillas in Afghanistan to Angola, the mining of Nicaragua's harbor during the Sandinistas' revolt, and to the destabilization of Muammar el Quaddafi's Libyan regime- all were William Casey's plans.

Ollie North also learned from Casey the CIA utility as a way of

---

[133] Ibid
[134] Ibid
[135] Ibid

executing quick moves "without the cumbersome process of asking- or even telling Congress and the American public." The code of a covert warrior's testimony to which he had subscribed states that "...a covert action in its nature is a lie." He insisted that "lying to Congress is justified as necessary to avoid betraying hostages, operational personnel, or whatever. When documents are shredded or altered, or even created, that is simply a part of 'Operational Security' or ...the 'Protective Mode.'"

"In office high or low- even Cabinet officers are kept out of the loop, that is because covert action must be compartmented. If memos go up to the President seeking authorization, but don't come back, that is because in covert operations, the President's 'plausible deniability' must be maintained."[136]

The chain of command for the Reagan Doctrine ran around most of the CIA and NSC, to Lieutenant Colonel Ollie North, who passed on documents of orders to be carried-out by four-star generals and Admirals in the Pentagon saying: "This is what the White House want's done." North was considered a hero of sorts after publicly delivering scathing attacks on radio and television, about Congress and its "irresponsible meddling in foreign policy," thereby causing public opinion to decisively shift in Reagan's favor.

Congressional investigative efforts produced nothing tangible, save for the fact that Congress could not, and would not, control the intelligence community. No one was really charged with crimes in a subsequent Independent Counsel Investigation. With Ollie North's campaign and crusades buttressing the President, "the people judged... and judged that Reagan had acted properly..."[137]

[136] Hayward Steven
[137] Ibid

27

A NEW WORLD ORDER

T HE WAYS OUR PERCEPTIONS WERE manipulated and managed in Washington, in more ways than one, the 1988 Presidential election outcome was a forgone conclusion and continuation of the Reagan-Bush era, with George Bush Senior now being President. With full force, Bush intended to focus his administration on foreign policy and international relations. His first order of business was to "get rid of all of the Reaganists as quickly as possible, substituting them with people who had mortgages rather than ideologies."

While there were ongoing challenges to American economic and political dominance and recklessness of its military policies in its Western hemisphere, and in the Middle East, Russian influenced and dominated nations were also fermenting with resentments, leading to the overthrow, or transformation of their economic and political systems.

Visions of a "New World Order" which Bush foresaw and embraced was well articulated at daily meetings at the White House, with the National Security Council members' presence. The administration's intentions to squish regimes that were on the verge of break-away, and were not likely to align themselves with the United States strategic position in economic and military affairs were carried over with Bush. The beginning and continuations of such incidents were carried on when 10,000 U S troops were ordered into the streets of Panama to take control of that country.

With tooth and claw, severe economic sanctions, and diplomatic moves during the Reagan years were used by the U S to remove President Manuel Noriega of Panama from office, but all attempts were unsuccessful. He had been indicted by the U S Courts for drug dealing and money laundering, and was a firm supporter of the Nicaraguan government that was in power, while Reagan had supported its opposition by supporting the Contras. [138]

In any case, the Bush administration called for Noriega to give it up after presidential elections for civilian rule were held in May of 1989; encouraging the Panamanians to overthrow the dictator. He then ordered a surprise night-time airlift of additional U S forces to take control of the capital. Noriega was captured and flown to the U S to stand trial on drug charges.[139]

With echoes from his inaugural address stating that "...the totalitarian era is passing, its old ideas blown away like leaves from an ancient lifeless tree," many did not foresee the rush with which the whirlwind was coming. Russian leader Michael Gorbachev had abandoned the doctrine by which Russia reserved the right to intervene militarily on behalf of its Soviet type communist regimes around the world.

Political upheavals must be allowed to run their course. With such freedom from a leash, communist governments of Bulgaria, Czechoslovakia, East Germany, Romania, and Yugoslavia gave up their manipulation of power and held popular elections; with the exception of Romania. Amazingly, very little violence precipitated in their transformations.

Boris Yelstin was elected to represent the republic of Russia in 1989; while the new Congress elected Gorbachev to the post of President of the Soviet Union when Russia held its first free elections in 70 years. A new Congress of Deputies were also elected. East Germany lifted the ban on travel restrictions to cross the Berlin Wall; and on November 23, the Brandenburg gate was reopened. Parliaments of both East and West Germany held free elections for unification, setting July 1, 1990 as the date for economic and social union.

Relinquishing all occupational rights, all four Allied Powers who defeated Germany in 1945 signed a treaty leaving Germany free to unite; which officially took place on October 3, 1990. A "Charter of Paris for a New Europe" was agreed upon, that significantly reduced the presence of troops and conventional weapons. Essence of the document proclaimed "an end to the era of confrontation as the first time in history, where there was a profound transformation on the European landscape that is not the result

---

[138]

[139] Ibid

of war or a bloody revolution." In signing on the Charter of Paris, Bush declared "The Cold War is over…We have close a chapter in history." [140]

The Warsaw Pact Military Alliance, which is the Russian bloc that had mounted a formidable perennial threat to Western Alliances for more than 40 years was formally disbanded in 1991. President Michael Gorbachev was awarded the Nobel Peace Prize for his efforts and policies in pursuing political change in Eastern Europe, as well as his initiatives in ending the Cold War.

But a peaceful change was quite elusive in Russia itself. A standoff had ensued between the newly elected government and the old regime staging a coup. The world was stunned to learn that on August 19 of the same year that Gorbachev had been removed from office. He had just reached historic agreements with the Russian republics that would have give them increased autonomy at the expense of Russia's central government. The day before the documents were to be finalized and signed for the official granting, the President was formally detained by the Communist Party while on vacation. Three days later on August 22, the attempted coup collapsed. Gorbachev was forced to resign from the Communist Party on August 25.[141]

On August 30 the Soviet Parliament voted to suspend all activities of the Communist Party. Eleven of the former republics agreed to form the Commonwealth of Independent States (C.I.S.), effectively dissolving and bringing the74-years history of the Soviet Union to an end.

While Russia and the rest of Eastern Europe were in the mood of independent alignment and peaceful reorganization, the nation of Iraq in the Middle East had taken a turn to wresting territory. Saddam Hussein, another son of the CIA alliance had launched a surprise military invasion of its neighboring country of Kuwait on August 2, 1990. Iraq had demanded compensation from Kuwait for drilling of oil on Iraqi disputed territory. It also demanded that the territory be given up, a reduction of oil output, and raising the price of its oil.

The invasion was swift. Within 24 hours the ruling Emir had fled to Saudi Arabia, and the Iraqi's took control of his kingdom. They then began amassing troops, strategically positioning them on the Kuwait border of Saudi Arabia. The Iraqi's aim was to wrest the oil fields that Western nations depend on.

---

[140] Ibid
[141] Ibid

MIDDLE EAST PROFILE

A BRIEF SCENARIO OF THE UNITED States involvement in the Middle-East began with an alliance between the U S and Britain shortly after World War I. Between 1919 and 1925, the Wahhabi Dynasty, a strict orthodox Moslem sect in East Arabia conquered Persia (now called Iran). In further conquest of the area by this Moslem sect, Britain, and France also wrested some territory, creating two more Arab monarchies. Iraq and Transjordan in 1921 were under British control; while Syria and Lebanon fell under French rule. Wresting eighty percent of Palestine, the British recognized Jordon as an autonomous and independent state, but still retained military and financial control over it.

Conducted by a British commissioner in 1921, an Iraqi plebiscite-which is (the direct vote of qualified electors of a state in regard to some important public question; or the vote by which the people of a political body determine autonomy, or affiliation with another country), had a ninety-eight percent approval of installing Syria's Fisal I as King. He was placed as King in Basara, Iraq and reigned until his death. He was then succeeded by his son who got killed in an auto accident in 1939, which many believed to be a suspected coup by the British. A three-year old grandson then reigned until 1959 as Fisal II. He created an Arab Federation in 1958, joining Iraq and Jordon; but he was also assassinated in a coup. King Hussein then succeeded Fisal II and dissolved the Arab Federation.[142]

IRAN

In a bloodless coup in 1921, Reza Khan Pahlavi expelled all Russian Officers doing business in Persia, then starts a new regime. Lenin willingly gave up special rights claims to Persia, granting it joint command to the Caspian Sea, and frees it of its obligation contracts with Russia.

---

[142] Ibid

Subduing his opposition, chiefs in the South-west region that included Sheik Khazal, who were supported by the British and Anglo-Oil Company, Pahlavi went on to establish government control throughout the country. He reigned with absolute dictatorial powers until 1941 when British and Russian troops (part of the Allied Forces fighting in World War II), invaded Persia in late August. Pahlavi abdicated after his sixteen-year reign, and was then succeeded by his son Mohammed, who cooperated with Allied Forces.[143]

In 1950, the Iranian Senate, which was once Persia, and Majlis named Mohammed Mossadegh as Premier. He was the leader of an extremist movement called the National Front Government. Breaking a 1933 treaty with the British, he nationalized the oil industry in 1951. Britain appealed to the international Court of Justice, which then ruled against Iran. U S President Harry Truman appealed for a compromise when Iranian forces began occupying the Arabian oil fields, while the Anglo-Oil Company completes evacuation of its personnel.

Through a CIA coup in 1952, costing roughly $200,000, and engineered by Kermit Roosevelt, grandson of Teddy Roosevelt with a covert operation code named Operation Ajax, Shah Mohammed Reza Pahlavi was put back in power from a brief exile and Mossadegh was imprisoned, supposedly "to prevent Soviet takeover." The Shah then "effectively un-nationalized" the British oil concessions, granting U S firms 40%, and reducing the formerly British-owned company's share from 100% to 40. The creation and structure of the authoritarian state was deliberately created. For the first time in world affairs, oil was now used as a political weapon by the Arab nations, Russia, Britain, and the United States.

The Shah began his brutal reign of terror with his police force called "Savak," and death squads, committing the most hideous and heinous crimes against humanity, from 1953 through 1979- with full approval of the United States. The Shah acted as a "Pentagon CIA surrogate agent to police the region."[144]

The United States and Britain were directly responsible for the repression committed under the Shah's regime- not merely for establishing his power, while encouraging and consenting to his policies, but also for

[143] Ibid
[144] Ibid

guiding the Savak secret police under his command. Savak was created by the U S and trained by Israel "with significant British input, and was even instructed in torture techniques by the CIA.

The British SAS were responsible for training the Shah's Special Forces. "The Federation of American Scientists reports that Savak, formed under the guidance of U S and Israeli intelligence officers in 1957 developed into an effective secret service agency; its job being the effective subjugation of the Iranian population to the rule of the Shah."[145]

In spite of his gruesome and cruel purge, with the highest death penalties administered in the world since Hitler's reign, where no valid system of civilian courts were established, the Shah of Iran retained a benevolent, dedicated, and humane image in the United States' ubiquitous press reports and perceptions. As a matter of fact, "head of the Savak agents in the United States operated under the cover of an attaché at the Iranian Mission to the United Nations with the FBI, CIA, and State Department fully aware of these activities..." The ends sought were "to spread a deep sense of fear, suspicion, disbelief, and apathy throughout the country. This objective was successfully attained." [146]

THE GULF WAR

I N 1963, IRAQ THREATENED TO nationalize the Iraqi Petroleum Company, which was also a foreign consortium doing business there, reaping huge oil profits. Once again, the CIA organized its favorite coup with the Secretary General of the ruling Iraqi Ba'ath Party who jubilantly claimed "we came to power on a CIA train."[147]

While doing business in Iraq in 1972, the Kirkuk Petroleum Company was nationalized. The Nixon administration then embarked on a campaign to "destabilize" the Iraqi government by arming its Kurdish population, through the CIA and other agencies, in order to harass and attack the

---

[145] Nafeez Mossaded Ahmed
[146] Ahmad p. 37, 38, 39
[147] Ibid

ruling government. Pentagon documents revealed by the House Select Committee on Intelligence Activities, claim that after a visit to Iran in 1972, Nixon, Kissinger, and the Iranian Shah reached an agreement where the Shah was free to purchase "anything short of nuclear weapons from the U S." Between 1973 and 1980, Iran and Saudi Arabia ordered more than $30 billion worth of American arms. By the mid-seventies, Iran accounted for more than half of all American arms sale abroad. "Arms sale became the central component in U S-Iranian relations."[148]

Intending to harass Iraq while maintaining Iranian supremacy, the U S continued to arm the Kurds in Iraq. Shortly after collapse of the Shah's regime, and seizure of the U S Embassy in Tehran with 52 American hostages, the U S abandoned the Kurds; and the CIA contingent that was operating there managed to flee to safety. Ninety-six members of the CIA-funded Iraqi National Congress were then rounded up and executed by the Iraqi government. [149]

The U S then began providing direct military aid to Saddam Hussein in Iraq, supporting its eight-year war with Iran that began in 1980, lasting through 1988. Russia, Saudi Arabia, and Kuwait also gave assistance to Iraq. Iraq was now considered a protectorate of Arab states opposing Iran's revolutionary intentions. "So enduring was America's gratitude... (for the war Iraq was waging with Iran) ...that Saddam Hussein was given almost everything he wanted up to the day he invaded Kuwait in 1990."

"Don't worry about what you see on TV, I have a special relation with the U S. ...I have been told to attack other Arab countries and keep them in their place. Just ignore what you see on TV and in the media." Saddam Hussein is being quoted by one of his confidants. Washington's support for him reached an extreme that it was even willing to overlook an Iraqi Air Force attack on the USS Stark that killed 37 crewmen (p.412-3) (p.395).[150]

The Bush administration's immediate response to the invasion of Kuwait was one of outrage and indignation. Hussein had become too powerful, deciding to ignore negotiations. Now members of Congress, Russia, Britain, Iran, China, and Japan united in denouncing Iraq's move into Kuwait. The United Nation's Security Council voted 13 to 0 in

---

[148] Ibid
[149] Ibid
[150] Ibid

August of 1990 to impose economic sanctions against Iraq. At the time, Kuwait was violating OPEC's oil production agreement by exacting excess amounts of oil from pools shared with Iraq, demanding payments of loans it made to Iraq during its war with Iran. The CIA is said to have assisted and directed Kuwait in its actions.

Negotiations broke off with Kuwait over these disputes; while the U S intentions was to provoke Iraq into action against Kuwait; justifying its mediations- since the U S showed no opposition to Iraq's increasing threats to Kuwait during the process. The real prodders were said to be big U S business companies hanging around in the wings for major contracts in Iraq.[151]

Whatever reality was at stake, largely at its urging for the first time in history, the United Nations later authorized the use of force against Iraq if it did not withdraw from Kuwait before January 15, 1991. Bush went on to rally a broad coalition of foreign leaders and international alliance in an unprecedented fashion. Twenty-eight countries sent military forces to the Persian Gulf region, adding impetus to the unanimity by which the United Nations Security Council voted to condemn the invasion.[152]

In the changing climate of Post-Cold War tensions, the cooperation and support of Russian leader Mikael Gorbachev was what actually enabled swift and decisive action at the United Nations. Addressing the nation, Bush declared that "The crisis in the Persian Gulf, as grave as it is, offers an opportunity towards a... period of cooperation, a new world order can emerge... free from the threat of terror, stronger in the pursuit of justice, and more secure in the quest for peace. An era in which nations of the world... can prosper and live in harmony... A world quite different from the one we've known. A world where the rule of law supplants the rule of the jungle. A world in which nations recognize shared responsibility for freedom and justice. A world where the strong respect the rights of the weak..."[153]

After heated and extended debate, and the deadline was drawing closer for Iraq to pull out of Kuwait, Congress voted on January 12, 1991 giving

---

[151] Ibid
[152] Ibid
[153] Ibid

Bush the authority to "use all necessary means to drive Saddam Hussein out of Kuwait."

About 500,000 U S troops were deployed to Saudi Arabia and surrounding areas in the Middle East. Emphasizing significance of the new status quo America had reached with Russia in the partnership that was forged, Bush stated: "Clearly, no longer can a dictator count on East-West confrontations to stymie concerted U S action against aggression."[154]

The United Nations Security Council's deadline for Iraq to withdraw from Kuwait expired on January 15, with no compliance from Hussein. The very next day the first wave of planes began raining bombs on Iraqi troops, its military instillations, and communications. More than 106,000 military flights were clocked in a span of 43 days of abject horror.

Operation Desert Storm began February 24, and ended in roughly 100 hours. It was the first war to be televised live around the world. A massive array of high technology weapons were unleashed that proved Iraq to be powerless and defenseless. Over 100,000 Iraqis were killed, compared to a little over 200 U S fatalities before Iraq surrendered, unconditionally on March 3. All the Nations around the Middle East continue to bleed profusely.

SOMALIA

Trouble asserted itself in the nation of Somalia in Africa. Its form of government had disintegrated into anarchy and chaos. Warlords dominated the streets and highways, crippling the nation's economy, as hundreds of thousands take their death toll from disease, malnutrition, starvation, and war wounds. On December 3, of 1992 the United Nations voted to authorize the use of force. Bush announced the deployment of U S troops to that country the following day on December 4.

One source claimed that "it was the first time American troops had been used in such a purely humanitarian effort in a foreign country where no strategic or national security interest of the US were involved." Another,

---

[154] Ibid

claims that "....Bush's decision to intervene in Somalia....supposedly for humanitarian reasons, was later proved....to be substantially oil driven. Four large oil firms- Chevron, AMOCO, CONSCO, and Philips- had exclusive concessions covering two-thirds of Somalia that were put at risk when the nation's pro-western government was overthrown."

The newspaper report noted that "....CONCO had allowed its corporate compound there in Mogadishu, Somalia to be made into a de facto U S embassy, a few days before the Marines arrived in the capital..." Stating further that the U S government's presence and claims to "peacekeeping" and purely "humanitarian relief" as plain "absurd" and "nonsense."[155]

SUMMARY OF THE ERA

Bush was a strong and compelling President among local and international leaders- having effectively led an international coalition against Iraq, hammering out international agreements on arms control, nuclear disarmament, and free trade. Communism had collapsed, along with the Warsaw Pact and military threat it had posed to the U S and its allies. The Cold War was declared over, and the United States emerged as the undisputed super power in the world of other nations.

When Bush took office in 1989, his administration was forced to face the consequence of Ronald Reagan's "voodoo economics" that resulted the scandal of massive failures of government insured Savings & Loans Banks. Billions of depositors' dollars were lost in fraudulent, shoddy dealings, snake oil loans, and investments.

After a decade of monetary soothsaying and granting risky loans, many banks went out of business, causing government to borrow billions of taxpayers' dollars to replace the lost money of depositors. A bailout plan of $166 billion over ten years was approved by Congress- supposedly the largest federal bailout in U S history. By August the same year, the bailout had swollen to $30 billion over ten years.

---

[155] Philips Kevin, *American Theocracy*

1992 was another national election year. In spite of all the success that Bush had accomplished as a powerful leader, the American public insisted on focusing on their own economic insecurities. The New World Order which the President had proclaimed also required changes in structural components of the country, which Bush's social reality could not articulate to the voters' satisfaction. Promotional popularity without substance won out. William J. Clinton, a jive-Democrat, "who methodically followed the Republican Party's agenda" with his narcissistic visions was elected President.

28

EYES IN OUR SKY

THE AUTHOR WOULD LIKE TO make a plea against potential charges of *plagiarism,* (if any so desire to pursue), in using research materials of various authors, with due credit. I believe that the sole purpose and intent of their publication is to *inform* or *educate* the public to be responsible and assertive citizens in controlling their own fates and destinies in the world they live in, and know very little about.

It is my firm belief that the following excerpts from their diligent, disciplined, and conscientious work, as well as their practical experiences, is of added service to their most fervent intentions- for all Americans to be a more informed and a better understanding people. The intended purpose of this treatise is to do the same. I take nothing away to discredit their assertions nor to aggrandize mine, but to shed more light on critical issues which concerns survival in our American society.

That said, my wish and hope, as I live out the rest of my social life, is that the leaders of our nation, however dignified or rotten the son-of-a-bitches are, that they are always given, or have at their hands and disposal, the best possible information and solutions, from the best possible sources, to resolve continuous contentious problems; and that the least amount of unfortunate people suffer as a consequence.

A SO-CALLED "BLACK RACIST" SENATOR FROM THE SOUTH

From 1945 to 1974, Senator J. William Fulbright of Arkansas chaired the Senate Foreign Relations Committee- longer than any other Senator in American history. He has produced a document in his own words, "to create a more comprehensive and sensitive America; to warn us of the *arrogance of power,* and the follies of empire, and to remind Americans of what is truly valuable in our national experience." Following are some selected excerpts from his treatise *The Price of Empire, (copy 1989)*:

On Communism: "Was the country better off with Truman elected? I think not. This fifth successive presidential defeat so frustrated the Republicans ... the atmosphere engendered ... created a kind of bitterness in our political system, a meanness... that come with Joseph McCarthy. ...the atmosphere engendered... by their irresponsibility, aggravated the Cold War, and contributed to the animosity toward the Russians that plagues us to this day."

"The surprise Democratic victory of 1948 so embittered the Republicans that they seize upon the threat of communism with uncommon ferocity."

"The highly emotional attacks upon communism and Russia that have become so familiar a part of our national political vocabulary suggest a lack of confidence in our own system's ability to compete effectively and peacefully with the Russians, and especially to do so without using violent oratory to mobilize our people..."

"Truman once commented that every time we started to make progress with the Russians, something seemed to happen. He had the idea that there were forces around us who just did not like the idea of our having normal relations with the Russians."

"When it comes to keeping treaties, I don't think the Soviet record is any worse than ours.... The Bay of Pigs in 1961 and the intervention in the Dominican Republic in 1965, to cite only two conspicuous examples, were blatant violations of the Charter of the Organization of American States. We ignored our treaty obligations and did as we pleased. We paid no attention then, and we pay no attention now when treaties and promises get in our way."

"We have not completely recovered yet. You see the periodic revival of the same kind of sentiment, this paranoiac anti-communism. Reagan's initial rhetoric was a virulent revival of the old McCarthy attitude that proved successful, politically, in so many cases. It has been the Republican Party's most reliable issue and avenue to power in the postwar era."

On Joseph McCarthy: His allegations left people embarrassed and humiliated. It didn't matter what the facts were. He destroyed the reputation of people and made them feel destroyed, even though there was little or nothing to his allegations…"

"I thought he was disgusting and irresponsible, trying to prejudice people by appealing to their worst instincts… "…"

"…I thought him to be a demagogue and ruthless boor. They use to have an old saying downhome: 'You don't engage in a pissing contest with a skunk.'"

The Foreign Relations Committee "is a forum of debate and dissent, removed the stigma of disloyalty from the raising of questions about the war and from efforts to end the war and the advocacy of peace. That was the main function, the practical outcome. It was to make opposition legitimate within the framework of democratic institutions.

On The Nation Entering War In Vietnam: "The Senate Foreign Relations Committee in 1967 conducted an exhaustive inquiry into the events of August 1964 in the Gulf of Tonkin. The investigation showed conclusively that the administration had already, by the time of the Tonkin Resolution, determined their policy…

They misrepresented the actual event. They knew there had not been an unprovoked attack…. the account presented to us was a misrepresentation of the facts for which the President has to be held responsible…"

"Only when we began those later hearings on the Tonkin Gulf did it really begin to dawn on me that we had been deceived. And I have had little confidence in what the government says since then… The preoccupation with a resounding affirmation of our unity overrode considerations of legislative accuracy and precision. They told me that delay was unacceptable, that it would destroy the whole thrust of determined and united action."

"… -before Vietnam …it never occurred to me that Presidents and their secretaries of state and defense would deceive a Senate Committee. I thought you could trust them to tell you the truth, even if they did not tell you everything. But I was naïve, and the misrepresentation of the Tonkin Gulf affair was very effective in deceiving the Foreign Relations Committee and the country, and me, because we didn't believe it possible that we could be so completely misled."

"...The Vietnam hearings showed that Ho Chi Minh had written to the State Department several times in 1946, pleading with us to assist him and saying he was modeling his constitution on our institutions. The Truman administration did not acknowledge his letters..."

"I don't know whether I was radicalized by the war... Certainly I thought more and more about our global policy and about our anticommunist obsession. And the more I thought about it, the more I became convinced that the obsession had distorted our perceptions and impaired the judgment of our leaders..."

"Looking back at the Vietnam War, it never occurred to me that President Johnson was guilty of anything worse than bad judgment. He deceived the Congress, and he deceived me personally, over the Gulf of Tonkin episode and his purposes in the election of 1964. I resented that, and I am glad the deceit was exposed, but I never wished to carry the matter beyond exposure..."

"The worst thing Nixon did was to continue the prosecution of the Vietnam War. ...I sent him a memo suggesting that it wasn't his original responsibility and that it would be to his advantage to bring the thing to an end. ...He said he needed a few months to survey the situation... evaluate the circumstances, to look into it."

"It was never a promising policy... it just widened the gap between the objectives sought and the means available for achieving them. So we went right back to where we were. And that interlude of believing that he was tending to end the war short of military victory was over."

"The whole period seems very odd and elusive. The administration practiced a kind of expert manipulation that I would attribute a large part to Kissinger. They kept emphasizing that they were going to reduce the American troop presence, all the while obfuscating the situation and finally invading Cambodia..."

"...Everybody who didn't support the President and the war was made out to be disloyal. Traitor is about it..."

"We had the Pentagon Papers before they became public. The Question was, what should the Committee do about them?"

"By then, I was not shocked by the revelations. The government, especially the CIA, had been involved in so many things- the misrepresentation was so common it was virtually routine. ...I thought there was no limit to what they were capable of doing."

"The invasion of Cambodia was a dreadful act. As best they could, the Cambodians had maintained their neutrality; and our attack was inexcusable. But we did it and the events that followed ruined Cambodia- and the consequences are still being felt in that part of the world. We've contributed to an awful lot of tragedy in the world."

"...we should restore diplomatic relations with Vietnam... Our conscience should impel us to conciliation at every opportunity..."

"I never did find the domino theory persuasive. ...In the first place, the conflict in Vietnam was an indigenous revolution against a colonial power, France. And the Vietnamese nationalists turned to whoever could assist them, just as Castro did- or as the Nicaraguan Sandinistas do today. When we are their enemy, they have no other place to go.

...it would have been relatively easy for us to have won the friendship of the Chinese as well as the Vietnamese if we had accepted the legitimacy of their revolutions. We didn't do that; we don't accept the legitimacy of the revolution in Nicaragua today. We are paying for this attitude once again in Central America."

"Obsessive anticommunism has impaired our ability to understand modern third-world revolutions..."

"We have to recognize that these upheavals are, in many instances, authentic efforts by members of a society to internally improve their lot, to overcome the terrible inequalities of wealth and power. ...It is this simple proposition that we have so much trouble accepting..."

"...Every time there has been a revolution in Latin America- not a routine military coup, but a real revolution- we have rushed to conclude it was communist, and if not, Soviet-dominated, at least a ready avenue for Soviet exploitation. We rush to that judgment erroneously in the Dominican Republic in 1965. And there in Nicaragua. I am impressed by our own historical responsibility. We were responsible for Trujillo in the Dominican Republic and for the Somoza family in Nicaragua, having trained and supported them. We had aligned ourselves with their brutal regimes and sustained them in power until their own people rose decisively against them."

On Interventions "…We have taken the alleged urgency of protecting our own people and used it as a pretext to send in our troops- and there they remain, for quite other purposes."

"As history has abundantly demonstrated, we are neither able nor much inclined to install the best people, nor to create honest, stable, democratic governments in the countries in which we intervene. It is a very difficult thing to do. We have difficulty enough with that task at home; why should we think we can do it in Nicaragua, or Grenada, or Iran, or Guatemala? It is like the old missionary impulse: if we can't solve our own problems we'll go abroad and solve someone else's…"

"…When people try to assert their rights against an intolerable status quo, the United States on all too many occasions sides with those who wish to retain the status quo. We align ourselves against those who would strike at the corruption and tyranny, on the side of the traditional elites and the militarists who have kept their people in line."

"…We gave them on a grandiose scale the weapons of destructive warfare, at the same time that we were miserly in our aid to meaningful programs to deal with poverty…"

"There is a tendency in all societies for people with power to exploit whomever they can exploit…"

"…It is simply common sense- and elementary justice- for people to feel that the national resources belonging to their country should benefit the people of that country. They should be able to benefit from their own resources. We cannot go round the world any longer exploiting them as was done in the past."

"…We still find it hard to recognize the deep drive of smaller nations for a meaningful independence, and harder still to come to terms with their revolutions. We still to a great degree claim the right to dominate them, as in Central America- not to incorporate them into the United States, but to have extensive control over them."

"We supported the United Nations as long as we controlled the General Assembly. But when the control was lost with the proliferation of members following decolonization, we started to say the United Nations was of no use. We downgraded its reputation and, in recent years, even refused to support it financially, as we are legally obligated to do."

"Since World War II, the United States has become a globalist interventionist power. As the greatest power in the postwar era, we acquired a tendency to think that we had a responsibility to intervene and keep order, and to promote and carry out worldwide programs..."

"...If we start to plan to assassinate leaders we don't like, as the CIA is believed to have done with Castro, you are only asking for trouble. It is self-defeating. It is against our interests. I don't think it ever succeeds. It gives others an excuse to engage in terrorism, to kill our ambassadors or citizens travelling abroad. You start a process of terrorism that has far-reaching and unpredictable consequences. There is a good case to be made that we initiated it. We and some of our friends have initiated some of the worst aspects of modern terrorism."

"While our overt interventions have gained us little, our covert interventions have gained us less. The gradual development of the CIA as an operator in the field and all of its various covert operations have been on the whole a disservice to the country. The Iran-Contra affair is only the latest in a long series of fiascos. I cannot think of a single covert operation of this kind that was necessary or in the long run really successful."

On Iran "...Displacing the nationalist Mosadeq and restoring the Shah to power in 1953 ...and supplying him with arms without much attention to the real needs of the people. It culminated in the explosion that drove the shah from power and installed the radical fundamentalist regime of Khomeini. ...and you get a Khomeini, it becomes almost impossible for Americans to think seriously about what really happened..."

From Nafeez Mossaded Ahmed, author of *Behind The War On Terror,* **on** Iran: "An agreement was signed the year following the coup establishing a new oil consortium in which the U S and U K both had a 40% interest. The consortium controlled the production, pricing, and export of Iranian oil. The British share was reduced from the level of complete control it had prior to Mosadeq..."

"For the shah to maintain power, he had to control an increasingly agitated and resentful populace, which implied brutal repression- policies that were supported, and indeed, directed by American and British governments..."

"The shah implemented economic policies in accordance with the interest of western investors, thus ensuring that political repression resulted in the siphoning of the country's wealth to a minority elite. .... the shah's reforms favored the rich, concentrated on the city dwellers, and ignored the peasantry..."

"American investors and the Iranian elite alike both profited immensely from the shah's 'white revolution'. Yet, while western investors enriched themselves on Iranian resources, the country's own population suffers horrendously."

"...Kissinger also described the tyrant as a 'pillar of stability in a turbulent and vital region'... a 'dedicated reformer' with the 'most noble aspirations'."[156]

From Turi Munthe, Author of *The Saddam Hussein Reader* on Iran, Iraq and Kuwait: "The American people and their democratic institutions were deprived of information essential to sound judgment and were regimented, despite profound coercion, to support a major neocolonial intervention and war of aggression..."

"The press received virtually all its information from, or by permission of the Pentagon. Efforts were made to prevent any adverse information or opposition views being heard. CNN's limited presence in Bagdad was described as Iraqi propaganda. Independent observers, eyewitnesses' photos and video tapes with information about U S bombing were excluded from the media."

"Throughout the 75-year period from Britain's invasion of Iraq early in World War I to the destruction of Iraq in 1991 by U S air power, the United States and the United Kingdom demonstrated no concern for democratic values, human rights, social justice, or political and cultural integrity in the region, nor for stopping military aggression there."(p.311)

"There is Douglas Hurd in 1981, then a Foreign Office Minister who came to sell Saddam Hussein a British aerospace missile system and to celebrate the anniversary of the coming to power of the Baath Party redemption- a largely CIA triumph in 1968 that extinguished all hope of a pluralistic Iraq and produced Saddam Hussein."

"Margaret Thatcher's Treasury Secretary, who, within a month of gassing the Kurds, was on the same white couch offering Saddam 340 million pounds of British taxpayers money on export credits. And there she was again three months later, back on the couch, celebrating the fact that Iraq was now Britain's third largest market for machine tools, from which a range of weapons was forged." (p. 354-5)

"....Because of Iranian battlefield victories and the growing U S- Iraqi ties, Washington launched 'Operation Staunch,' an effort to dry up Iran's sources of arms by pressuring U S allies to stop supplying Tehran. Proceeds from the arms sales had been directed to Nicaragua."

Accounts by Secretary of State George P. Schultz on the Iran-Contra 'Arms for Hostage Deal':

"Our credibility is shot, we have taken refuge in tricky technicalities of language to avoid confronting the reality that we have lied to the American people and misused our friends abroad. We are revealed to have been with some of the sleaziest international characters around. They have played us for Suckers."

"So it must be stopped. How?"

"'Ultimately,' I said, 'the guy behind it, who got it going, and the only guy who can stop it, was and is Ronald Reagan.'"

"....My main fight was with the NSC Staff that had developed an operational capability and a fervent will to use it- often unwisely with authority ambition, and power, the NSC Staff could operate without anyone's full knowledge, even the Presidents,' and was not subject to Congressional oversight. Laws that limited the behavior of regular government agencies could be read as not applying to the NSC Staff..."

"What Poindexter had described was absolutely outrageous. The arms transfer could not be justified. I could not support this program in public, and I could not acquiesce with its continuation. President Reagan in his desire to free the hostages, had allowed himself to be sold a bill of goods.

Poindexter had fabricated a high-toned rational for a sordid swap, and the President had accepted it. 'Iran is playing us for suckers,' I said, 'and we are paying extortion money to them.'"

"...The U S government had violated its own policies on anti-terrorism and against arms sales to Iran, was buying our own citizen's freedom in a manner that could only encourage the taking of others, was working through disputable international go-betweeners, was circumventing our constitutional system of governance, and was misleading the American people- all in the guise of furthering some purported regional political transformation, or to obtain in actuality a hostage release. And somehow, by dressing up this arms-for-hostages scheme and disguising its worst aspects, first McFarlane, then Poindexter... with the strong collaboration of Bill Casey, had sold it to the president all too ready to accept it..."

"Casey did not want the state department 'to be briefed on what happened.' At this point I felt I could have no confidence in any CIA 'briefing.' ....Casey's people at the CIA were scrambling to try to back up Poindexter's assertion that Iran had abstained from terrorist activity over the past eighteen months."

"I shook my head. 'The facts are to the contrary. They can't rewrite reality." Three more hostages had been taken by Iranian-backed groups."

"....I had detailed material on statements that the President had made that was wrong. He had accepted as accurate information provided him by the CIA and the NSC Staff that was in fact laden with error- all coordinated, in so far as I could see, by Poindexter...."

"....The President's staff was continuing to deceive him, but he was allowing himself to be deceived, He eagerly bought the sophistry of Poindexter and improved it in the telling. He felt sure that if he explained it to the American people, they would agree that everything had been done the right way..."

"....I presented to the President detailed factual material... three new hostages has been taken.... There was much more..."

"'This is news to me.' Reagan said."

"...There were lies: Poindexter's statement that he had heard of the November 1985 shipment only yesterday and Casey's assertion that he thought it was a shipment of oil drilling bits. There were also omissions...."

"....Bill Casey's testimony had been 'altered' from the draft I had read just a few hours before. The CIA and NSC Staff were apparently changing their story to indicate that they did not know what the shipment contained...."

"....The situation was still unraveling. The President was roped in and refused to see the real picture. Bill Casey had the bit in his teeth...."

"Casey was not to be trusted. He had now changed his story in testimony to Congress.... And admitted that he *had* known about the arms-for-hostage trade described by Bud McFarlane..."

'Bill Casey is bad news,' I said to Vice President George Bush as we left. Casey had grossly distorted the proper conduct of government, and I was going to make it my crusade to stop him from continuing these renegade operations."

Attorney general "Meese had now publicly declared not only that the President had no knowledge of the diversion of funds, but also that he did not know of the November 1985 arms shipment and was not informed of the operational details. I was disturbed because the president had told me he knew about the 1985 shipment..."

Excerpts from *Nations of Nations, Copy. 1994:* Reagan's National Security adviser Robert McFarlane suggested opening a channel in some faction of the Iranian government: "If the United States sold Iran a few weapons, the... moderates might use their influence in Lebanon to free the hostages..."

"This is almost too absurd to comment on,' Secretary Weinberger replied, upon hearing of the idea to supply Iran with arms. Still, the President ...approved the initiative- ....In August 500 missiles were shipped to Iran from Israel, while the United States replaced the missiles in Israel's arsenal."

"Over the following year, three more secret arms shipment were made to Iran. The man who pulled the necessary strings so effectively was Colonel Ollie North, McFarlane's junior officer in the NSC.

"In the most dramatic initiative to Iran he and McFarlane flew to the capital,... in May 1986, using false Irish passports, carrying .357-caliber pistols, a chocolate layer cake, and poison pills for themselves, in case the mission went awry. Despite four separate arms shipments only one hostage was released."

"McFarlane's successor as NSC adviser, Admiral John Poindexter, had the President sign a secret 'intelligence' finding.' Henceforth, he, Ollie North, and others could pursue their missions without informing anyone in congress or even the secretaries of defense and state...."

McFarlane rallied Saudi Arabia and seven other friendly allies declaring that the Contras desperately needed funds. "The Saudi's obligingly deposited at least $30 million in Swiss bank accounts set up to launder the money. North then recruited Richard Secord, a former Air Force General, to buy the weapons with the laundered money and deliver them to Central America. In addition Ollie North illegally helped conservative fund raisers within the United States find money for what he nobly referred to as "project democracy."

Ghorbanifar, Ollie North's Iranian weapons-dealer connection: "I think this is now.... The best chance, because.... We never get such good money out of this.... We do everything, we do hostages free of charge; we do all terrorist free of charge; Central America free of charge." (P.1282 all quotes).

"The operation remained hidden from view through the fall of 1986. But that changed abruptly after another American hostage was released in return for a fifth hostage shipment of arms... As the inquiry into the Iranian affair continued, the link between the arms sale was discovered."

"The President defended the Iranian arms sale as negotiations unrelated to the release of hostages.... Reagan praised Ollie North as a national hero. Still, the president seemed uninterested in discovering what his subordinates were doing in his name..."

"....It is a deadly embarrassment to the United States that the war in Afghanistan was in part funded by rebels in the heroin trade- similarly, pro-US Contra rebels in Central America supported their operations by running cocaine and other drugs. ...General Noriega, apparently had been a key part of the South American drug traffic that connected Colombia,

the Contras, and Panama with markets for cocaine in the United States…"
(p. 82 from *The World Affairs Companion*, by Gerald Segal).

Attorney General Edwin Meese III: "To restate, at the outset, this was not a criminal inquiry, but rather an effort to reconcile conflicting statements about a complex covert, compartmentalized effort that few people understood in full. Knowing the Iran initiative of 1986 was authorized and lawful, though covert, I had no reason to assume that I was embarked on a criminal investigation. Rather, my effort was to deal with honorable colleagues, in the president's behalf, so as to pull together fragmented facts about a confusing situation." (P.294-5).

"….Whatever his critics say about Bill Casey, nobody questions his knowledge of intelligence matters, or his political horse sense…."

"Bill knew I was gathering information on the Iran-Contra matter and wanted me to know about a recent development. A few weeks previously, he said, he had been approached by a former business acquaintance …. With a story about some businessman who had been involved in the Iranian transactions. These businessmen, according to Bill, alleged that they had not been paid for their services. If they were not reimbursed, they would go public with accusations that money from arms deal was being used by the U S and the Israelis for 'other purposes.'" (p.290).

"….I questioned John Poindexter about what he knew about the diversion, since I had not yet had a chance to talk with him. He confirmed he did know of the diversion, but said he had told no one about it nor done anything to stop it. He was so angry with congress…. For what it had done to the Nicaraguan Freedom fighters that he just decided to let it happen. Poindexter said he was telling me this because he felt I was the only person he could trust; and that he would be guided by my advice…." (p.300).

"Whether it was technically legal or not, the funds diversion was a tremendous error that should never have been allowed to happen. That it did happen was a failure of the administration." (p.286).

"….The insiders called it the 'enterprise:' Private money, raised through the sale of government favors and property would go to fund private armies of 'freedom fighters' operating overseas. The ultimate aim of the enterprise as envisioned by CIA director Casey, was privatization on the grandest scale imaginable: the construction of a foreign policy instrument that was free from the meddling of Congress, financed by the sale of weapons and other precious commodity that government had in abundance…. –access."

"….it was a serious mistake by men who, in their zeal to advance legitimate national interests, took steps that were both unauthorized and unwise…." In terms of intelligence doctrine, the diversion represented one of the most fundamental errors in the book: crossing or combining two different covert operations…. This aspect of the Iran-Contra affair will undoubtedly be cited in future intelligence annals as a case study of how *not* to do it."

"….When national policy is conducted in a deliberate and routinized fashion, such as through approval at a formal meeting of the National Security Council, where an issue is clearly presented in all its alternatives, the President can sign off one of these, or a combination of them- providing a clear-cut executive decision."

"In 1986, the World Court condemned the United States for "unlawful use of force" against Nicaragua, demanding that it desist and pay extensive repatriations, and declaring all U S aid to the Contras, whatever its character, to be 'military aid,' and not 'humanitarian aid.' The terms of the World Court judgment were unfit to print, and were ignored."-

Fulbright: "President Reagan was basically contemptuous of Congress. His particular version of the imperial presidency amounted to a belief that he could do anything he liked as commander-in-chief and chief executive. The Reagan administration defied the war-powers resolution; violated the Boland Amendment regarding aid to the Contras; 'reinterpreted' the ABM treaty to give it a whole new meaning; and preached a doctrine of presidential prerogative that amounted to a claim that he had the right to ignore virtually all restraints."

"…presidents have felt free to act on their own in Lebanon in 1958, the Bay of Pigs in 1961, the Gulf of Tonkin in 1964, the Dominican invasion of 1965, the blockade of North Vietnamese ports in 1972, not to mention Grenada, and the Persian Gulf. Not one of these instances even remotely resembled a clear and present danger to our national security."

"The Reagan years were an irresponsible economic era, people thought the economy was doing relatively well, but they were wrong. …few leading political figures- have been willing to raise the question of the militarization of our economy as the key to our global economic deterioration..."

"To Question this militarization is portrayed as an attack on our very security and survival. It has become the sacred cow of our politics. You don't talk about it for fear of being unpatriotic, soft on defense. It used to be 'soft on communism;' now it's simply 'soft on defense.'"

"The ABM treaty codified the central strategic reality of the nuclear age: that neither we or the Russians have, or can reasonably be expected to acquire effective defenses against intercontinental missiles, and that, therefore, there is no useful purpose, and a high destabilizing risk, in trying to build such a defense. That is a sound deterrent principle. It worked, and it still works..."

"Acceptance of mutual vulnerability was the principle of the ABM treaty. That is how it was clearly stated at the time, and you see it clearly expressed in Nixon's and Kissinger's memoirs..."

"President Reagan, as I have said, had the right under the treaty to propose amendments or to withdraw from the treaty. But he did not have to perform radical surgery by tortured interpretation."

"...But they have preempted the terms of debate so as to scare off the rest of us and convince us that only they- the experts- are entitled to talk about national defense, when it is just plain common sense that this great multiplicity of weapons is nonsense. As Mikhail Gorbachev and, belatedly, Ronald Reagan came to recognize, we have accumulated weapons systems far beyond their usefulness. They are redundant. Yet the defense experts talk about these matters with utmost gravity... which is usually provocative and dangerous as well as erroneous. But the nonsense defines the terms of debate. And a serious discussion of what can be done to change the attitudes and the intentions of the two superpower countries towards each other is effectively squelched."

"Do any of our political leaders dare to say, 'look, this arms race is absolute nonsense,' that our perceived defense needs are built largely on fantasy?

"Consider Star Wars. By my reckoning the so-called SDI is a fantastic concept suitable only for Hollywood. That sort of thing works fine in movies, or in early-morning television cartoons..."

Gerald Segal author of *War In Space* from *The World Affairs Companion*: "SDI is peculiar in that it is a doctrine in search of a capability, rather than the more usual opposite way around. Taking the most benign view, SDI is a bit like the French folk story of the Pope's mule. The pope offered vast sums of money to anyone who could teach the mule to speak. One day a simple peasant went to see him and returned with the prize. He had promised to teach the mule to talk within ten years. When asked how he could make such a pledge, knowing well mules cannot speak, his reply was: in ten years either the pope will be dead, the mule will be dead or I will be dead. "Indeed the Bush administration has quietly smothered SDI, until some other perceived threat and new technology receives the debate about defense in the nuclear age."

Robert Gates, former Secretary of Defense: "….As I joked at the time, there appeared to be only two people on the planet who actually thought SDI would work- Regan and Mikhail Gorbachev..." (Robert Gates from *DUTY*, p.159)

Fulbright: "...it is a new game we are playing in the nuclear age-irrational, inhuman, and suicidal- a game with no possible winners, and a game we can avoid losing only by refusing to play."

"...To many Americans the Soviets remain an abstraction- an evil abstraction embodying a feared and alien ideology- and to many Russians, no doubt, we appear the same, in a kind of mirror image..."

"...The Soviet economy is stagnant and unproductive while ours appear to be booming- but the boom is based on budget deficits and borrowed foreign money. We are living well today by mortgaging our children's future..."

"The idea of the Reagan era that 'government is the problem' just isn't going to get us anywhere. In such a complicated society as we have, you have got to have some kind of responsible, representative national authority to define priorities and allocate resources. That we can get government of our backs' and privatize everything is at best an illusion, at worst an invitation for rapacity by selfish private interest..."

"...Now we are part of a complex international economic system- but we lack an institutional context in which we can effectively shape a sense of direction and a sense of responsibility. The privatization of so much of our American way of life is the way of shedding any sense of responsibility for the welfare of the public…"

"…We are *much* more likely to loose our democratic system through printing money, radical deficits, inflation, and the distortion of our economic and political life here at home, than we are through any external aggression by the Russians…"

Michael Parenti: "It has been argued that a strong intelligence system is needed to gather the information needed by policymakers. But the CIA and other agencies have been unlawfully involved in covert actions that go beyond intelligence gathering: economic and military sabotage, disinformation, campaigns directed against the U S public itself, drug trafficking, mercenary wars, assassinations, and other terrorists' acts…" p. 157-8

Fulbright: "…But the America I have believed in cannot last forever in a militarized environment. The greatest threat remains, as it so often have throughout history, form internal follies, not external enemies…"

"In earlier years we spoke a lot in this country about the need to not bankrupt ourselves, of the great strength we had because of our strong balanced economy. The Reagan administration undercut that. Calling itself 'conservative,' the Reagan regime, in a veritable orgy of fiscal radicalism- or 'voodoo economics' –poured funds recklessly and prodigally into the militarization of the entire system…"

Robert Gates from *Duty*: "Nineteen-eighty also saw the beginning of an eight-year war between Iraq and Iran, which began in September with an attack on the Iraqis. The U S approach during the Reagan administration was ruthlessly realistic- we did not want either side to win an outright victory; at one time or another we provided modest covert support for both sides. This effort went off the rails with the clandestine sale of antitank missiles to the Iranians, with the profits secretly being funneled to help the anti-communist Contra Movement in Nicaragua. This was the essence of the Iran-Contra scandal." (p.178).

Turi Munthe: "....in 1992 a congressional inquiry found that President George Bush senior and his top advisors had ordered a cover up to conceal their secret support for Saddam and the illegal arms shipment being sent to him via third world countries. Missile technology was shipped to South Africa and Chile, then 'on sold to Iraq,' while Commerce Department records were altered."

"Meanwhile across the Atlantic, this mirrors the emerging scandal which saw British weapons technology being illegally shipped to Iraq, by way of Jordon being listed as the 'end user' certificates. Within weeks of the Iraqi invasion of Kuwait, the CIA was still funding abundance of intelligence to Bagdad..."

"During the Gulf War Bush senior called on the Iraqi military and the Iraqi people to take matters into their hands and force Saddam to step aside. So successful were they, at first that within two days Saddam's rule had collapsed across southern Iraq, and the popular uprising had spread to the country's city of Basra. Then Washington intervened... the opposition (who were the Kurds) now found themselves confronted with the U S helping Hussein against them..."

"...There were no passionate calls for a military strike after Saddam's gassing of the Kurds in March 1988; on the contrary, the U S and U K extended their strong support for the mass murderer, then he was also 'our kind of guy.' When ABC correspondent revealed the site of Saddam's biological warfare programs 10 months later at Halabaja, the State Department denied the facts; and the story died."

"The two guardians of global order also expedited Saddam's other atrocities- including his use of cyanide, nerve gas, and other barbarous weapons..." (p 392-3).

"...To obtain Security Council votes, the U S... paid nations billions of dollars, provided them arms to conduct regional wars, forgave billions in debts, withdraw opposition to a World Bank loan, agreed to diplomatic relations despite human rights violations and threatened economic and political reprisals. The U S paid the U N $187 million to reduce the amount of dues it owed to the U N; to avoid criticism of its coercive activities."

Don R. Pember: from *Mass Media Law*, p78: "….Because of the censorship there was frequently little important news coming from reporters in the field. To fill their vacuum and satisfy the American appetite for news, the press reported information handed out at news briefings in both Saudi Arabia and the United States. These reports carry the illusion of news, but actually contain little important information. Worse, military briefing officers sometimes give out incorrect or misleading information. Many Americans were shocked after the war to discover how seriously they had been misled by the nation's military leaders…"

"The U N created to end the scourge of war then became an instrument of war and condoned war crimes…"

BIBLIOGRAPHY

INFORMATION SOURCE AND AUTHORS' WORKS CONSULTED

Chapter. 23

Whitney/Whitney: *Carter's Presidential profile:* pages 391, 394, 399. foreign affairs. Footnote 104,105, 106

Chapter 24

Joel Brenner: *Glass Houses,* p. 164

Robert Hughes: ***Culture of Complaint.*** Topic: *Culture and the Broke Polity.* P. 46, 40, 41, 45 footnote 107, 108, 109 110.**Thomas Frank:** ***The Wrecking Crew.*** Topic: *From Paranoia to Pretoria.* P. 103, 102, 104, 105 Apartheid and South Africa. Footnotes 111, 113 **Allen Wheelis:** ***The Moralist.*** Topic: Goodness And Morality. P. 52, 53. footnote 112

Chapter 25

George P. Schultz: Topic: *Revelation: Arms Sales to Iran.* P. 822, 803. NSC Act. Ollie North. P. 848 footnote 113 114,115, 116 117, 118, 121, 131, 132, 134, 135. Grenada, 120, 121, 124

Steven Hayward: Topic, *Executive Privilege.* P. 223. Footnote 133. 136, 137 Iran-Contra

Michael parenti: Topic: *CIA: Capitalism's International Army or Cocaine Import Agency?* P. 156. Footnote 125, 130.

David Hunt: *They Don't Get IT.* Topic: *The Intelligence disaster* footnote 138,139

Whitney/Whitney: Collapse of USSR. Footnote 140, 141

Schultz: Topic: *No Arms For Hostage Deal.*

Edwin Meese III: *Edwin Meese III.* P 294-5, 290, 300, 286

Robert Gates: *Duty.* P. 159, 178

Michael Parenti: Topic: *Watergate and Iran-Contra.* P. 157-8.

Turi Munthe: P. 392-3

Don R. Pember: *Mass Media Law. P.*

PART V

EXPERIENCING

**CHALLENGES AND COPING WITH
AN EMERGENT WORLD DISORDER**

29

CHICKEN IN THE ROUGH, EXPERIENCING

The enormous popularity that Bush had at the end of the Persian Gulf War did not match economic imperatives on the home front. Public interests focused exclusively on the economic malaise caused by voodoo economics. The President did not seem to grasp the immense rippling effect of mismanagement of the domestic economy by dishonest businessmen who were bilking the government billions of taxpayers' dollars to clear their indebtedness. Meanwhile, belief and faith of citizens in their government's ability to demonstrate its military might by the nation's strongest leader of our time- to date, was unquestionable. But more than anything else, he lacked the input and capacity from competent sources to articulate, intimate, and initiate badly needed changes on the home front.

As a consequence, the election of 1992 placed hope in Bill Clinton, a person with no substance, to remedy the internal situation. The soothsayer Democrat President, who played the saxophone to woo his sheep, turns out to be the maturity figure of media propaganda, misguided youth fantasy, and epitome of the immature display of American masculinity- a moral behavior model that the nation needed to heal its economic imperatives, escalating into mass homelessness.

People throughout the nation shouldered economic social strife the best they knew how, in spite of an unresponsive and pleasure-seeking, sociopathic President. Here are a few summaries of character assessments from reliable sources:

"Clinton was, in fact, an untrustworthy low-life who use people for his own purposes and then discard them," (the New York Observer).

A note from lawyer Cliff Jackson, from the book *Blood Sport. Copy,*

297

1996, to Bill Clinton concerning the circumstantial death of Vince Foster read, "....I am talking about your fundamental nature- seemingly in-bred and long-polished- and your casual willingness to deceive, to exploit, and to manipulate in order to attain personal and political power. I am talking about your willingness to compromise principle until there is no longer any principle left to compromise. I am talking about your expectations that others around you practice these same tactics to cover up for you....

...Without trust and integrity there can be no covenant, new or otherwise between the governed. There can be only a perpetuation of the current pandemic distrust and cynicism which now eats like a cancer at the very fabric of our society.... I believe in these values not because they are old, but because they are timeless; not because they are traditional; but because they are true; not because they are American; but because they are universal. Moreover, these values are not the exclusive domain of either Republican or Democratic parties.... Universal values are ideologically neutral...."[i][ii]

From a notable female reporter:

"....The many accusations of sexual misconduct involving Bill Clinton- everything from exposing himself in a hotel room to fondling a woman (in the White House) who desperately needed a job, to rape (when he was Attorney General of Arkansas) were very serious matters..."

"He was an arrogant no good son-of-a-bitch. A dirty rotten scoundrel..." From a managing editor of the Arkansas Democrat-Gazette.[iii]

Realities about the internal structure of American social life surfaced in the most disturbing events that were to unfold during the administration:

Less than a month after Bill Clinton's inauguration in 1993, two Moslem terrorist exploded a bomb in a parking lot under the World Trade Center in New York City on February 26, killing 6 people. They were later convicted and sentenced in1997.

Negotiations were going on for weeks before February 28, 1993 when four members of the American Tobacco and Firearms Bureau were killed at Branch Davidian Compound near Waco, Texas. 33-year-old Vernon Howell, known as David Koresh, leader of the Branch Davidian religious cult was wounded in the action, while two of his followers were killed.

This followed a 51-day standoff before the FBI moved in on April 19. Cult members then set fire to their compound killing more than 80 true believers.

From June of 1994 after the murder indictment of O. J. Simpson, through the time he was acquitted of the charges on October 3, 1995 and beyond, it became a media sensation of exaggerations and extraordinary proportions, overshadowing practically every other meaningful event, and every other hideous and heinous acts by the American people that occurred. Exploited for stereotype ethnic group sexuality, ethnic group hero-worship, the commercial marketing of products, television ratings, and fantasy relations.

Seriously harboring anti-government sentiments, were a trio of Gulf War veterans: 27 year old Timothy McVeigh, Terry Nichols 40, and 27-year old Michael Fortier conspired to blow up the Alfred P. Murrah Federal Building in Oklahoma City.

Around 9am on April 19, 1995 McVeigh parked a rented Ryder truck loaded with ammonium nitrate, (the most active ingredient in his homemade bomb) in front of the building. Two minutes later the bomb was detonated and the truck exploded bringing down the building and 300 others in the immediate area were reported damaged. Over 168 people were killed, and 600 or more injured. This was the deadliest terrorist attack yet, by homegrown Native Americans.

McVeigh was convicted on June 2, 1995, and executed on June 11, 2001. His partner, Terry Nichols was convicted on related charges on December 23, 1995 and sentenced to life imprisonment without parole. Michael Fortier received the lightest sentence of 12 years imprisonment for his connection with the affair.

On the unsettled issue of abortion, John Salvi was convicted in 1996 for the murder of receptionists at two abortion clinics in Brookline, Massachusetts. In 1997 bombs were detonated at abortion clinics in Tulsa, Oklahoma on January 1; in Atlanta on January 16; and again at the first site in Tulsa on January 19.

Looking for another way out of this all-engaging world, on March 23, of 1997 an apparent mass suicide had taken place at Rancho Santa

Fe, California when 39 members of a religious cult called Heaven's Gate were found dead-

Today's youth come of age: In 1998 two kids ages 11 and 13 killed four school girls and a teacher at a Jonesboro AR School.

Also in 1998, the House Judiciary Committee recommended and concurred on Clinton's impeachment, voting 258 to 176 in favor of. Clinton settles suit on November 13, 1998 by agreeing to pay Paula Jones for having made unwanted sexual advance on her in 1991.

On April 20, 1999 two kids, ages 17 and 18, killed 12 fellow students and a teacher at Columbine High School in Littleton, Colorado, then fatally shot themselves.

Falling in line with Clinton's administration's new domestic welfare reform measures, I was among the disadvantaged poor pushed to the fringe of homelessness. Prior to the administration's Welfare Reform measures taking effect in California, welfare for a single person was a safety net in cycles of prolonged unemployment- especially for black males. A disadvantaged recipient could have maintained his/her housing or rental costs, as the person develop skills, or try to find permanent or suitable employment.

The average monthly rental costs for a bachelor-type single unit in Los Angeles, up to this time, was between $300 and $350 in just about any lower middle-class neighborhood in the county. A welfare recipient must do some kind of mandatory work for the county, between 9 to 12 days, and must show proof at the end of each month that the person is actively looking for employment by securing the signature of a potential employer.

The cash grant for an average recipient was about $385 dollars a month. All this changed. With the new reform handed down by the Clinton administration, this cash grant was now reduced to $225 a month and $120 dollars' worth of Food Stamps for a single male recipient.

Landlords don't accept Food Stamps for rent. In fact, you could go to prison for selling or exchanging them things for anything other than food. During this period food stamps used to be issued like coupon books. As a direct result of reduction in cash grant awarded, very few people were able to hang on to their rental units. So the rest naturally fell into homelessness.

Meanwhile, young black males found the welfare cash Grant of $225 appeasable enough to provide an incentive for crack cocaine investment. Decent neighborhoods were then invaded and plagued; attracting converts engaging in the most vulgar forms of behavior that satisfy their mental pleasure cravings. Relatively comfortable and manageable lives were wrecked in weeks, creating a whole new culture of abuse, meanness, and decadence. All moving to the popular and vulgar beat of Hip Crap- so-called "Hip Hop music," movies, videos, and television programming.

In their mental pleasure-seeking pursuits, the reality of homelessness was never a fear for users from middle class families or even the riffraffs. In fact, for the chronic users it was a welcome vacation from a boring existence. These were booming years for niggers in the business of crack cocaine manufacturing, pushing, wheeling and dealing. The vast majority commanding bankrolls of ready-cash money on hand in their pockets.

Both them and the local policemen in my neighborhood- niggers themselves, completely transformed my identity into one of their own making; after serving 3months of jail time for being used in a case of entrapment by a policewoman to solve their so-called "war on drugs" campaign.

(Note: in the overground of political analysis then and now, most Americans, both Democrats and Republicans, believe that the Clinton years were very prosperous and booming years for the overall US economy).

From here on- 1993 through the years 2000, because of that 3-month incarceration, I was never again able to pay my rent on time. I was always at least two-and-half months behind. What a drag on the little guy landlord in them days! Angry. But not more than me for what legal law had done in using me for their own convenience.

Angry? The local law compensation I got was, "we're sorry, we got the wrong guy." This is what the manager had told me the police told him about my arrest and incarceration. Now I am left to pay my rental, and other bills with that!

"We're so sorry."

These were grinding years of real poverty, misery, privation, and humiliation for me. Undergoing radical changes just to maintain or acquire basic necessities of survival. In my distress, I was comforted as being host to dozens of other victims at this hotel-motel, daily-weekly-monthly rental.

The pervasive hopelessness in them and their trust in the local economy of work was aligned with mine. The crucial difference was that I considered mine to be more acute. This gave both management and the local police the idea that I was a dope pusher.

My company at this juncture of my social life were ragged, rejects, and misfits. College professors with PhD's, murderers, thieves, riffraffs, and what-nots- but we were all intimate in self-disclosure. Their futures which thrive in professions, trades, and various work specializations they had acquired or taken up was now going to new Mexican invaders, automation, and the emergent computer world.

There were no immediate answers other than a call for political action, on both state and national levels. The computer world as we know it today was in its transition stage of perfection as a common tool. Frustrations, divorces, dissatisfaction, and discontentment were commonplace around me. Recreational drugs, recreational sex, and recreational sports involvement filled the gap of unemployment or temporary work.

My identity transformation was not so much about the de-skilling processes, immigration, the emerging computer world, nor shaping of the new economy. It was rather about a rejected, struggling, disadvantaged person, doing odd-jobs, and trying to acquire some kind of marketable skill, which I never was able to establish at this point in my social life. In spite of formally being in and out of colleges for about six years, I could never qualify for an entry-level training job in the local job market.

I was just too fucking dumb! I rectum. I mean, reckon.

In any case, this being my true fate at the time, I am now looked upon as a "king pin" crack cocaine pusher of the neighborhood, who can't even afford a rickety $500 car, to drive himself to a job that pays $5-an hour whenever a crumb is handed out of the State Unemployment Office, Casual Labor section, that I hang out at daily!

I would always be found here between the hours of 7am and 10am every work-day of the week when the office would be open, and whenever there were no job offers. Meanwhile, paranoid black rock cocaine users and dealers would drop in and hang around us honest working rejects of industry. They were never interested in work as we were. They just needed a place to hide. And as they hid amongst us, their identities merged with ours.

They often show their bankrolls of cash to prove to any of us that we were really fucking stupid for working at $40 a day, or a few dollars more. Their main gripe for joining our company were cries of *racism* for any who, who was willing to hear. Most of my co-working white buddies were sympathetic and taken by them. The most vexing, angering, and pervasive behavior was their use and abuse of people. In fact, they still do.

The real inside world of my identity was the recreational time I used researching the nature of human existence. At age 38, sometime in 1989, in my very last bout with the heaviest depression I have ever experienced, in my search for the meaning of my own existence. In spite of all adversity and obstacles, my taking up this research turned into trails of discoveries that gave me the urge to publish the harsh realities in the struggle for existence, within the contingencies of human survival, in a state of privation.

I could have stifled with my ragged company, whose only alternatives were to live a subversive form of social life. That is, to add and continue the vicious and unbroken cycles of arrogance, ignorance, decadence, and poverty. This was no alternative for my frustrations, anger, and despair. These choices are way too chancy and suicidal.

It took 19 ½ years of honest self-searching research to write and publish *We Know Who God Is, Country Free USA;* my first book. A book that chronicles and show the nature and nurture of ultimate authority, formal authority, territory, boundaries, power, force, as well as where they or it are vested, and always entrusted. The enterprise of research welcomes every, and anybody. One failure and rejection after another in trying to secure a decent paying job pushed me deeper into the research bag.

Having accepted, acknowledged, and understood the things I could not do from my social position and status by existence, I set out to explore and experiment with what I have learned, attained, what I can do, how to do them, and get results.

There were whores, tramps, decent, law-abiding, reckless, and low-life women- women beyond my deepest imaginary lusts at my disposal; engaging me in all my ultimate sexual bonding fantasies, other than helping me land in an otherwise executive position in government, a private firm, or corporation's board of directors.

To transcend the brewing of resentment, hurt, hatred, suffering, persecution, circumstance, and everything else, I again affirm my complete

Steven Swazo

humanity or status by existence with the dominant contingent forces of my immediate social environment. Making an absolute commitment to subordinate all surrounding circumstance to the success values I had achieved, attained, and embodied up to this point in my social life.

Nobody really gives a damn about what you have accomplished, if and when there is no outward display of some commercially valuable artifact, such as an expensive car, house, barnyard, pig sty, or what-have-you. So, if you haven't accomplish these visual displays of success, then you are a failure. The other display is knowledge. It must be published or shared. Individual fulfillment is then accomplished through affirmations. It is what you can enjoy with what you have accomplished to this point in social life.

Yes. Indeed, emotional resilience is needed and must be developed to maintain psychic health. Especially when we are torn away from the objects, places, people, and goals we esteem and value; consider dear, and meaningful to us. I never surrendered nor gave myself up to the surrounding crack regime and mentality, nor the socially bestowed identity I was living under by the force of my definers.

I used my full intelligence faculty doing social science research, setting myself up to explore the full scope of human existence through written human history, gathering tools and techniques from a vast pool of available knowledge and personal encounters. And most important of all, through this frill of experiencing, there is loss of frustration from failure in achieving goals I once thought to be meaningful.

Patience may be a thing or virtue others would contend to be the central discipline. To me, in most practical situations, that's just an afterthought. No person in a state of privation is ever conscious of being patient. Hunger for the ever-present goal of desire and self-fulfillment just foments deeper. There is no patience there!

What route you're goanna take is the real thing. Creation, destruction, submission, or go along? Research's inherent fulfillment and affirmations gave me the drive and energy to reach one of my main intended goals, successfully accomplished in 2009, the year *We Know Who God Is, Country Free USA* was published. Pushed hard to submission and destruction, I always chose *creation-* not procreation.

30

WHERE IS MA?

Q UALITY CHANGE IS SLOW FOR the enlightened who must live out their lives or great parts of their lives amongst the ignorant poor. What changes for the ignorant poor is not the intensification of quality progress. Rather, it is the exaggeration and multiplication of bullshit-the primitive or elementary state of things, by merely marking time. They ceaselessly pile up confusing dichotomies, ideologies, additions, exaggerations, and intensifications of real, pseudo, or mythological events-the net output of television programming, movies, and every aspect of surface or popular culture.

Economic, political, religious, and associational paradigms or principles through which individuals and people of different ethnic groups have competed for favorable positions and prestige in American social life engenders a kind of status rivalry. This is generally based on common interests, ascending degrees of loyalties of association to rule of law, political, or ideological affiliations. Further, every individual strives to be more than a mere statistic or cog in the production of self and goods.

The enlightened poor who have seen through the illusions and delusions of religions or some other associational paradigm must now re-think the whole foundations of their social lives, or world taken for granted. They must find meaning and purposes in human terms alone. These terms are fundamentally driven by economic necessities. Small wonder, a poll taken around 1979 found that 94% percent of Americans believe in the "invisible hand of God," while only 24% take to regular or routine religious worship.

Although they may not frequent the churches and synagogues, it remains inconceivable for others to abandon their own religion and other non-progressive beliefs, handed down, or inherited from parents and the dictates of other authority figures, artificial, surface, or pop culture that gives them meaning and purpose in social life.

According to Anthropologist Joseph Campbell, "The function of a living mythology is to offer an image of the universe that will be in accord with knowledge of the time, the sciences, and the fields of action of the folk to whom the mythology is addressed." He goes on stating that "In our day, the world pictures of all the major religions are at least two thousand years out of date, and in that fact alone there is ground enough for a very serious break off."

In reference to religious practices today: "They are inviting their flocks to enter and to find peace in a browsing-ground that never was, never will be, and in any case is surely not that of any corner of the world today..."[iv] When major economic conditions and paradigms of carrying-on shifts or breakdown, the "unholy," people like me, center our lives on timeless unchanging principles. One such principle is the practice of science.

People's belief in a God never Changes. And every human being search for a way out when we reach a dead-end. When we reach a dead-end, any *body* or any *thing,* triggered by our full feelings and beliefs, and our inability to do for ourselves, could be, and is often our savior- That God of ours or higher power. And we call it, him, her, or the circumstance God, because it is always more competent than our failing powers.

The scientific method is meant to be progressive and impartial. The inroad to all Gods, their practice and worship, on behalf of none or no religious beliefs. It is the most trustworthy tool, authority, and inroad to all creations, Releasing energies by unlocking the unknown and so-called *secrets* of *nature* and *nurture.* What we know as a species, and what we don't know.

Pseudo-science such as myths, superstition, religion, and art, by contrast are not progressive. Progress is not their purpose. They do not correct the past of their predecessors- they perpetuate them. These cocksuckers, (pseudo-scientists) repeat, interpret, and teach them. Such paragons of the cloth or religious nonsense, and mumbo-jumbos are priests, rabbis, and ministers interpreting and re-interpreting their bibles as God's words.

As Carl Sagan pointed out in his book *The Demon-Haunted World,*

Copy. 1996: "Pseudoscience speaks to powerful emotional needs that science often leave unfulfilled. It caters to fantasies about powerful powers we lack and long for..." It is easier to present pseudoscience to the general public than science, since it is embraced in equal proportion as real science is misunderstood. "Religions are often the state-protected nurseries of pseudoscience..."

In failing powers, "Nancy and Ronald Reagan relied on an astrologer in private and public matters- unknown to the voting public. Some portion of the decision-making that influences the future of our civilization is plainly in the hands of charlatans. If anything, the practice is comparatively muted in America; its venue is worldwide."

The pursuit of education in a specified field of study leads to professional specialization, expertise, the formal or conferred-upon identity of a scientist, expert, or specialist; while other pursuits leads to a greater awareness of, or on the human condition. However, the fact remains that the deeper we probe into the nature of things and events, the more adept and expert we become in handling and using them, and the less we attribute anything to the workings or doings of any kind of religious God for our salvation.

Thus, the general public must be assumed to be a lay authority of the understanding of the works of science, simply by striving to know more about their community or immediate environment. This much could be attributed or credited to positive existence or survival regardless of a person's status. As members to the pact of trustworthy authority, it must also be assumed that each individual on the planet knows a little bit more than the other, in one area of social life or another. This knowledge is the power to enhance social life in whatever form livable.

Inherent power is thus our individual *ability to do.* What you and I know and is able to do. When we can't do, we need the expert, the professional, or the able-bodied-know-how person. Because tentatively, we haven't the least idea, notion, concept, or energy of how to proceed with our tasks, or manage the dilemmas that living conditions are now posing for us in our limited capacity to act.

CLINTON'S GLORY YEARS

Disturbance theory claims that only when human interests and valued resources are threatened in the social and economic environment, or in government policy, the formation of interest groups seems to happen. In my case of severe privation it happened. I became the center, sort of a neighborhood psychologist to a ragged company of structurally unemployed peer group members, undermined by illegal migration and deskilling process brought on by technology.

Some were well-educated, some divorced, others from broken homes or decent family life, some searching for a niche, a new career, or a clear-cut foreseeable pattern in which they can reorganize their social lives and continue to live and grow. There is the desperate need to be wanted for their various skills, work, and type of professions, to earn an income, feel worthy and competent of themselves again. Their anxieties tweaked with a need for orientation and training in the emergent economy.

It was a long-ass, dull, grueling, aching pain during those Clinton years when tangible material benefits and options for opportunities for people on the home range living on a fringe of the economy dwindled, and became almost non-existent. While the new illegal immigrants burgeoned and prospered.

Values of solidarity in sharing the taboos of society, such as the benign use of recreational drugs, and free consensual sexual encounters; frequent discussions of ideologically oriented issues surrounding the nation's people' heroic deeds- a few exaggerated, became stale and pastime conversations.

Sporadic employment and watching ball games became a substitute pastime for me and my disenfranchised interest group, or ragged company. These activities compensated for our inadequacies, frustrations, and allayed our anxieties about our uncertain, fucked-up economic future.

During these high periods of uncertainties for lower working-class citizens, and prosperous times for those who benefitted immensely on the other side of the social coin, one source claim that the greatest single act of statesmanship that Clinton accomplished in his two administrations was the vision of an economic free trade area stretching from Canada through Mexico.

The outgoing Bush administration had signed an agreement of open boarders of trade between the two countries, but needed Congressional approval to get the deal going. In spite of fierce opposition from the AFL-CIO, which would have been enough to kill the agreement, Clinton and his staff pressed on to convince Congressional Democrats to support the agreement.[v]

There were widespread sentiments that this would result in an unabated flow of illegal Mexicans and other undocumented illegal immigrants flowing into the United States. Californians passed proposition 187 because of illegal immigrants', including their offspring's impact on all aspects of its economy. Anti-immigrant sentiments were ebbing at its highest levels of intolerance by citizens who voted for some forms of government action.

The widespread notion that American manufacturing plants and jobs would move toward cheaper labor, which Mexico has an endless supply of was a fact; as the rust belt states continued to lose manufacturing plants. This overall threat to the national economy was not posed by Canada.[vi]

Compounding alienation of working-class Americans was convergence of information into the emergent computer technology and telecommunications, forming a global economy. The making of this new economy has been, and is, competition for the best information- sniveling; replacing farmlands, coal mines, or mineral deposits. "The rules, customs, skills, and talents necessary to capture, produce, preserve, and exploit information are now humanity's most important," states Walter Writson.

The new wave technology requires a reevaluation of moral values, ideas, culture, its institutions, and political structure; implying a transformation and some forms of upheaval in human affairs. We cannot go back to our customary ways of doing business. The conformity, uniformity, bureaucracy, and the forces of yesterday's consensus just doesn't exist anymore.

The former laxity in uniformity has turned into a globally diversified hustle-market. Arising from the fact that the entire human quest in social life has been, and still is *to know*, because if we know we can foresee, remedy, build, avoid, and we will always be right- Information, images, symbols, culture, ideology, and values are now the central resource of society's *knowledge-based* system. It is not that a knowledge-based system is anything new in human affairs. In fact, this has always been the case going back to our most primitive human ancestors.

We ourselves have borne witness to human progress in our time, demonstrating that for example, one of the main reason nations used to ship huge amounts of their raw materials across the planet to other nations is mostly because they lacked the *knowledge* to convert their local materials into usable substitutes. Once that know-how is acquired, there are drastic savings, monetary, employment boom, and so on in that nation state.

While land, labor, raw materials, and capital can be regarded as finite resources, *knowledge* is for all intents inexhaustible. The new changes in society's knowledge-based system is the most pervasive part of every firm environment- more than the banking system, political system, or energy system. There is the deeper fact that of all the resources needed to create wealth, none is more versatile than *knowledge*. "The new technology will not go away- it will only get better in accordance with Moore's Law, which postulates that microchips will double in density and speed every 18 months. Bandwidth will grow even faster,"[vii] according to Writson.

MORE OF THOSE PROSPEROUS YEARS

Besides the goof with NAFTA, what else did Bill Clinton accomplish in the eight years that he was President? "He encouraged 10 of the worst accounting scandals of all time if there is one thing to rival terrorism...." In the management of business and finance, his massive permissive deregulation created a speculation boom. Enron, a company that deals in energy, and WorldCom in telecommunications "became poster children of speculative havoc that created illusory earnings during the boom....The energy and telecommunications sector issued roughly one trillion dollars' worth of new debt...[viii]

To ship to Mexico tens of billions to pay off his bond holders at Citibank and Goldman Sachs, President Clinton had to act by executive order. This deal represents our first payment on NAFTA and GATT. "The looting of America on behalf of the new world order has begun," states Kevin Philips. "This deal isn't a loan. It isn't an investment in the future. It is a $48billion wash rag to wipe the egg off the faces of the politicians who marched us into NAFTA and GATT."

Presidential candidate Pat Buchanan had declared: "....the infamous bailout of the Mexican peso have resulted in the continued surrender of American sovereignty to the institutions of the new world order.... an order defined and administered by the bureaucratic minions as the World Trade Organization, the Trilateral Commission, the Council of Foreign Relations, and the United Nations."[ix]

Some goofy political actions were handed down to the nation on Clinton's way out:

Their concessions took in some $ 7 billion. Both Marc Rich and Picus Green, aluminum and oil traders were indicted in a case called the largest tax fraud in US history pulled off on the IRS. Both men fled the country, while Clinton turned down all deals that would have had both fugitives returned to US authorities. In this interim, Marc Rich's ex-wife lobbied the president while he and Picus Green stayed out of shooting range- giving more than "$1.5million to causes related to the Clintons.... She loaded the Clintons with gifts, including a gold saxophone...." and both IRS fugitives got their pardon.[x]

Is this a political conscience of national leadership? Or is this a moral Crack/ rock to smoke? ".....They robbed banks, killed police officers, and bombed the US Capitol, the Naval College, the FBI office in Staten Island and other targets.... Rosenberg was apprehended with 740 pounds of explosives and an arsenal of weapons. She was sentenced to fifty-eight years in prison. ...Clinton not only granted Rosenberg clemency but also commuted the sentence of Linda Sue Evans, convicted in the 1983 plot to bomb the capitol."[xi]

In September of 1999 Clinton gave clemency to fourteen members of the FLAN organization, a Puerto Rican homegrown terrorist group responsible for more than 130 bombings and attacks in the country from 1974 through 1983, killing 6 Americans and wounding scores of others. The FBI and Attorney General opposed their release. Clinton choose to bypass the Justice Department, felt no sympathy, compassion, or sense of duty to consult with any of the victims surviving relatives, and gave clemency to fourteen of the sixteen members of the terrorist organization.[xii]

With radical change in the nation's overall economic structure, certain skills became obsolete overnight. Large numbers of the middle class, including highly trained people, find themselves thrown out of work and legitimate opportunities. All aspects of social life being so, things went much, much better with the national cocaine use epidemic that empowered a low-life class of black rock-cocaine pushers.

Lower middle class tensions were also kept cool with the commutation of the sentence of Carlos Vignali, the son of Horacio Vignali, a wealthy Los Angeles developer and major donor to Democratic politicians. His *misdemeanor* crime was for shipping nearly half a ton of cocaine to Minneapolis for processing into the niggers' delight-Crack.[xiii]

"Headache", his half-brother Roger Clinton, as the Secret Service dubbed him, also got pardoned for his conviction in the cocaine business. He was once a driver for Dan Lasater, said to be a restaurant magnate and cocaine distributor whom Bill Clinton had once pardoned while he was governor of Arkansas.[xiv]

And a little something more about our exalted leader's moral behavior: Bill Clinton's blow-job modeling affair with Monica Lewinsky and other women in the White House, led to his impeachment as President of the United States on December 19, 1998. His wife Hillary Clinton, who would later seek the presidency twice, went on national TV blaming the whole Lewinsky blow-job affair as a "vast Right-wing conspiracy." And what did Bill had to say for himself?

"I tried to walk a fine line between acting lawfully and testifying falsely, but I now recognize that I did not fully accomplish this goal, and that certain of my responses to questions about Ms. Lewinsky were false."[xv]

Well Bill, em niggers love you- black, white, and everything in between, and they never give up on you and your wife Hillary to be America's first ruling dynasty.

TOWARD THE NEW ECONOMY

For about seventy-five percent of the American workforce, activities of the new wave global economy has become widespread, nationwide, dramatic, and irreversible. The storms of takeovers, divestitures, mergers, consolidations, reorganizations, start-ups, joint ventures, and internal reorganizations- the entire economy takes on a new structure that is diverse, fast-changing, and more complex. It is unintelligible to most Americans how their country has been invaded, and how even members of lowest class have lost our once cherished manageable independence.

The globalization of business and finance routinely rupture and erode this national sovereignty that we once held so dear, pushing our accomplishments into insignificance. Our values, standards, and meaning to social life are vigorously challenged by the uncontrolled flow and birthrate of invading migrations.

With the nation's industrial knowledge-base dominance and increasing stagnation of the Middle class, restless capital can no longer find a lucrative return in investments that produced real tangible wealth that could be sold abroad or consumed at home, so innovative ways were found to pump up the phony value of image and assets, and more business fled to different countries. The structurally unemployed, deskilled, other hangers-on, had more than their share of economic malaise, because of enforced idleness, and a lowered standard of living that now began to upset the balance of meaningful social life they are accustomed to.

Several features of the new global economy now limits the role of older, ordinary working-class citizens' participation, because standardized use of a home computer had not quite come into its own until the beginning of 2000. The lay's thinking about the global economy was dumbed-down, not serious, and was directed more at the rampant examples of corporate manipulation and failures in trade, oil, oil, oil, and more fucking oil.

Meanwhile, hideous crimes, new wave of mass murders, the influx of refugees, mass migration from third world countries, beginning with Mexico- their sheer complexity as a distinct social force, and remoteness from familiar everyday social life began to stifle the relatively free-flow of familiar relations amongst members of the host culture, placing an undue burden and strain, with more and more falling out of the labor force.

31

BUSH-CHENEY

OIL-BASED FOREIGN POLICY PERSISTED UNDER the Clinton administration. Major attacks with aircrafts and cruise missiles were launched in Iraq in January and June of 1996, and in December of 1998. Troops were also deployed near its boarders in 1997 and 1998 with Operation Phoenix Scorpion and Desert Thunder, when Bagdad dropped oil concessions to Russia, China, and France. The administration signed the Iraq Liberation Act of 1998 on October 31, calling for a regime change.

Two months earlier, Clinton signed off on a finding that accused So Damn Insane of building chemical weapons and others of mass destruction, of failing to cooperate with the United Nations, and "being in material and unacceptable breach of its international obligations." This insistence was essential to keeping Hussein hogtied by United Nations' sanctions, and was thus able to implement the oil concessions it dropped.[xvi]

If the outgoing Clinton Presidential leadership proved that we were a nation of people who are as promiscuous as dogs, the incoming Bush-Cheney administration proved that we could also be technically chaste. The impact of religion on domestic policy—making became intense. Religiosity became the Republican Party's badge of honor and hallmark "for linking policy statements to scripture and prophecy. ....By 2001, theology- the yardstick of belief, not judgment- began to displace logic and realpolitik in official Washington..."[xvii] asserted one Senator.

While in the Senate, Senator John Ashcroft, later nominated and confirmed by the administration as Attorney General, successfully authored legislation to let the states turn over welfare and other social services to religious providers. As former Governor of Texas, Bush had embraced this legislation which he, now as President, proposes for federal faith-based institutions.

"Where possible, religious agencies would take over the provision of social services." When this measure stalled in the Senate, Bush used his executive order to establish faith-based initiative units in the departments of Justice, Education, Health and Human Service, Housing and Urban Development, Labor, and Agriculture.[xviii]

"....The GOP increasingly fell under the influence of theocratic fundamentalist eager to use the resource of the state to regulate private behavior, and of neo-conservative chicken-hawks, some of them ex-Democrats- who never saw a war they didn't want somebody else's kid to fight."[xix]

Bush's administration embraced an "oil forward" policy with instant intensity in the early summer of 2001. Plans were discussed for "convincing the Taliban in Afghanistan to accept construction of an American pipeline for UNOCAL from Turkmenistan through Kabul- to Karachi, Pakistan. Talks continued through the summer of 2001, but later collapsed. Multiple sources suspected a double-dealing was in the catbirds seat. And indeed. ".... Washington had the American government planning to attack Afghanistan sometime in autumn. And Clinton's 'regime change' in Iraq became code for a second invasion."[xx]

Then came a dramatic surprise, when the world as we know it, changed. Besides intensifying existing oil pursuits and the application of Mid-Eastern pressures- September 11th, the day of the attack on the Pentagon and World Trade Center, gave Washington an all-inclusive commitment and justification: "Fighting terror was about everything, and everything was about fighting terror..."

"If you ever wondered how the United States come to be embroiled simultaneously in two major wars and half dozen covert ones in the past decade (since 2002)," Senator Lofgren continued, "the cheerleading of Washington's laptop commandos, with their disproportionate influence in major media, has been a major factor. .... During 2002 and 2003, right up to the Iraq invasion, the flow of secrets became a geyser. A very serious matter...yet, somehow that didn't matter when the objective was to provide a pretext for war. The deeper injury.... lay in the flood of cues about US intelligence operations recklessly revealed by the Bush administration during its advertising blitz. The official conclusions that justified the pretext for war were of course nonsense..."ˣˣⁱ

There was no question that the value of Afghanistan transcended the oil pipeline issue. With the collapse of the Soviet Union, "It has become an important potential opening to the sea for the landlocked new states of Central Asia. The presence of large oil and gas deposits in the area has attracted countries and multinational corporations, Russia, China, not to mention Pakistan and India."

In turn, American policy represented certain geopolitical beliefs connected to the economic interests of particular groups; while its "foreign policy elite saw a need for the United States to dominate Central Asian energy resources as it had dominated the Persian Gulf oil fields. ....But control of the area would also enhance US global power, and such control was thus a critical part of a geostrategic strategy to maintain global primacy."ˣˣⁱⁱ

OUR WAR INVOLVEMENT

According to former Secretary of Defense Robert Gates: "We had no idea of the complexity of Afghanistan- tribes, ethnic groups, power brokers, village, and provincial rivalries.... and our initial objectives were unrealistic. And we didn't know that either. Our knowledge and our intelligence were woefully inadequate."

"....When we landed, I couldn't help but reflect that a little over twenty years before, as Deputy Director of the CIA, I had been on the Pakistani side of the boarder looking into Afghanistan and doing business with some of the very people we were fighting now. It was a stark reminder to me of our limited ability to look into the future or foresee the unintended consequences of our actions."

On the invasion of Iraq: "The façade of Saddam's regime misled us with regard to what we were letting ourselves in for...."

"....From early on we had underestimated the resilience and determination of our adversaries as the situation on the ground changed for the worse- In Afghanistan it was- and is- a massive endeavor made significantly more difficult because no one knew what anyone else was doing. Each country and organization worked strictly within its own sector on its own projects. There was very little sharing of information on what was working or not, little collaboration, and virtually no structure....

"Decades of rule by Saddam Hussein who didn't give a damn about the Iraqi people; the eight-year long war with Iran; the destruction we wreaked during the Gulf War; 12years of harsh sanctions- all those meant we had virtually no foundation to build on in trying to restart the economy, much less create a democratic Iraqi government responsive to the needs of its people...." xxiii

Former US Army Colonel David Hunt: "I am a soldier, trained to be a manager of violence; I'm a killer with two college degrees and a year at Harvard. I am a Ranger, Paratrooper, and Mechanized and Special Forces qualified officer with more than twenty-nine years of service to his country. I have been sent all over the world. I have led men and women in peace and war. I have worked with our national intelligence services and such amazing men as Navy SEALs, Rangers, and Special Forces. I am one of them and proud of it. We are the ones charged with killing the bad guys, we have lain in wait for days and killed them. We have hunted them down and killed them. We have dropped bombs on them and killed them. That's what we do. We kill bad guys..."

The situation: These people we support tend to be from fanatical Muslim religious schools called Madrasses that "have only one purpose: they Create Islamofascists. That is, they make terrorists and disguise them as religious nut jobs."

"These guys don't think like us. To understand the nature of our enemy, you have to understand what they believe; and to do that, you have to look at their guiding principle."

"It was never a question that the United States would win the war in Afghanistan and Iraq; neither country had an army worth a damn. What was in question was how many soldiers we would need to keep that peace in both countries once the military victory was realized. And now it is crystal clear that the United States blew it on this one."

"Put bluntly, thousands of men and women have died because of the misguided, arrogant, and immensely stupid decisions not to take the Generals recommendations."

"Leading takes guts, something in short supply with those who left Rumsfeld's office with their balls cut off and went to war with a plan they knew was wrong...."

"....General John Abizaid, the MMC.... (Main motherfucker in charge) has two days of actual fighting in Grenada. General George Casey, the head guy in Iraq has.... let me count them.... zero days in combat...."

In spite of this command "it took less than three weeks for our soldiers to get to Bagdad, many of my great friends, soldiers with whom I have served were among the first into Iraq and Bagdad, and they have told me over and over that there was no plan for the peace. .... Generals, Colonels, Captains, Sergeants, Navy SEALS, Special Forces soldiers, you name it.... They say they weren't given a scintilla of guidance of what to do once they won the war. They never had any doubt that they would win, but none of them were told what to do the morning after."

So Damn Insane abdicated, was captured, tried, and hanged by his people's court. American-educated Ahmed Chalabi was elected to be the new leader of Iraq. This guy, according to Colonel Hunt, "someday somebody will produce a made-for-TV movie about the whole situation, how we come to love, hate, then just tolerate Ahmed Chalabi while turning Iraq into a chaotic mess."

"The truth is what we got from this guy is what we should have expected- screwed. Sleeping with devil gets you horns in the ass all the time." [xxiv] – Colonel David Hunt.

Gates: ".... We have never gotten it right. Not in Grenada, Haiti, and Panama, Libya (twice) Iraq (twice), Afghanistan, the Balkans, or Somalia.... We need a lot more humility" [xxv]

32

RADICAL CHANGE & THE GOD BUSINESS

W ORLD-WIDE COMMUNICATION AND INFORMATION EXCHANGE, its efficiency, transparency, being almost instant with full-blown images, has now dramatically transformed our consciousness, compelling us to surrender part, or even all our sovereignty, and to accept increasing tensions from one another, willy-nilly. This database underlies what has become universally accessible as a global enterprise, with *information* being the universal solvent of secrecy, causing the erosion of barriers and boundaries- legally, behaviorally, electronically, in language or speech, in public and private interaction, decorum, and so on.

We are now stuck with two giant waves of change in the United States that it is increasingly becoming difficult to sort out meanings from the conflicts that arise. The massive wave and blitzes of information and misinformation exchange through the internet, social media, twitter, and other new wave mediums is one thing.

The other is the unprecedented flow of refugees, illegal migration and their proliferation of children as an industry all by itself, specifically in California, and their presence as a competing language and culture, rather than an assimilating one. This is invasion. Migration without assimilation. These two elements of dramatic change has been creating social tensions, dangerous conflicts, and is producing strange new ideologies that cuts across traditional bonds of class, ethnic groups, gender, political party affiliations, and all our loyalties.

Former NSA intelligence and counterintelligence director, Joel Brenner notes that "Within the American security establishment, the vocabulary of conflict is also warlike in the absence of declared war; we are stocked with self-declared cyberwarriors who for the most part are not soldiers in the usual sense, but geeks employed by a military or intelligence organization..."

Brenner further talk about the blurring which creates genuine confusion about who is a soldier and who is not. Who is an American citizen and who is not. Simply by being in possession of a hand-held computer, rather than tanks, artillery, and grenade launchers. The geeks are equipped with computer viruses and microrobots as the tools of warfare and invasions.

Resulting collisions sharply affect differing needs of two radically different civilizations. (*Civilization* as meant here, is how we become citizens in a culture, which in this case is our Americanization). This "could provoke some of the worst bloodshed in years to come," noted Alvin Toffler in 1995. It is a condition that has created a mockery of the familiar mirrors of political personalities and authority figures through which we once align and integrate ourselves. The collusion of both major political parties not to enforce immigration rules and laws have mostly hurt lower working-class Americans in more than a thousand-and-one ways.

When rules and laws are made in the interest of one social group or category of people, the host culture's civil rights are encroached upon. There is no way around it.

There is the splintering of a younger generation of the middle-class, drawn by a blend of personal alienation from meaningful and tangible models of orientation and relationships. What they absorb like sponges are synthetic TV, Videos, and motion picture heroes and heroines. Resultant effects are shallow idealism, a propensity to embrace the cause of any mass movement of discontent that may arise out of boredom, the lack of a coherent sense of identity, and the need for excitement in their restless empty social lives. A need for belonging, or being a part of something greater than themselves. And believe me, this is a major one. As media shapes their image of the world with toxic disinformation, it simultaneously hinder their capacity to feel, think, and act properly.

The unemployed and distraught who have lost their faith in the economy, have also lost their certainty that their lives are significant. Having inherited the kingdom of this world they sought, they are dissatisfied and haunted by the need to believe in something that is lasting.

Their loss of cohesion, vitality, and creative powers is followed by uncertainty, and with uncertainty, a loss of balance, since social life demands life- supporting and sustaining illusions. Where these have been dispelled something secure is needed to hold on to. They then give credence to the cries of preachers for conversion and a return to the old religion- giving rise to vice, crimes, disorders, addiction, and suicides.

Alternative information pathways that the internet and other modern-day mediums provide, tend to bypass older structures of exercising self-restraint, control, and command- further lacking any unifying purpose of shared citizenship with peers, elders, or members of their own host culture.

This new wave of social splintering is quite similar to the wave of disunity brought on during the late sixties and early seventies when psychology, sociology, and philosophy became prominent sciences, validating a mass institution in the study of lesser known unpopular religions and spiritual views of other cultures, which were once taboo, that now provided coherent pathways to identity formation and purpose. These evoked an exciting and dramatic shift of perceptions, pursuit, and adjustments that produced radical alternative pathways of being in our society. These were the new seeds of my generation who are today's children's' fathers and mothers.

What had been a fervent prayer to an unseen deity to solve the nation's problems became angry shouts at political and institutional leaders. Behind all the display of the nation's power and wealth, there was something that is commanding as it is substantial. These were new sets of ideas, attitudes, and convictions, with the confidence that the ideas and convictions generated were viable.

Those who tried to maintain and defend the old status quo, responded with continuous polarization of viewpoint toward the emerging change in the crystallization of events that they saw and interpreted as runaway chaos and uncertainty- even to the total dis integration of their entire ways of social life. For them, the Bible's prophecies were to be understood literally in some quarters. What this progressive generation of traditional American views saw in the uncertainty of those days was the long awaited apocalypse preparing to descend on our ass.

As a Judeo-Christian society, the Bible is usually held up to us as our ultimate source of morality. But where else should we go, or what else should we look up to, in search of a higher power and impartial reasoning, considering the national chaos that was marred with protests, anger, and mean violence in trying to right the prevailing injustice?

Is the Bible story of the destruction of Jericho and the invasion of the Promised Land morally distinguishable from Hitler's invasion of Poland, Saddam Hussein massacres, or the notorious and odious business of the CIA?

Absolutely not! Evil has no independent existence. It is merely the negation or absence of good.

Laws can be moral. They can also be immoral- and usually they are. All human-made laws, including the many attributed to God, (and not those fixed in *nature*) have a dual relationship in the living conscience of the human world. Their relative value of good and bad, good and evil, right and wrong, are all culturally defined, conventionally expedient and biased, with no universal agreement on any specific human act.

If we were to insist on connecting morality with justice and the law, as we often do, then we would have to be willing to admit, or state that at least prior to 1865 in the United States, slavery was moral, according to (Article IV, Section II, Clause III of the Constitution). The moral conscience of our American norms are derived from our interpretation of the constitution.

MORE ABOUT THE GOD BUSINESS

Humans are driven hard to seek meaning- even in an otherwise considered immoral system. And meaning can only be found by discovering a necessary relation between our lives and whatever forms of undesirable irritability our human environment is offering us. As we have seen throughout human history, and still bear witness to today: divine ordination can breed very dangerous ideas, beginning with the justifications of slavery, and today the gruesome Moslem's ideology that is with us.

There is no stronger belief position on which people are immovable as their religious faiths or ideas. Further, every, and anything could be incorporated into a religious faith, with reference and proof of the most pious reasoning in their tenets of belief.

Every one of us make a stand in social life, and that stance is an unquestionable belief we confide in- whatever the consequence may be-win, lose or draw. This stance is religious by nature. This stance is individual. This stance is our true religion.

Civilizations everywhere interpret their own symbolic figures literally, regarding ourselves as favored in a special way of being in direct contact with the absolute- our ethnic group, country, nation, state, or locale. The youth, as well as the innocent truth livers and seekers of society will discover that "....it has always been on myths that the moral orders of society have been founded, canonized as religion..." and many other forms of moral concepts and precepts, according to anthropologist Joseph Campbell. The human mythic imagination represents facts of the body-mind; while this body-mind is made manifest in a fictional manner such as a book, narrative, work of art, or film production.

This is the *God of forms* that dominate us throughout our entire lives. According to the blueprint of the US Constitution, we can all aspire and be a part of this goddamn *God forming* enterprise, if we are successful at making a living. Regardless of what we may produce, these facts of the human body-mind, which are *God of Forms,* or goods, must reckon with the social world's outward order of facts- what already exist as common currency of exchange, and what is culturally beneficial. Like growing corns or wheat, producing logic or illogic.

Continuing throughout all of human history, the majority of us, irrespective of country, nation, state, locale, or human gathering have always been dominated by a relatively small number of persons producing these God-forms or goods we consume. People who understand the mental processes and social patterns of masses, are the ones "who pull the wires which controls the public mind,"[xxvi] noted Marshal McLuhan. Vast numbers of human beings must cooperate in the dominant organized forms that this minority class dictate in virtually every act of our social lives, ethical thinking, conduct, business, work, or politics. And mainly through needed consumption.

This minority social class and category of people, because of their dominant social and economic hold and endurance in any society, it is, and has become exclusively *the place* where everybody else below struggle to be.

Our habits, collected from almost any commercial action of

consumption today, provides a wide variety of information on our buying patterns and lifestyle choices- from buying groceries to buying cars. This information provides fodder for the conscious and intelligent manipulation of our random and organized habits, consensus, and opinions. "Those who manipulate this unseen mechanism of society constitute an invisible government which is the true ruling power of our country..."[xxvii] observes John C. Stauber and Sheldon Rampton in their book *Toxic Sludge Is Good For You.*

MORALITY & MEDIA-POLITICS

Countless research, as well as authors, and journalists have claimed that there is a gullible side to the American people by which we can easily be misled, and religion is the best device used to mislead. Since invoking God as the highest base of morality has always been a habit of American Presidents throughout our nation's history, within narrow or the widest breath of understanding to their audience "....George W. Bush made a specialty of it... With God's approval you need no human standard of morality."

And believe me, this God business bugged the fuck out of me. From the beginning of the Clinton era, when strings of hideous crimes were being committed nationwide, by perpetrators who were pardoned in one form or another, but deserved eternal imprisonment or the death penalty, blaming it all on their Christian beliefs and image of God that inspired them to do what they actually did. It was no small wonder that the title of my first book morphed into *We Know Who God Is, Country Free USA.* Country-Free USA is predicated on our national consensus- which is the *US Constitution*, reached by the nation's founders, with respect to the *Old World* dominant orders, working philosophies, and ideologies.

Since time immemorial, humans have continuously justify their most hideous, insane, barbaric, heinous, egregious acts and behavior in the name of their religious God and beliefs. Here is Adolph Hitler, world renown as one of the world's most compassionate and hideous figures, as compared to Josef Stalin and Vladimir Lenin, who slaughtered more than 80 million Russians.

Perhaps influenced by Martin Luther, since Martin Luther is said to have been "virulently anti-Semitic," Hitler is herd repeating several times that he was a Christian: "My feeling as a Christian points me to my Lord and Savior as a fighter... Today, I believe that I am acting in accordance with the will of the mighty creator by defending myself against the Jew, I am fighting for the work of the Lord...." Nazi storm troopers had "Got mit uns" inscribed on their military belts- meaning, God be with us.[xxviii]

Taking it for granted that at least 94% of Americans believe in a God or higher power, and at least 75% make no connection between religion and their judgment of right and wrong is commendable. What it means is that we have a greater population of people, however misled, whose judgments are based on intelligent choices, actual social events, experiences, and interaction with other humans, rather than on a mysterious, imagined religious God doing the calling of what each of us is designated to do. It is what Allen Wheelis has referred to as *negative morality*.

"Negative morality accepts the existence of strangers, knows that there will always be a "they," that "we" and "they" will be divided at times on the most basic issues, unable to agree on the nature of good. Because of the inevitability of such decisions and opposition, negative morality urges the mutual acceptance of abstract rules of fair conduct in order that individuals and groups of divergent values, and conflicting purposes may live together without destroying each other."[xxix]

Is this not the purpose of all our written laws? If not, wherever you find them, they must be repealed and replaced. Take Action!

Although existing side-by-side by contrast, *Positive morality* is based on human groups and groupings. By their very organization's structure, norms, consensus, or conscience, they cannot stomach or tolerate strangers. A baseball team, college football team, social club, some corporations or companies, cliques, gangs, some churches, some agencies in law enforcement and so on, are common social structures, groupings, institutions, or systems that employ or practice *positive* morality. For them to remain cohesive, or exclusive as a social group or organization, all members must subject themselves to the regulatory norms of the social group, grouping, business, or organization to meet its expectations and objectives. Otherwise, they would not exist.

In other words, even in the absence of religion, in-group and out-group hostilities will always exist. One explicit purpose of the existence of American government rule and its preference for law has always been to neutralize hostilities and provide avenues for further negotiations of hostile relations and contentious issues. As pointed out earlier, true democracy is compatible with science, as in a court's decision when all relevant facts to be considered are in.

Negative morality as in a decision made in the rule of law exist outside the realm of social institutions and human organizations with restricted or loose boundaries, allowing an individual to act more freely once he or she have met their contracts, commitments, or obligations inside their grouping.

Goddamit! I'm free from work. I can do what I want now! How many times have you felt this way?

The "we" these wide variety of human organization and institutions exude is one of exclusiveness requiring certain commitment from their members, and does not include all other members of society, but would like its "we" feelings to prevail for all the rest of the members of society. The positive morality of social groups, groupings, and organizations, and their endurance through time are ever-dependent on loyalties, allegiances, and practices. Their growth further depends on positive rewards that members draw.

None of us as members of society outgrow our need for a place of refuge. That is, a social grouping that shares our individual concerns and needs. This definition of home is a place of belonging and growth. It is a place where we enjoy our status by existence- what we have accomplished and now wish to accomplish, a place for repose and comity. The knowledge and feeling of playing a useful part in the human community. For those looking for one, and have never been able to win one in any satisfying way, some status of accomplishment of esteemed value, the longing to establish their identity as something more than a statistic, or labor unit of sale is indeed overbearing.

The drag and pull back for many toward the old okay elementary way of home existence as in childhood socialization is often strong and irresistible. There are endless varieties of ready-made fantasies provided by mass media too. Believable myths that have been perpetuated through ignorance, envy, or the desire to control the lives of others. The vain search for power or competence. Their easy, available and accessible consumption will now allow the powerful creative *godhead* producers of *God-forms* to germinate in a fertile breeding ground of "another brick in the wall," another dunderhead, another arrested development.

We are not eager to be fooled nor deceived. But if we are unconsciously, or uncritically following popular mass media publications, manias, and delusions, then we have set ourselves up for it. Marshal Mc Luhan alerted us to the fact generations ago that, "once we have surrendered our senses and nervous system to the private manipulation of those who would try to benefit from taking a lease on our eyes, ears, and nerves, we don't really have any sense of rights left,"ˣˣˣ more so, a solid sense of identity.

The most popularly and frequently mentioned and shown things will sway our attention and awareness. This American citizen now lives in a world where fantasy is more real than reality; where images carry more dignity than their original contextualization- all from being bombarded or blitzed with well-researched means of attraction, ambiguous forms of truths, and sentiments that thrives on the viewer's, listener's, or reader's sensibilities and honest desires to be informed of all the facts.

In the end, these presentations only harp on the factual basis on which an individual, social grouping, or target audience are supposed to make up their minds. The rest of the content of the messages and information are superfluous, meaningless, and are mere attractions, for cajoling and soft-soaping the consumer into compliance or acceptance.

"The mainstream media's toxic symbiosis with our entrenched political parties, and the permanent shadows of government, have made it difficult for the average American to assemble an accurate and coherent picture of the world, much less make informed judgment about our foreign and national security policies..." states Mike Lofgren in *The Party Is over.*

The unanimity of this statement among the common populace is indeed staggering. Since, the Judicial, political, military, academic or pro-active scientific enterprise, and the all-encompassing mediums of communication have misled and misinformed us on many occasions. Others, having vested interests in doing so, have deliberately betrayed our senses and better thinking.

Each of us are now left with an independent faculty to cultivate for ourselves new forms that match our needs and social realities. The cry to return to biblical revelations and elementary non-issues of importance are indeed strong for the incompetent. Science as a habit of thinking is the only tool-kit readily available for recognizing twaddle, nonsense, and cruelty that prey on those least able to protect or defend themselves; people most in need of our compassion, and those offered very little hope.

"...If we don't practice these tough habits of thought (which are the principles of science), we cannot hope to solve the truly serious problems that face us- and we risk hope to solve the truly serious problems that faces us- and we risk becoming a nation of suckers, a world of suckers for grabs for the next charlatan who saunters along," states Carl Sagan.

33

ARABIAN WEDDING, US STYLE

SINCE 9/11, TERRORISM, AN OFFSHOOT of mass murders; (I'm not really sure if here is any difference between the two), has replaced communism as the nation's number one international and domestic enemy, as well as its justifications for re-tooling its defense apparatus. Terrorist groups or individuals, mostly Moslems today, or those who associate themselves with the religion, win support from young idealists frustrated with their inability to bring change in their country. While others seek revenge for the havoc our nation has wreaked in their country, and personal ways of social life.

Further, there are individual members who subscribe by vows or fantasy, and want to change the remainder of the human world they have, or have not experienced through failure, incompetence, or loss of expected esteem among their human communities. A loss from the once okay feelings and sensations of their personal cultural institutional socialization. Something every growing swinging dick or cunt would like to have and retain forever!

Incidentally, to these Moslem cultural socializations, whatever they inherit and sew in their beliefs, and however ooold or ancient these claims may point to, from the initial formation of the United States as a distinct culture with its own form of constitution serving as the supreme law of the land- every immigrant, regardless of religious belief or practice, instinctively know that from the moment they step on U S soil, they have stepped into a complete time zone of freedom, restrictions, and tolerance, quite different from their own, or the ones they are accustomed to.

The real Moslem avengers, such as Bin Laden, have witnessed "Patterns of covert operations undertaken mainly by the CIA, and eventually our own military involvement, (in other cultures) have often disclose a general disregard for the sovereign rights of other people, justified in part as being a wider struggle with Russia or national security." Noted Richard Falk, *Revolutionaries And Functionaries,* Copy. 1988.

"Political leaders led us to wars where the wars have their own historical roots in nationalism, anti-colonialism, and civil strife. Then also there is the intriguing triangle of Iran/ Israel/ United States. Each is part terrorist, part opportunist, part terrorized. Beyond this is the structural role of secrecy."[xxxi]

The most deadly, overt or covert terrorist to the United States, and all its allied sovereign nations today is the individual who has taken up a commitment to Osama bin Laden's declaration: "We-with God's help- call on every Muslim who believes in God, and who wishes to be rewarded, to comply with God orders to kill the Americans and plunder their money whenever and wherever they find it."[xxxii] A complete declaration of war.

This international terror is traced to the United States wedding into this guy's family. "They had been involved in the Iran-Contra scandal and in secret US aid in Afghanistan War that gave birth to Osama bin Laden... ...horrifying as it sounds, the secret relationship between these two great families, helped to trigger the age of terrorism and give rise to the tragedy of 9/11," noted Craig Unger, in his book *HOUSE of BUSH HOUSE OF SAUD.*

THE STORY

Oil was discovered in Saudi Arabia around 1938. Thereafter a lucrative concession was granted to a consortium of giant American oil companies and the Saudis, Called ARAMCO (Arabian American Oil Company). Money poured into the Saudi's kitty for the next twenty-five years, as "roughly 85,000 'high net-worth' Saudis invested a staggering $860 billion in American companies- an average of more than $10 million a person...." These investments went into banks, defense, energy, technology, and media companies.

"....the Bushes and Saudis had pulled off elaborate covert operations and gone to war together. They had shared secrets that involved unimaginable personal wealth, spectacular military might, the richest energy resources in the world, and the most odious crimes imaginable. They had been involved in the Iran- Contra scandal, and in secret US aid in the Afghanistan War that gave birth to Osama bin Laden."xxxiii

According to Unger, Bush was pursuing a very different agenda from the one written about in the media when he went to the Middle East under the pretext of a peace plan between Iran, Israel, and Iraq. "The former CIA director was now actually working as an intelligence operative.... to facilitate the arms-for-hostages deal with Iran, and to set in motion the delivery of military intelligence to Saddam Hussein."

The United States relationship with our blood brother Saddam Hussein is said to have started somewhere back in 1959, when at the age of 22 the CIA hired him as an assassin to shoot, then Iraqi Prime Minister, Abd al Karim Qasim, who survived the assassination. However, "....In the ensuing two decades, the agency saw him as a cutthroat and a thug, but at least he was their thug- one who would be called on to fight Soviet expansion in the Middle East. In 1963, that meant that the CIA officers in Bagdad provided Saddam with lists of 'communists' whom he then assassinated."xxxiv

In 1979 Saddam began his rule in Iraq By purging out political opponents. A "double-policy" is said to have been maintained towards Iraq throughout the entire Regan-Bush era- specifically in the line of using Geneva Convention-banned biological weapons. The United States publicly denounced Iraq's use of the weapons, but covertly supplies them to our blood brother, Saddam. The poor guy needed them.

Beginning in 1984 the centers of disease control began providing him with biological materials. "The Reagan administration knew that Iraq was using mustard gas, saran, VX, and other poisons. But privately, senior officials supported a covert program in which the defense intelligence provided Saddam with detailed planning for battles, air strikes, and bomb-damage assessments" against Kurds and Iran.

Conversely, by early 1982, the US government knew Israel was providing US arms to Iran. "Israel and American intelligence officials acknowledged that weapons, ammunitions, and spare parts worth several billion dollars flowed to Iran each year during the early 1980's."

The Reagan administration secretly began allowing Saudi Arabia,

Kuwait, and Egypt to transfer U.S. weapons, including howitzers, helicopters, and bombs to Iraq, even though Congress never would have approved such transactions. In the meantime, as the official propaganda machine throughout the United States continued to criticize the use and horror of chemical weapons, covertly, "the administration wanted to make certain that Saddam knew such pronouncements were merely for public consumption. ....Rumsfeld was to assure Saddam that the U.S. concerns about chemical weapons were nothing more than posturing."[xxxv]

Secretly arming both sides, the United States participation in both the Iran-Iraq, and the war in Afghanistan, taking place simultaneously, never registered on the analytic screen of the American electorate, perhaps other than "the eternal and defining pillars of American policy in the Middle East: *Oil* and *Israel*." The United States, sworn defender of Israel, is also the guarantor of security to the guardians of Wahhabi Islam, the fundamentalist religious sect that was one of Israel's and America's mortal enemies."

More than a military build-up, the Saudi alliance constituted a major shift in American foreign policy in the Middle East that took place with virtually no public debate in the press or Congress. ....Even more secretive was the new understanding that Saudi Arabia would become a U S partner in covert operations, not just in the Middle East, but all over the globe."[xxxvi]

Unger asks: "How can the president reconcile this solemn vow with his alliance with a state that bears more responsibility for 9/11 than does any other nation? He does not." Charges about Iraq's role, or its link to Al Qaeda turned out to be baseless and wildly exaggerated. But "....The Bush administration had succeeded in switching villains to the extent that 70% of Americans ultimately believed Saddam Hussein was linked to 9/11, simply because there was no political pressure to change American policies in the Middle East."

Bypassing government officials who knew most about Iraq, and certain CIA analyst who had studied it for years noted that "The United States went to war with Iraq on March 19, 2003, based on a variety of startling false assumptions."[xxxvii]

Today we are witnessing and experiencing terrorism as a religious global warfare for world domination, with an intact afterlife belief and fantasy, and rituals that are performed daily as a way of social life, which all free-thinking people must, or ought to live by. Those who take to Muslim religious beliefs, or the beliefs of Islam, have staked the claims for this senseless warfare. As of the date of this treatise, nine acts of various forms of terrorism has been committed in the United States by these people living among us Christians, Jews, Buddhists, and other practicing religious faiths.

According Richard Falk, "the terrorist is someone who is responding to deprivation and perceived or real injustice; sometimes using political means to reach desired personal goals, sometimes acting in a desperate spirit of revenge and retaliation, making those who have caused the suffering pay."

A much more acute form of terrorism confronts us on the home front, and it has to do with the quality of social life we are leading. Mass murders have become commonplace nationwide, through a spirit of sheer injustice, meaninglessness, and the frustrations of realistic or extravagant hope in an economic system that doesn't deliver. Revenge and retaliation, using any random member of society as their victims or hostages. Since the turn of the century, thousands of Americans have been killed, murdered or maimed by home-grown terrorists.

We grows em too. And we grows our own with good manure.

There is the utter disregard in the uprooting of people from vocational stability without viable alternatives, owing to rapid job obsolescence, and the continuous churning out by technology. This is compounded by accelerated external migration from other nations, engineered by interests of the members of our very ruling body- Congress! Social upheavals, and the disruption of familiar patterns are net results.

About 120 million of us Americans at the bottom of the economic ladder have become strangers to each other- just one step away from the shit-pit of homelessness, where social life has become wretched. Opportunity is not ours, other than incentives to get locked-up by joining the otherworldliness of illegal activity.

Besides the loss of confidence in political leaders; trusts have been betrayed by swings with the media, people have come to doubt the reliability and freedom, once the backbone of many legal institutions. For my generation of believers in the political system, confidence eroded in the law making body of the land (Congress) all the way back in 1980 when a high-level undercover sting operation called AB-SCAM, targeting public corruption and organized crime was publicly acknowledged.

In a trail of corruption and purchased favoritism, FBI investigations and trap caught a Senator, five Congressmen, two former judges, and two more lawyers deep in the lifestyle. The dodo. Loui Galambos in his book, *The Creative Society*, noted that ever since the pursuit and conclusion of this investigation "the public standing of the profession, as well as congress went into a free fall."

We must face up to the fact that unacknowledged injustice exist as an open painful wound for survivors everywhere. An article titled "Deadly Familiar Tragedy" published by the Los Angeles Times on 12/4/2015 noted that between 1999 and 20013, over 1500 people were killed in mass murders. Congressional Research defines mass shootings as one in which there are four or more victims, excluding the killer.

Anthropologist Joseph Campbell defines terror as "...the feeling that arrests the mind in the presence of whatever is grave and constant in human sufferings...."

Former Secretary of Defense Robert Gates experienced the hardest part- "....visiting the wounded in hospitals which I did regularly...got harder each time. It tore me apart to see young men who had limbs blown off, trauma to their bodies and brains, wounds both visible and invisible"

"I began to lose my composure. ....I simply could not go on. Press accounts would say that I was clearly struggling and suffering. I was."

"This was the real face of war."

34

HOPE & CHANGE

W EARY OF WAR CASUALTIES AND wounded loved ones, the nation decided to elect a president whose mandate was peace. Peace, or compromise he did pursue with other nations by a spirit of atonement for the hell, havoc, and horror that America had, or might have wreaked in their ways of social life as the dominant power force. I am not sure what programs the Democrats had planned for domestic implementation, other than a much-feuded Affordable Health Care Bill.

The Election of Barack Obama as the first black, half-breed President of the United States was a welcoming change of great expectations in domestic relations. And boy, what a change we've had! A new gender identity complex, and the old competing ethnic group superiority/inferiority complexes has risen again from the dead, and is again asserting itself with a culture of tattooed ignorance, politically correct, and deadly violence.

In the most protracted period of economic distress since World War II, Tax and Health Care legislation, both issues central to improving the economy were the main issues of the day in Congress. Barely beginning his term in office in 2009, Eric Cantor, Republican leader of Congress in the lower House noted that the two major issues will not be decided until the 2012 election. Contending, "...he would obstruct major legislation that might affect our economic recovery for an entire congressional session," noted Senator Mike Lofgren.

From the very top of our political social structure, Senate Majority Leader Mitch Mc Connell, rather than pledging a spirit of benign co-governance with the new incoming President to make things work out for the nation, he admitted his hatred, "...more than he wanted to pull the country out of a deep crisis."

"Both Houses were now prepared to operate on 'a Leninist Principle' of the worst, the better." According to this principle, if both House held fast against every one of the Democrats attempts at restarting the economy, the Presidency and both Houses of Congress will fall into their laps in 2012. Republicans did win both Houses of Congress in 2012, but lost the Presidency.

".... the congressional directory now look like a cookbook of lunacy. This is not to say that such specimens represents all, or even most Republicans; but they have engaged, through their shrillness, dogmatism, inflexibility, and belligerence, to become the center of gravity of the party." Republicans, trying to act like Democrats "now resemble a barnyard of chickens scurrying around in every direction frantically searching for worms."[157]

These worms are the meaningless issues that surface as strategic ambiguities. Fundamentally, Lip. The defense of illegal immigration and chain migration. Hot air emotional balloons. Endless oscillation of justifications for doing nothing while the flames of erosion burn relentlessly in the hearts and souls of the poorer classes of the host culture form illegal and legal migration, joblessness, insecurity, and pervasive meanness.

"Rebranded under the rubric of hope and change, Obama and the Democrats essentially stepped into the shoes of the former Republican administration's policy lines, only with modifications of emphasis, while some of the most egreous aspect of the previous administration were downplayed, but there was more continuity than change."[158]

All absorbed in making amends for the nation's world dominance, the President ignored the mass disenfranchisement of poorer classes of the host culture- his own fucking people, the very ones the Democratic Party pledges to liberate. But I guess we were not his people. The Party's entrenched relation with the defense of illegal immigration and tyrannizing of the publics' body-mind only escalated a culture of alienation.

The unprecedented influx of refugees, promoting the false ideology of Global Warming, climate change, or whatever name it may morph

---

[157] Lofgren Mike The Party Is Over p. 28
[158] Ibid

to next; the sordid issues of radical Islam, Isis, and other terror groups, marred focus of the remainder of Obama's administration. Politics became well-blended with popular culture. In fact, politics was popular culture itself, with Obama as the star of pre-visions. Things to come. He was the Medias' plowboy.

All the props of news, press, and political reports were now entangled with the entertainment industry and its schizoid personalities. No "intelligent" Democratic Party voter could or would dare make an attempt to separate the two. Simply because focus of the President was their real personality figure of ultimate defense, frame of *live* reference as progress, and American success model. Owing specifically to his token ethnic group background.

Besides a few sound political actions typically taken by any past U S President, today's mass media- written, visual, auditory, and tactile, plays the most important role in the forming and shaping people's attention, awareness, and perceptions of what is important, even though it ain't, or they might not be, and what issues merit their concern.

Both the ruling Presidency (Obama's), and the media actually merged in a kind of compulsive dictatorship as it climaxed with swamp creatures at the highest levels of the nation's intelligence departments of the FBI, and CIA, doing everything they can to continue the dictatorship, and to ensure that Hillary Clinton wins the US Presidency.

Only citizens of substance really knew what was going on beneath this superficial grandeur state of affairs. And mostly those who listened to Sean Hannity, the most positive, the most vocal, the most confident, trustworthy source and broadcaster about Donald Trump winning the 2016 presidential election.

But I'm getting a little bit ahead of the ruling administration here. There are the serious matters of boarder security, homelessness, illegal migration, and joblessness for the home range. While, on the other side of the sleaze curtain of entertainment about this serious state of affairs are the stand-up TV comedians and anti-Trump movement, faithless and vain women, the experts, the selective hosts that convincingly conform their twisted and warped views- softening, obscuring, and deluding their audience and nation's social feelings about real issues which should concern them.

The whole goddamn nation was mesmerized and dabbling with values and cultures of the Moslem world of religious nonsense, purge, violence, and privileges. The Moslem world had superseded all focus of attention for remedying serious economic problems on the home front- the homeless men and women who are continuously displaced by immigrant populations in Border States, others through flight of companies and corporations to other nation states, and the rest through the deskilling process often brought on by new technologies.

Since there are multiple competing Medias for audience attention, these reports deserving serious attention are often tainted, laced, or douched for share of the greatest numbers of the audience. This includes trivialization of American Presidency and very important political issues of national security on local and national levels through TV shows.

The larger the audience ratings, the more the commercial advertising businesses are committed to them, while stations and corporations reap larger margins of financial profit. More serious than this bankrolling are its demented effects on the innocent, inquiring, and aspiring body-minds of the young. Their honest curiousity about their nation's state of affairs.

Media coverage of, and the harping on issues and events, legitimizes any existing random and selective problem of focused attention and route that controllers have embarked upon. The decisions about which stories of "importance" will be ignored or covered. Furthermore, strong absolute professional norms approve and help in this definition of *what is important*, significant, and worthy- locally and nationally; "something for which national leadership can be fairly held accountable," according to sociological forensics.

Consider this statement from a former NSA operative Joel Brenan: "Secrecy and openness just cannot get along in the same organization... If we are going to protect what must be kept secret, we must separate it from what is not. A salutatory effect of that separation would be to stop funding secret organizations that produce mere journalism."

The pursuit of news or information that conforms to peoples' common simple beliefs- those that conform to their convictions are specious, but taken in as substance, or the real thing. While interest is lost in more meaningful events taking place within their immediate communities and their own personal lives.

On any given day, mass media coverage nowadays is mostly selective and skewed, and can be very harmful if taken in for granted without being first examined by a critical faculty of history, science, and context. This leads us now to the understanding of forms.

35

FORMS

T HE INTEGRATION OF INFORMATION AS usable units for the projects or goals we have chosen or set up for ourselves involves the wise use and conservation of our human energies. Our energies are drawn by the gravity force of attraction- what seems plausible and real to our senses. Attraction holds our attention, leading to absorption and interaction with various forms and substances of human and non-human objects, creations, and productions.

The Attention that we give any *form* we are interacting with automatically narrows our perception. We automatically ignore everything else. Attention is to take notice of. To notice is to select, choose, or disregard. We are choosing onn, and onn as we have always been all along. Some trials, some failures, and some hits here and there, some modifications, and some misses. Whatever our situation may be, and for the vast majority of simple choices we face in everyday social life, we are sure of their quality yield and consequences without a fuss.

The hum-drum of live culture, or cultural life attracts us like flies on shit or sweets. It provides stable income and opportunities for job-seekers, the talented, or skilled people. It provides status, positions of power and charisma. It is the prime feature attraction of the day from which we draw the satisfaction for our common personal welfare.

If the overt temperament, air, aura, or social feeling of society can be defined by the heroes, heroines, and success models it revers and admires as symbols and images of attraction, then you can also size up the identity problems of persons in that society by those success and model images that a random member might emulate, yap about, worship, aspire, or choose to become.

This modeling medium is surface or popular culture. Popular culture is also information culture. There is no difference other than *forms*. The infinite variety which holds our influence are historical. Identification with historical elements such as *forms,* forms of human or non-human attraction shapes our personalities by producing semblance of behavior between persons and characteristics of the objects. A biased or influenced behavior orientation. That is, we give our highest regards to those who convincingly disprove established beliefs that doesn't fit our social reality.

The very act of this understanding is a cereberation of joining, merging, and acting, even on a modest scale in the magnificence of the social world and its constant build-up in stocks of knowledge. How to do.

The stability of our society is based largely upon this identification that the younger generation and others make with the ideas and artifacts produced by peers, or by the older and dominant generations. The most powerful and dominant forms in culture are mostly manufactured and produced by a special class of people, or an ascendant class with adequate resources, educated beyond their audience' ability to understand.

These are people of high income, status, and influence, producers of valued artifacts in our society- as well as public and private administrators who put the elements of our assurances together, such as the routine function of bureaucracy, which all or most members of society can depend on.

To maintain status-quo, it stays preoccupied with all the elements of surface culture. They are basically gossip, personalities, sexuality, ethnic group feuds, feeding on trivia, and episodes of crisis and incidents of the moment produced through every possible media of communication, and gathered from every possible source of interaction.

With a constant dose and blitzkrieg of this drama, it is very difficult- if ever, for a young, inquiring body-mind to look in depth at an issue straight on for clarification. And even though a person may have all the necessary tools at his or her disposal, they don't know intuitively where to begin. The roads, and avenues of honest inquiry are hermetically sealed. Shut tight with nonsense and meaningless issues.

Conditioning the individual's inner-control system in making choices is more convincing when the external is not explicit, as when somebody tells an irrelevant story that serves as a point, hint, or suggestion. Setting examples by urging and persuading people to act exerts a similar kind of control, exploiting the general tendency to behave imitatively, according to Psychologist, B. F. Skinner.

Let us do a little philosophy by trying to understand *form* or forms.

To understand what the whole human and non-human world of forms is made of, we must look at *matter* as our basic element.

We could say that the entire universe or world is made of *matter*. Yet, *matter* is not a thing. In this short philosophy it is not a thing yet.

It becomes a thing when it is in a state of organization with a level of human understanding by an individual, social group, community, or members of the whole nation. These *matters* are shaped forms, where we reveal our individual properties of solidity in our reasoning, interactions, expressions, and experiences of creating, doing, and satisfying needs. Basically, the shaping our lives.

Thought is the primary constructor of Forms. The very beginning and shaping of *matter*, which simultaneously, and automatically occupies *space*.

Changing or manipulating the content of our body-minds is a probability of action in belief preferences, perception needs, purposes, and humble opinions.

Space, whether real or imaginary- a blank or vacuum in our heads for meaningful action is the medium for *Form*. Therefore thought is the shaping of space. Thoughts are therefore shaped forms occupying the earth's surface.

Shaped Forms are the manufactured currency of the drama we all now know and experience as social life- communication, institutions, surrounding structures, roads, cars, mules – every, and any physical object or artifact. The organization of *matter* into these *forms* involves a creative, and specific, objective form of action production. Shaped forms thus involve how, and what individuals think, relate to, and do. Mental Effort or work must be done to create form from moment to moment.

Each is free to create his or her own form from whatever sensation or attraction may have been aroused in us. These sensations that draws our influence and attention are exactly what it is that influence thought motion for the organization of *form* or forms in a sequence of whatever seems advantageous for our survival, convenience, and security, from moment to moment.

These involve the greatest influence, the greatest Gods, the greatest Devils, and the greatest spirits of gravity that pulls us in, swaying our sentiments, and ultimately our choices. Going simultaneously with these are habits, patterns, logic, and all the notation symbols which we have learned, internalized from others around us, greater society, and culture as an appropriate response. End of philosophy on what forms are all about.

Compared to citizens of other nation states, material success beyond mere subsistence is commonplace in the United States since Post-World War 11. Again, private property, citizenship, migration, education, profession, craft, specialization, expertise, talent, or labor are the legitimate means of self-aggrandizement, elevation, and maintenance of status. There are other means, but these are the core perennial standardized means.

The paradox of existence and liberty guaranteed by the constitution demands that we give or surrender part of our allegiances to many aversive forms of image production or *forms*, simply because we need to earn income for survival, self-development, chosen identities, goal fulfillments, and a whole lot more. Generally speaking, our fates are sealed when we are unable to create the necessary forms for our own convenience, self-development, or legitimate self-aggrandizement.

We must be aware that every social, corporate, entrepreneurial, and industrial enterprise in the United States, including ones in the planning, and making stages, has, and is entitled in making its own rules and establishing its own prerogatives in their operation, as longs as they're not in conflict with the states' or nation's existing laws of infringements.

We, the lower class majority in the population, need the courts and political action to see to it that they operate fairly in their own interests as well as the public's expectations. "The courts are our bastion of sanity in this constitutional system, because they can take a long view, free from popular passions..." notes Philip K. Howard in his book *Collapse of The Common Good. Copy. 2001.*

Whatever our beliefs are, and however we may acquire them, they need affirmations of right or wrong behavior from leaders of society. Those who inspire our chosen ways of social life, in the sense that they have attained something material or immaterial of lasting value, some greater than our individual selves. Our values and freedoms hinge upon them because of the responsibility they show and uphold in making choices that affect the greater population.

We require that those who have achieved this influence in our society conduct themselves with a commitment to the common good; values which we hold in common that enlarge the peace of antagonistic cooperation, and a sense of obligation to the community. When this is not the case of the people we identify with, we experience a negative quality of reality anxiety.

Reality anxiety is a painful experience resulting from perceptions of danger and sense of insecurity in the external world of individuals. This danger happens to be a condition which threatens to harm, invalidate, or discount the worth or production of a person, impede his or her progress, and to behave in demeaning ways.

The person feels un-free of the powerful controls exercised by those "others," who comprise the smart-asses of economic and social controls, or aversive dominant form producers. These forms are to ridicule, criticize, invalidate experience, blame, censure, and suppress unwanted behaviors in others.

There are powerful interest groups who don't want us to resolve our own social issues and national problems. These are the people who actively promote meaningless issues deemed as important, issues that are well understood by an ascendant generation or social class, now presented as novel to an older or younger ignorant generation, tacitly accepted as a part of "human nature."

The tendency toward these social problems we have experienced, deeply rooted in our interaction with the inside and outside world of others, is that if anyone could eliminate every trace of them today, they would begin to creep back again tomorrow. This inertia and sluggishness is expected to some degree, based on the reproductive cycle in the rearing of children, and limited rewards available to masses in society.

All forms of social organization grow out of something enduring that we fully recognize in our environment in the process of our adaptation and survival. Given appropriate circumstances, this something enduring could easily re-create meaningful patterns we had forgotten. Patterns can be easily found in feelings about our various institutions and various reinforcers that these institution use.

Following Skinner's behavior patterns discoveries, beliefs and trust in a system or institution are often built when the probability of action is undeterred through reinforcement behavior. While, punishments for non-believers are usually confined to intentionally arranged circumstances by the dominant controllers of forms, because the results they get are reinforcing to them.

Meanwhile, new cultural patterns evolve when new forms of practices further the survival of those who practice them. In other words, a person could be persuaded to change his or her behavior pattern by making a situation more favorable for action, or dissuaded by making it highly intolerable.

A final word about forms, and forms to come into being. American culture has produced the science and technology it needs, as well as the wealth needed for effective action in remedying its own problems. We have the physical, biological, and behavioral techniques needed. The problem question is: how to get people to use them and induce others with lesser resources to act, in order to increase the chance that their cultural ideals will survive or will be realized.

36

WE'RE FINALLY HERE!

"YOU WILL BE CHALLENGED, ATTACKED, or threatened. This culture war is not for the timid." – Culture Warrior Bill O Riley.

A new form of American civilization was delivered in a reindeer's package: The New York slimes, MSLSD, better known as MSNBC, The Washington compost, better known as the Washington Post, african americans, white niggers, also called "black caucasians;" chicans, the mexican poverty plague, clintons, and the hussien obamas. The nation's arterial and venal lines of political lunacy. These basket-weavers and their chapter imposed in American political social life is at reckoning point.

As you may have gathered from what you have read throughout this treatise: a useful complexity is not nonsense. But nonsense could easily be manufactured as complexity for intentional aversive intelligence use. Invidious comparisons has produced serious confusion in shoddy educational objectives, dangerous erosion of standards, cheap politics, decadence, and tyranny of the lowest common denominator.

A clue might suffice for the solution: A notable religious scholar observed that when the biblical character Moses, after meeting with God- the Man Upstairs- on Mount Sinai, and trudges back down to deliver the message to the people awaiting him, Moses told them: "I've beaten Him down to ten. But *fucking* is still a problem." Human sexuality and our desires for constant fulfillment is never-ending.

"I know of no safe depository of the ultimate powers of society but the people themselves."

"The people must develop the political experience... the moral education, and the stimulus that comes from correcting their own errors," -Thomas Jefferson.

In the world of forms, "Thermonuclear politics is here!" From his book *The B S Factor, The Theory and Technique of Faking It in America.* Copy. 1975, Arthur Herzog zeroed in on the aversive conditioning and the main controllers of our supply of meat and pertatoes- the mass media.

"Light (on meaningless selective issues) is converted to heat. The Thermopolitical crucible softens the old, hard-edged forms (of our social reality) so that they can be twisted into new, sometimes grotesque shapes. Thermopolitics tends towards what physicists call 'the heat death,' the melting down of everything into the same liqueous mass." Perceptions are astronomically massified on some selected issue of conflict, event, data, person, social group, or category of persons. A new form of deception is then handed down from the top of the nation's, states', and local administrative heap. And we all get to believe when the whip comes down.

"In the Theermopolitical process, light, in the form of an idea, is fed into a special prism, (an image, imagery, or expert) called a spokesman (or woman), which bends and distorts the light so that what emerges bears no resemblance to that which originally entered. The product is hotter, flatter, mushier, massier, messier."

"Oh it's one big mess!" President Donald Trump would say, before he furiously dubbed the whole carrying-on *fake news.*

"....errors may make news where accuracy won't. Errors can be advantageous. A misquotation may be better than no quotation. Or suppose a couple of punks are trading shots. ...you've got the makings of a story or a riot." Max Singer states that "....The system of reporting ensures that errors of fact and interpretation may be repeated, compounded, and reformulated as myths."

A central reason is that reporters want to be on the front page, and another that There must be a front page."

"News can (and does) make news by contradicting itself."

"... The endless appetite of the media for news puts a premium on novelty, excitement, and conflict." Bill O'Riley has referred to this media lot as a "Fascist Organization. They seek to impose their world view on us Americans, not by popular vote, which is the way it should be done in a democracy. ...by 'gaming' the legal system, this strategy is to rely upon activist left-wing judges to bring about secular changes in our laws, not by popular vote, but by judicial fiat."

These are the "establishment players who can change your life with the stroke of a pen, an activist court ruling, or a dishonest article in the press. Most media people are well-educated and come from affluent homes; some are urban dwellers who see themselves as sophisticated gatekeepers of the common good." A great portion of these people were the people in the first paragraph. The ones who fervently supported and forged everything they can, and voted for Hillary Clinton to be President of the United States in November 2016.

The fixation of public attitude was uttered by the outgoing President, putting his bag of ballyhoo in Hillary when he robustly stated: "Hillary Clinton was the only person qualified to be President of the United States." She is caught red-handed by the general public too as a compulsive liar, forger, cheat, or sociopath at best when FBI Director, James Comey was questioned about her state of affairs while she was serving as Secretary of State. Indeed, conclusions drawn when Comey was questioned publicly by a Senate Investigative Committee, makes her the best person available to perpetuate America's aversive control and conditioning of its people.

The surprised election outcome produced pandemic hatred that lead to the total undermining, and undoing of our trusted national security system. Former CIA Director John Brenan, FBI Director James Comey, and as of the day of this book, Robert Muller who is assigned to a highly dubious "Russian Collusion investigation," all cooked-up by Hillary Clinton's campaign camp are all parties of the Obama train-load. The other portion of the train-load are neutered Republicans, with no balls or guts for their less fortunate country men.

And so the devil incarnate was chosen over her, nonetheless. His election to the Presidency has liberated national awareness beyond the reach of these highly polished, and well-educated God-form producers. *The establishment players* as O Riley has them. More real to us "bigots and trolls," as some of them refer to us Donald Trump voters who elected him, was the significance and real meaning of our national freedoms. Its erosion from worn-out and meaningless conventions, as well as a refusal to go along to get along, by doing the same as the opposition in "gaming" *the legal* system.

The devil incarnate has brought to light the souls of phony living earth angels and God-forms of our world views. "The politics of anger, mistrust in the establishment and expert opinions."

"Never has the political class/ industry/ elite so misread the electorate and so misunderstood American priorities..."

"And now, the political establishment has been toppled. But it is possible to catalog some of the pillars that have fallen: the entire political-consultant industrial complex has collapsed, political parties... now seem utterly archaic."

"Suddenly we don't know what is going to happen?" Was the expression of the Hillary Clinton followers. (Quotes from Time magazine).

Well, I'll be damned! Was this national election supposed to be a child's play? A TV, video, or well-rehearsed feature-length movie of some dingleberry's fantasy? Or, was it not about the American heart-felt desire for trust and strength in a competent, realistic leader?

Libraries of books can be, and are written about the ripple effects of Donald Trump's election to the presidency, from the moment he made a formal announcement that he was going to take up the challenge for a nation going adrift and awash with deception, neglect of its citizens, and the erosion of public trust.

We now have a President who is pure in motives, unencumbered by worldly ambitions, and dedicated to the well-being of the country's people. "America first!" The opposition Democratic Party is trying to turn this into a battle cry of racism and worst things to come.

Donald Trump's election to the Presidency has proven that both political Party members benefit themselves and their circle of suckers by ignoring the electorate's need, while satisfying their money contributors' demands. We cannot admire these two-faced, mindless, public servants of the state anymore, suckering the electorate for votes, while satisfying the corporate cause, or their own organizational good. And at the cost of all citizens.

The games of: football, baseball, basketball, and so on, are the extension of our inner and outer social lives. They are a media of values and meanings of interpersonal fulfillment, whether we actually participate in them or, from mere identification for those who participate as an audience. These games are dramatic models of our social lives providing satisfaction, psychological release of tensions, a sense of patriotism, and the lessons of winning and losing as participants or spectators.

But political life as a "gaming system" is one of seriousness and deserves our adult attention- for it involves who gets what, and how much- Beginning with industry and its individual lifeblood, the worker. How we find work, how to hold on to my job, where to find the best paying jobs; and who is going to hire me? Furthermore, can you meet your lease or rental costs, or can you afford to maintain your own property without much of a struggle? This is the basic American mind-set I know. Those who have been surviving beyond this mere subsistence level worry about other things.

Under these compulsive conditions of the political state, a person struggles, a person protests, feels indignant when jolted unnecessarily, tripped, pushed around, or forced to behave in demeaning ways, owing to needs of securing basic survival necessities.

The unavoidable purpose of this treatise has been to induce others to act on a code of social justice, based on the United States Constitution. To free themselves from the viciousness of their environments, the various kinds of intentional aversive conditioning or control by the overwhelming and all powerful media, which we all participate in, inducing all of us at one time or another to feel, think, and act unconsciously, and accordingly to its own agenda.

While its deliberate purpose is to face challenges of the present, and challenges of future times to come. To insist on an *inner education*, so that a person identifies his or her self with humanity- the entire human race or species, rather than with whatever in-group the person belongs to, the wit and whims of media, swing and sway of programming, propaganda, politics, crisis, or the visible dissolution of things.

President Donald Trump has been, and is the best American leader of the day- undeterred in offering clues, and clearly showing us how the controlling powers of *aversive-form* producers may be weakened or destroyed- to MAKE AMERICAN GOVERNANCE GREAT AGAIN!

BIBLIOGRAPHY

INFORMATION SOURCE AND AUTHOR'S WORKS CONSULTED

Chapter 31. **Steven Hayward:** *The Politically Incorrect Guide to the Presidents.* Copy. 2012. Character assessments. P.246-248. Pardoning, p.251. Impeach, p.254-257. **William A.McGeveran:** *The World Almanac, Copy. 2006.* Chronology of some misfortunes during the Clinton years. *1992* through 2001. O.J. Simpson. Oklahoma City bombing. 1996, 197 Abortion clinic bombing, AR School and Colombine. 1998 Clinton impeached.

Chapter 32. **Joseph Campbel**: *An Open Life. Copy 1989.* Hell, p.78. Mythologies and Religious beliefs. Joseph Campbell: *Myths To Live By.* Topic: Living mythologies. **Steven Hayward:** Clinton's trade deal with Mexico. Immigration. **Walter Writson:** *Bits Bytes, And Diplomacy. Copy.* p.175 Convergence of computers and telecommunications, p. 202. **Alvin and Heidi Toffler:** *Creating A New Civilization. Copy. 1995.* Topic: Super Struggle. Knowledge. Dangerous conflicts from waves of migration. Inchorence of political life. Social disintegration. Intrusion on sovreignty, p. 24, 31, 33, 42.

Chapter 33 **Kevin Philips:** *American Theocracy. Copy. 2006.* Operation Phoenix and Desert Thunder in Iraq. Oil Concessions, p.83. UNOCAL. Oil-Forward policy, p. 81. **Mike Lofgren:** *The Party Is Over. Copy. 2012.* Pretext for war. **Robert Gates**: *Duty. Copy.* Comments on war in Iraq and

Afghanistan, p. 178, 391-2. Colonel David Hunt: They Just Don't get it. Soldier, p8. **Hunt:** *On The Hunt.* Winning the War, Rumsfeld. p. 39-43 Ahmad Chalabi, p. 48.

Chapter 34 **Joel Brenner,** *Glass Houses.* Topic: Bleeding Wealth. **Alvin and Heidi Toffler,** Topic: Collision of Culture. **Allen Wheelis:** *The Moralist.* Copy. 1973. Nihilism, p.11. Goodness and Morality, p.39. Negative and Positive Morality, 46, 49, 50, 52-3. **Richard Dawkins:** The God Delusion. Copy. 2007. On Adolph Hitler being virulently anti-Semitic, p.312. **Marshal Mc Luhan:** *Understanding Media: The Extensions of Man.* Copy. 1964. Media & Identity. **Joseph Campbell:** *Myths To Liive By:* Religion and Mythologies

Chapter 35. **Richard Falk:** CIA Covert Operations. **Kevin Philips:** *American Theocracy,* copy. 2006: ARAMCO, US oil firms in Somalia. **Craig Unger:** *House of Bush House of Saud. Copy. 2004.* US sworn defender of Israel and Saudi Arabia, p.3. Bush's direct connection, p.15."... Bush's direct connection to the Saudi's, Saudi's investments in the US. The Houston-Jeddah connection, from topic: Great Escape, p. 9-28. Saddam Hussein at age 22. Rumsfeld's conceding reply to Saddam about chemical weapons use, p.65-69.

Chapter 36. **Mike Lofgren:** *The Party Is Over. Copy. 2012.* Republican Party's Profile, p.28. Eric Cantor. Mitch Mc Connell on Obama's Presidency and Health Care legislation, p.40. Why we were embroiled in three wars simultaneously, p.107. World picture of American youth. The flow of information leaks, p.119. Pretext for war, p.120. American youth's world view, p. 121.

Chapter 37. David Foster: The Philosophical Scientist. Copy. 1985. Forms, p.164. **B. F. Skinner:** Conditioning. Reality Anxiety. Re-enforcements. **Philip K. Howard:** *Collapse of The Common Good.* **John W. Gardner:** *No Easy Victories. Copy. 1969.* Commitment to the common good.

Chapter 38. **Stephen Breyer:** *Active Liberty Copy. 2005.* Thomas Jefferson's quote, p.3 .**Arthur Herzog:** *The B. S. Factor Copy. 1973.* Topic: Thermonuclear Rhetoric, Thermonuclear politics, p. 166. **Bill O**

Riley: *Culture Warrior. Copy. 2006.* Establishment players. P. 15. Fascist Organization, p. 16. Judicial fiat, p. 18. Media people's profile, p. 22. Rush Limbaugh: "black Caucasians." Mark Levine: "the Washington compost. MSLSD. The new York slimes."

Endnotes

i

ii

iii   Stewart, James, Blood Sport p.364-5

iv   Campbell, Joseph

v   Galambos, Louis: *The Creative Society*

vi   Ibid

vii   Writson, Walter:

viii   Kevin Philips *American Theocracy* p. 293

ix   George Grant, *Pat Buchanan* p.78, 104

x   Steven Hayward, *The Presidents* p.250

xi   Ibid p.251

xii   Ibid p.244-5

xiii   Ibid

xiv   Ibid p.249

xv   Ibid p.246

xvi   Kevin Philips, *American Theocracy* p.82

xvii   Ibid p.237

xviii   Ibid p.234

xix   Mike Lofgren, *The Party Is over* p.12-13

xx   Kevin Philips p.83

xxi   Mike Lofgren p.119-120

xxii   Kevin Philips

xxiii   Robert Gates, *DUTY* p. 589, 200, 35

xxiv   David Hunt, *ON THE HUNT* p. 40, 41,43,48

xxv   Robert Gates, *DUTY* p.554, 590

xxvi   John Stauber/Sheldon Rampton *Toxic Sludge Is Good For You.* P24

xxvii   Ibid

xxviii   Howard Zinn *Political Issues.* P14

xxix   Joseph Campbel

xxx Marshal Mc Luhan, *Understanding Media*
xxxi Richard Falk *Revolutionaries And Functionaries, The Dual Face of Terrorism.* .135
xxxii Craig Unger *House of Bush House of Saudi.* P.184
xxxiii Ibid P.15,17, 28
xxxiv Ibid, p.66
xxxv Ibid p.68
xxxvi Ibid p.61
xxxvii Ibid p.276, 277, 272

Printed in the United States
by Bookmasters

Printed in the United States
By Bookmasters